U.S. BOLT TORQUE

W9-CZN-796

U.S. BOLT TORQUE

CHILTON'S REPAIR & TUNE-UP GUIDE
FIESTA 1978 to 1980

Covers all Fiesta models

Vice President and General Manager JOHN P. KUSHNERICK
Managing Editor KERRY A. FREEMAN, S.A.E.
Senior Editor RICHARD J. RIVELE, S.A.E.
Editor JOHN M. BAXTER

CHILTON BOOK COMPANY
Radnor, Pennsylvania
19089

SAFETY NOTICE

Proper service and repair procedures are vital to the safe, reliable operation of all motor vehicles, as well as the personal safety of those performing repairs. This book outlines procedures for servicing and repairing vehicles using safe, effective methods. The procedures contain many NOTES, CAUTIONS and WARNINGS which should be followed along with standard safety procedures to eliminate the possibility of personal injury or improper service which could damage the vehicle or compromise its safety.

It is important to note that repair procedures and techniques, tools and parts for servicing motor vehicles, as well as the skill and experience of the individual performing the work vary widely. It is not possible to anticipate all of the conceivable ways or conditions under which vehicles may be serviced, or to provide cautions as to all of the possible hazards that may result. Standard and accepted safety precautions and equipment should be used when handling toxic or flammable fluids, and safety goggles or other protection should be used during cutting, grinding, chiseling, prying, or any other process that can cause material removal or projectiles.

Some procedures require the use of tools specially designed for a specific purpose. Before substituting another tool or procedure, you must be completely satisfied that neither your personal safety, nor the performance of the vehicle will be endangered.

Although information in this guide is based on industry sources and is as complete as possible at the time of publication, the possibility exists that the manufacturer made later changes which could not be included here. While striving for total accuracy, Chilton Book Company cannot assume responsibility for any errors, changes, or omissions that may occur in the compilation of this data.

PART NUMBERS

Part numbers listed in this reference are not recommendations by Chilton for any product by brand name. They are references that can be used with interchange manuals and aftermarket supplier catalogs to locate each brand supplier's discrete part number.

ACKNOWLEDGMENTS

The Chilton Book Company expresses its appreciation to the Ford Motor Company for the technical information and illustrations contained within this book.

Copyright © 1979 by Chilton Book Company
All Rights Reserved
Published in Radnor, Pennsylvania 19089, by Chilton Book Company

Manufactured in the United States of America
7890   87654

Chilton's Repair & Tune-Up Guide: Fiesta 1978-80
ISBN 0-8019-6846-1 pbk.
Library of Congress Catalog Card No. 78-20258

CONTENTS

1 General Information and Maintenance

1 How to Use this Book
2 Tools and Equipment
3 Routine Maintenance and Lubrication

2 Tune-Up

15 Tune-Up Procedures
15 Tune-Up Specifications

3 Engine and Engine Rebuilding

21 Engine Electrical System
29 Engine Service and Specifications
44 Engine Rebuilding

4 Emission Controls and Fuel System

66 Emission Control System and Service
70 Fuel System Service

5 Chassis Electrical

77 Accessory Service
81 Instrument Panel Service
82 Lights, Fuses and Flashers

6 Clutch and Transaxle

85 Transaxle
88 Clutch

7 Drive Train

90 Driveshaft and U-Joints
93 Rear Axle

8 Suspension and Steering

95 Front Suspension
98 Rear Suspension
100 Steering

9 Brakes

106 Front Brakes
110 Rear Brakes
114 Brake Specifications

10 Body

119 Repairing Scratches and Small Dents
123 Repairing Rust
129 Body Care

11 Troubleshooting

134 Problem Diagnosis

166 Appendix
171 Index

74 Chilton's Fuel Economy and Tune-Up Tips

Quick Reference Specifications For Your Vehicle

Fill in this chart with the most commonly used specifications for your vehicle. Specifications can be found in Chapters 1 through 3 or on the tune-up decal under the hood of the vehicle.

 ## Tune-Up

Firing Order_____

Spark Plugs:

    Type_____

    Gap (in.)_____

Point Gap (in.)_____

Dwell Angle (°)_____

Ignition Timing (°)_____

    Vacuum (Connected/Disconnected)_____

Valve Clearance (in.)

    Intake_____   Exhaust_____

Capacities

Engine Oil (qts)

    With Filter Change_____

    Without Filter Change_____

Cooling System (qts)_____

Manual Transmission (pts)_____

    Type_____

Automatic Transmission (pts)_____

    Type_____

Front Differential (pts)_____

    Type_____

Rear Differential (pts)_____

    Type_____

Transfer Case (pts)_____

    Type_____

FREQUENTLY REPLACED PARTS

Use these spaces to record the part numbers of frequently replaced parts.

PCV VALVE

Manufacturer_____

Part No._____

OIL FILTER

Manufacturer_____

Part No._____

AIR FILTER

Manufacturer_____

Part No._____

General Information and Maintenance

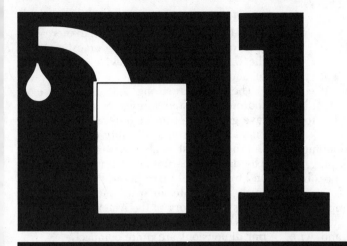

HOW TO USE THIS BOOK

This book is organized so that the most often used portions appear at the front, the least used portions at the rear. The first chapter covers all the information that may be required at a moment's notice—information like the locations of the various serial numbers, and proper towing instructions. Chapter 1 will probably be the most often used part of the book because of the need to carefully follow the maintenance schedule which it includes to ensure good performance and long component life. Chapter 2 covers tune-up and will be used regularly to keep the engine running at peak performance and to restore operation in case of failure of any of the more delicate components. Chapters 3 through 10 cover repairs (rather than maintenance) for various portions of the car, with each chapter covering either one system or two related systems. Chapter 11 covers Troubleshooting of the various systems on the car. This chapter should be checked first in the event of trouble. The appendix then lists general information which may be useful in rebuilding the engine or performing some other operation on any car.

In using the Table of Contents, refer to the bold listings for the beginning of the chapter. See the smaller listings for information on a particular component or specifications.

In general, there are three things a proficient mechanic has which must be allowed for when a nonprofessional does work on his car. These are:

1. A sound knowledge of the construction of the parts he is working with, their order of assembly, etc.

2. A knowledge of potentially hazardous situations.

3. Manual dexterity, which includes the ability to put the right amount of torque on a part to ensure that it will not be damaged or warped.

This book provides step-by-step instructions and illustrations wherever possible. Use them carefully and wisely—do not just jump headlong into disassembly. Where you are not sure about being able to readily reassemble something, make a careful drawing of it before beginning to take it apart. Assembly always looks simple when everything is still assembled.

Cautions and notes will be provided where appropriate to help keep you from injuring yourself or damaging the car. Therefore, you should read through the entire procedure before beginning work, and make sure that you are aware of the warnings. Since no number of warnings could cover every possible situation, you should work slowly and try to envision what is going to happen in each operation ahead of time.

When it comes to tightening things, there is generally a slim area between too loose to properly seal or resist vibration and so tight as to risk damage or warping. When dealing with major engine parts, or with any aluminum component, it pays to procure a torque wrench and go by the recommended figures.

TOOLS AND EQUIPMENT

The suggested list of tools below is what you would have under ideal conditions. If your budget won't allow such a complete tool kit, you can probably make do without the tools that are marked with an asterisk.

1. A set of metric sockets, including a deep well socket suitable for spark plug removal. Includes socket drive and, if possible, various socket drive extensions.

*2. A set of metric combination (open-end and box) wrenches.

3. Feeler gauges (both blade and wire type).

4. A spark plug cleaning tool.

5. Various standard and phillips head screwdrivers.

*6. Various angled standard and phillips head screwdrivers.

7. A timing light (preferably battery powered).

8. A dwell meter.

*9. A torque wrench.

10. A grease gun, preferably with a flexible hose.

11. An oil filter wrench.

12. An oil can spout.

13. A bulb/syringe designed for adding fluid to manual transmissions and axles.

14. A remote starter switch.

HISTORY

The Ford Motor Co. began importing the Ford Fiesta in 1978 in response to increasing sales of small imported and domestic cars in the U.S., as well as worldwide fear of crude oil shortages in the future.

The Fiesta's strong suit is the use of thoroughly tested foreign components that give good performance and mileage in combination with the availability of Ford Motor Company's vast dealer network for service. The design incorporates a transverse engine and front wheel drive in order to most effectively utilize interior space and produce a car that is satisfactory to the American market in terms of interior room, even though the exterior dimensions are quite compact.

All Fiestas are three door (hatchback) sedans; there are four levels of trim available.

SERIAL NUMBER IDENTIFICATION

Vehicle

The serial number is broken down as follows:

1. There is a six letter prefix (for example, G C F B U G) which is interpreted as follows:
The first column represents the country in

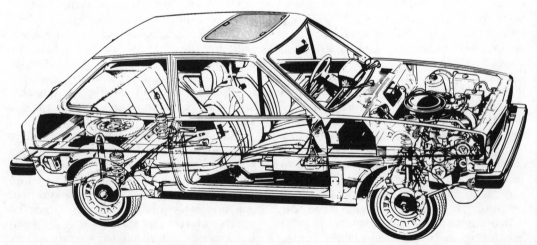

X-ray view of Fiesta shows front wheel drive and transverse engine layout; note how short the engine compartment is compared to the overall length of the car

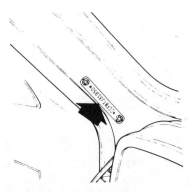

The serial number tag is located on the driver's side windshield pillar

The vehicle identification plate is mounted above the right/front headlight just under the hood hinge

which the car was manufactured, G referring to Germany.

The second column indicates the assembly plant, S in this case S for Saarlouis.

The third indicates the car model, in this case F for Fiesta.

The fourth indicates the body style variation, in this case B for three door sedan.

The fifth represents the build year, for example U for 1978.

The sixth represents the build month (G for December).

2. The five numer suffix represents the position of the vehicle in the sequence of assembly (for example, 42263), starting with the number 10001.

ENGINE

The engine code may be found on the vehicle identification plate. All models use the L4 engine, which is an overhead valve, inline four of 1600 cc capacity.

Transaxle

The transaxle code may also be found on the vehicle identification plate, and on all models

is identified by code: T, referring to a 4 speed manual design.

Axle Ratio Code

The final drive axle ratio code is also shown on the vehicle identification plate, and is P for all models, referring to a ratio of 3.58:1.

ROUTINE MAINTENANCE

Replacing Air Cleaner and PCV Filter

The air cleaner keeps airborne dirt and dust out of the air flowing through the engine. Proper maintenance is vital, as a clogged element will enrichen the fuel/air mixture, restrict airflow and power, and allow excessive contamination of the oil with abrasives. The air cleaner and PCV filter are replaced every 30,000 miles or 30 months, whichever comes first.

1. Pull the two spark plug wires, that run through the retaining clip under the air cleaner duct, out of the clip.

2. Remove the two support bracket bolts at the air cleaner tray and the bolt attaching the bracket to the valve cover. *Do not loosen the air cleaner support bolts at the EGR valve and intake manifold!*

3. Remove the two nuts which fasten the cover to the air cleaner tray and remove the cover.

4. Inspect the grommet on the carburetor for deformation and replace it if necessary.

5. Inspect the new element and make sure the filter paper is intact and the seals have not been damaged. Wipe clean the sealing surfaces on the tray and cover with a clean rag. Put the new element into position on the tray.

6. Put a small amount of clean engine oil on the new crankcase filter pack. Then, remove the old pack and put the new one in position.

7. Replace the air cleaner cover and install cover nuts and the various support bracket mounting bolts. Reposition the spark plug wires in the retaining clip.

PCV Valve Cleaning

1. Disconnect all hoses from the oil filler cap, noting their locations, and remove the cap from the rocker cover.

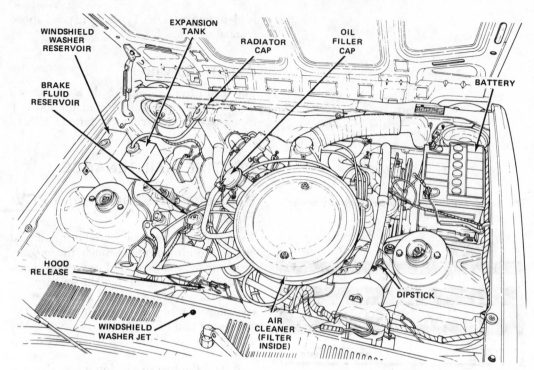

WINDSHIELD
WASHER
RESERVOIR

EXPANSION
TANK

RADIATOR
CAP

OIL
FILLER
CAP

BRAKE
FLUID
RESERVOIR

BATTERY

HOOD
RELEASE

DIPSTICK

WINDSHIELD
WASHER JET

AIR
CLEANER
(FILTER
INSIDE)

Locations of various items to be checked during routine maintenance

2. Soak the cap in a suitable (non-volatile) solvent. *Do not use gasoline!* The cap must not be taken apart, or soaked for more than 30 minutes.

3. Remove the cap from the solvent and shake dry (do not use compressed air). If it is still dirty, repeat step 2.

4. There is a calibrated orifice in the end of the oil filler hose connection in the colored insert. If the orifice is dirty, clean it as described above (in step 2). Handle gently to avoid damage to it. If it cannot be cleaned, replace it with a part of the same color.

5. Reinstall the orifice, and then reinstall the oil filler cap and connect all hoses.

Belts

CHECKING AND ADJUSTING

Belts should be checked at 1,500 miles and every 15,000 miles thereafter.

1. Remove the air cleaner as described above, to gain access to the belts.

2. Carefully examine the belts for cracks, a glazed (very smooth) appearance, or exposed and torn reinforcing cords and replace the belt where condition is poor or doubtful. See step 5 for replacement instructions.

3. Press firmly on the belt in the center of a free span. The belt should stretch or deflect ⅛ in. to ¼ in. if about one foot or less of belt spans the distance between the pulleys, and ⅛ to ½ in. if the span is longer than one foot.

4. If adjustment is necessary, slightly loosen the bolt on which the accessory pivots, and the adjusting bolt (which runs in a slotted bracket) and pull or pry the accessory away from the engine to tighten the belt, or allow it to move toward the engine to loosen the belt. Tighten the bolts and then recheck tension.

CAUTION: *If possible, put tension on the accessory with your bare hands. If a prybar must be used, pry carefully as close as possible to the belt pulley. If the engine uses an air pump with an aluminum housing, do not pry on the pump housing. Be very careful not to overtighten bolts that run into an aluminum housing. If you're in doubt about how much torque to use, use a torque wrench and torque to 15–18 ft lbs.*

5. To replace a belt, loosen the accessory's pivot bolt slightly, loosen the adjustment bolt (the one which runs in a slotted bracket) until there is no longer any tension on the bracket, and then push the accessory toward the engine until the bolt is at the inner end of the slot. *Do not attempt to install a belt by prying*

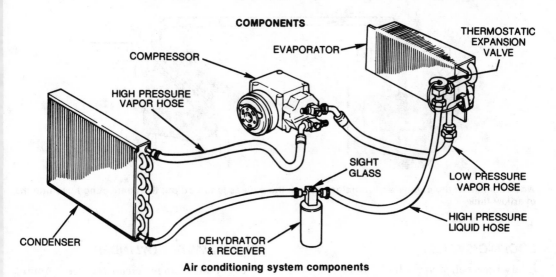

Air conditioning system components

it onto the pulleys. Then, adjust the belt as in step 4, but to the minimum deflection (⅛ in.)

6. Replace the air cleaner.

Air Conditioning
SAFETY WARNING

Do not attempt to tighten fittings or otherwise repair the system unless you have been trained in refrigeration repair as the system contains high pressure.

SIGHT GLASS CHECK

When placing the unit in service at the beginning of the summer season, make the following checks:

1. Operate the engine at approximately 1,500 rpm. Locate the sight glass, located on top of the receiver-drier, a small, black cylinder which is in the engine compartment.

2. Have someone turn the blower to high speed and switch the AIR lever to A/C position while you watch the sight glass. The glass should first become clouded with bubbles, and then clear up. Operate the unit for five minutes while watching the glass. If outside temperature is 68° F or above, the glass should be perfectly clear. If there is a continuous stream of bubbles, it indicates that the system has a slight leak and will require additional refrigerant. If the system starts and runs and no bubbles appear, the entire refrigerant charge has been lost. *Stop the system and do not operate it until it has been repaired.*

3. Inspect all lines for signs of oil accumulation, which would indicate leakage. If leaks are indicated, have the leak repaired by a professional mechanic. Do not operate the system if it seems to have leaks as this can aggravate possible damage to the system.

4. Check the tension and condition of the compressor drive belt and adjust its tension or replace as necessary.

5. Test the blower to make sure that it operates at all speeds and have it repaired if it does not.

In winter, operate the air conditioner for 10 minutes with the engine at 1,500 rpm once a month to circulate oil to the compressor seal, thus preventing leakage.

Fluid Level Checks
ENGINE OIL

At every stop for fuel, check the engine oil as follows:

1. Wait until the engine has been turned off for several minutes, so that as much as possible of the oil will have returned to the crankcase. Then, remove the dipstick.

2. Wipe the dipstick clean with a clean rag.

3. Reinsert the dipstick and push it down until it has fully seated.

4. Remove the stick and check the level. If oil has fallen to the lower mark, add 1 quart.

5. If you wish, you may carefully fill the oil pan to the upper mark on the dipstick with less than a full quart. Do not, however, add a full quart when that will overfill the crankcase, as this could cause engine damage. The excess oil will generally be consumed at an excessive rate even if no damage to the engine seals occurs.

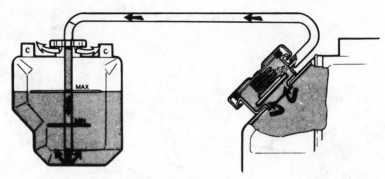

When coolant in the engine and radiator expand, the excess is forced out the connecting hose into the overflow tank

COOLING SYSTEM

Every time you stop for fuel, check the level of coolant in the reserve tank. If coolant level drops to a point slightly below the "MIN" label on the tank, refill the tank with a 50-50 mixture of water and ethylene glycol antifreeze (use a stronger mixture where required by extreme cold temperatures). If the level drops to near the bottom of the tank, air can be sucked into the radiator, and the only way to be sure of how much water is in the system is to remove the radiator cap. The cap should be removed about once a month, anyway, to make sure that the radiator is full. Make sure the engine is cold when removing the cap. The coolant level should be no lower than one inch below the filler neck.

Fill both the radiator and the reserve tank (do not fill the reserve tank above the "MAX" line). Then, as the system heats and cools, air will be purged from the top of the radiator and the hose connecting radiator and tank.

BRAKE MASTER CYLINDER

At every oil change, clean the area around the master cylinder reservoir cap, and then remove it to observe the fluid level. If the fluid is not above the minimum level mark, add DOT 3 or DOT 4 type fluid, or Ford part number ESA-M6C25-A. Do not overfill the reservoir, as air space must be left in the top of the reservoir to allow for fluid expansion.

TRANSAXLE

Each time the car is lubricated (at engine oil changes) the transmission fluid should be checked. The car must have been sitting still on level ground for a while before making the check. Remove the filler plug with an open end wrench and, if fluid does not flow right out, insert your finger into the hole to check for fluid. The level should be within ¼ inch of the lower edge of the hole. If the level is low, refill the transaxle with manual transmission fluid which meets Ford specification ESW-M2C-83C. Because of the difficulty of getting fluid into the transmission, it might pay you to buy a bulb and syringe unit de-

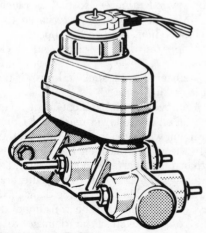

Brake master cylinder

Transmission oil level is checked by removing this plug, located on the side of the unit under the hood

Capacities

Year	Engine Displacement (cc)	Engine Crankcase (Quarts)		Transmission① (Pints)	Gasoline Tank (Gallons)	Cooling System (Quarts)
		With Filter	Without Filter			
1978–80	1598	3.5	3.0	5	10	6.6②

① Includes final drive
② Add one quart if a cooling reservoir is used

signed for just this purpose, if fluid level is low.

Add the fluid until it reaches the bottom edge of the hole, and then reinstall the plug. Make sure that if any dirt gets onto the plug, you wipe it clean before installing it. Do not force the plug when turning it back into the hole, but try to hold it perfectly straight and then turn gently until the threads of the plug and hole fit together smoothly and without force. Tighten the plug until it is just snug with the open end wrench.

STEERING GEAR

No periodic lubrication is required.

BATTERY

Check the fluid level every three months in mild or cold weather, and about every month in temperatures over 80 degrees F. The battery case is made of a translucent plastic which will show the water level on the outside. "MAX" and "MIN" marks are placed on the case to let you know whether more water is required.

To add water, remove the cap or caps of the cell(s) needing water by unscrewing them. Clean tap water may be used if the water in your area is not unusually hard. Distilled water is better if you can get it and must be used if only hard tap water is avail-

able to avoid formation of deposits on the battery plates. Add the water slowly to avoid splashing the water/acid mixture out of the cells and to avoid overfilling, which could excessively dilute the mixture. Make sure to screw the filler caps back on snugly. In winter, run the engine for a few minutes after filling the battery in order to mix the new water with the acid in the cells or it may freeze and damage the battery plates or cells. If the battery requires frequent addition of water, have the battery and charging system checked for mechanical or electrical problems.

WINDSHIELD WASHER TANK

The windshield washer tank is in the left/front corner of the engine compartment. If you have a rear window washer, the tank is located in the spare tire area. You can use plain water in summer weather, but the premixed solvents available will not only provide protection against freezing, but will dissolve grime better than plain water. Every fall, as soon as freezing weather threatens, fill the tank or tanks with solvent and run the system through several cycles to flush plain water from the system.

Tires and Wheels

TIRE ROTATION

Check the tires periodically for wear. If there is an uneven wear pattern (such as wear on one edge of a tire), have the front suspension inspected and aligned, and then rotate the tires. Tires should be rotated every so often (about 6,000 miles) to equalize wear, even if all suspension components are in good shape.

Rotate tires front to rear (do not X them) as shown in the illustration. If a high pressure temporary spare is provided with your car, do not use that tire in the process.

CHECKING TIRE PRESSURES

Use an accurate tire gauge to check tire pressures-gauges used on air pumps are not accu-

The battery. Each of the six battery cells has its own screw-on type filler cap

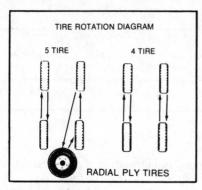

Tire rotation pattern

rate enough for optimum tire life. Tires must be inflated cold (after less than a mile of driving). The decal on the right hand door lists the required pressures. Make sure to change pressures as required after tire rotation.

Check tire pressures about once a week until you establish that a longer interval (say two weeks to a month) will still not result in a substantial change in pressure. Remember that in the fall, cooler weather will cause tire pressures to drop, causing a need to add air more frequently. With a sudden increase in temperatures, as in the spring, pressures can go too high.

TIRE REPLACEMENT/USE OF SNOW TIRES

Replace original equipment tires with tires sized and rated for weight as shown on the tire sticker. When using snow tires, make sure they too are of the same type and rating, as mixing of radial and bias ply or bias belted tires will cause improper handling of the car. Mount the snow tires on the front wheels.

Fuel Filter

The fuel filter should be replaced immediately in case there is any evidence of dirt having gotten into the fuel, or about every 30,000 miles. If the engine seems to be suffering from fuel starvation, remove the filter as described below, and blow through it to see if it is clogged. If air won't pass through it fairly easily, or if there is a lot of dirt visible in the inlet passage, replace it.

FILTER REPLACEMENT

1. Make sure the engine is cold, or spilled fuel could ignite and cause serious injury and/or damage! Open the hood. If you have fender covers, install them. Otherwise, be careful not to spill fuel on the paintwork. Place a rag under the filter and connections.

2. Use a pair of pliers to squeeze the ends of the crimp clamps together and move them toward the center of the hose connecting the fuel line and the outer end of the fuel filter. Then, use an open-end wrench on the flats of the filter to turn it clockwise and remove it from the carburetor.

3. Screw a new filter onto the carburetor, starting the threads carefully and without force to prevent cross threading. Tighten the filter snugly with the wrench.

4. Install a new hose, with two clamps at its center, onto the filter connection and the fuel line. Make sure the hose is on tightly at

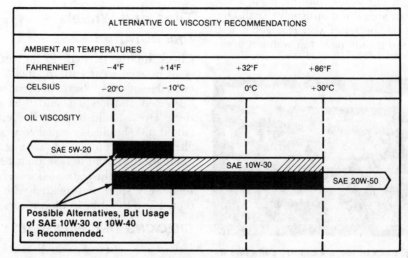

Oil viscosity chart

both ends, and then position the two clamps right near either end of the hose.

5. Remove the rag and dispose of it in a safe place (such as a sealed container).

LUBRICATION

Oil and Fuel Recommendations

Oil meeting API classification SE (the best type available) is recommended for use in your Fiesta. Viscosity grades 10W-30 or 10W-40 are recommended, but you may also use 5W-20 in very cold weather, or 20W-50 in very hot weather. See the chart below.

Multi grade oils are also advantageous in that they eliminate the need to change oil merely because of a change in the weather. If you are using the very light 5W-20 grade, and the weather goes above 10 degrees F. for more than just a couple of days, make sure to change your oil to one recommended for use in warmer temperatures right away.

The only fuel recommended for your Fiesta is unleaded gasoline. Use of leaded fuel will quickly interfere with operation of the catalytic converter and in just a few tankfuls render it useless. This will cause the emission of much greater amounts of hydrocarbons and carbon monoxide from the exhaust system. The fuel should have a Research Octane Number rating of 91, or an Antiknock Index of 87. Most commercially marketed unleaded fuels meet these specifications. Ratings are usually posted on the pump.

1978 Maintenance Intervals Chart

Maintenance Operation	*Service Interval (months/miles in thousands)*
Change Engine Oil [1]	1.5 and then every 7.5
Replace Oil Filter [1]	1.5 and then every 7.5
Check Engine Valve Clearance	1.5 and then every 15
Check Coolant Condition and Protection	30
Replace Coolant, Check Hoses and Clamps	36 months/45,000 miles
Check Drive Belts	1.5 and then every 15
Check Air Cleaner Temperature Control	45
Replace Spark Plugs [2]	G:15, H:30
Clean PCV Valve Assembly	G:15, H:30
Check and Adjust Fast Idle	1.5
Check Curb Idle	G:1.5 and then every 15 H:1.5 and then every 30
Check Carburetor Bowl Vent	G:15, H:30
Check Choke	G:15, H:30

1978 Maintenance Intervals Chart (cont.)

Maintenance Operation	Service Interval (months/miles in thousands)
Replace Air Cleaner and Crankcase Filter [3]	30
Check Cylinder Head and Intake and Exhaust Manifold Bolt Torques	1.5
Inspect Brake Linings	15
Inspect Brake Lines and Hoses	30
Lubricate Parking Brake and Clutch Cables	15

Note: The passenger side door pillar bears a code letter which refers to a particular maintenance interval in some of the operations listed here. Note whether the car bears the code "G" or "H" and follow the interval for the code if a distinction is made in the listing.

1. Change engine oil and filter every 7,500 miles or six months, whichever occurs first. If you are driving less than 10 miles in weather colder than 10 degrees F. most of the time, doing a lot of idling or running mostly at very low speeds, or the air is very dusty, change oil every 3,000 miles/3 months and change the filter every other oil change.

2. If the weather is colder than 10 degrees F. and most of your trips are less than 10 miles, you are idling or driving at low speeds most of the time, or the air is very dusty, clean and gap spark plugs every 6,000 miles.

3. More often under very dusty operating conditions.

1979–80 Maintenance Intervals Chart

Maintenance Operation	Service Interval (months/miles in thousands)
Change Engine Oil [1]	1.5 and then every 7.5
Replace Oil Filter [1]	1.5 and then every 7.5
Check Engine Valve Clearance	15
Check Engine Coolant Protection, Hoses, Clamps	At 12 months
Replace Coolant	50
Checks Belts and Belt Tension	At 1.5 and then every 15
Check Air Cleaner Temperature Control	45

1979–80 Maintenance Intervals Chart (cont.)

Maintenance Operation	Service Interval (months/miles in thousands)
Replace Spark Plugs [2]	F:15, B:30
Clean PCV Valve	F:15, B:30
Check Curb and Fast Idle Speeds	At 1.5, and then F:15, B:30
Check Choke	F:15, B:30
Replace Air Cleaner and Crankcase Filter [3]	30
Inspect Brake Pads and Linings	7.5
Inspect Brake Lines and Hoses	30
Lubricate Parking Brake and Clutch Cables	15
Check Thermactor Delay Valve	F:15, B:30

Note: The passenger side door pillar bears a code letter which refers to a particular maintenance interval in some of the operations listed here. Note whether the car bears the code "B" or "F" and follow the interval for the code if a distinction is made in the listing.

1. Change engine oil and filter every 7,500 miles or 12 months whichever occurs first. If you are driving less than 10 miles in weather colder than 10 degrees F. most of the time, doing a lot of idling, or running mostly at very low speeds, or if the air is very dusty, change oil every 3 months or 3,000 miles, whichever comes first, and change the filter every other oil change.

2. If the weather is colder than 10 degrees F. and most of your trips are less than 10 miles, you are idling or driving at low speeds most of the time, or the air is very dusty, clean and gap the spark plugs every 6,000 miles.

3. More often under very dusty operating conditions.

If your car is properly tuned and yet exhibits a tendency to knock slightly under load, a switch of gasoline brands may enable you to find a fuel which performs better in your particular engine.

CHANGING ENGINE OIL AND FILTER

1. Drive the car until the engine is hot (this promotes complete draining of old oil). Shut off engine.

2. Apply parking brake tightly and block the wheels. Put a pan of about 1 gallon capacity under the oil drain plug. Then, crawl under the car and with the proper size open end wrench, remove the oil drain plug.

3. Clean the oil drain plug with a clean rag and install a new gasket.

4. Using an oil filter strap wrench positioned so it will tighten as you turn counterclockwise, turn the filter off the engine mounting until it is loose. Unscrew the filter the rest of the way, holding it with a heavy

Removing the oil drain plug

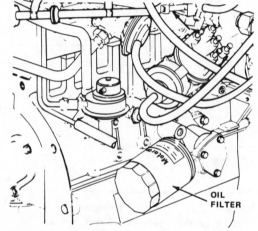

The oil filter is located on the side of the engine, as shown, and is accessible under the hood

rag to keep it from burning your fingers. When the unit comes loose, turn the mounting base upward to avoid spilling hot oil.

5. Wipe clean the filter mount on the engine with a clean rag. Coat the rubber gasket on the new filter with clean engine oil, applying it with a finger. Carefully start the filter onto the engine mount and turn it until it just touches the engine mounting surface at the gasket. Then, turn the filter just ½ turn farther.

6. Install the oil drain plug into the crankcase, and tighten it just snug (15–23 ft lbs).

7. Remove the oil filler cap from the top of the engine and *slowly* refill the crankcase with the specified amount of oil.

8. Reinstall the filler cap. Start the engine and run it at idle (not faster) until the oil light goes out. Continue running engine as you check around the filter base and drain plug for leaks.

9. Stop the engine, allow it to sit for several minutes, and then recheck oil level and add if necessary.

Body Lubrication

A number of spray lubricants are available in pressurized cans, such as WD-40, CRC, or Ford part number D7AZ-19584-A. These kits include a small tube which fits in the orifice at the top of the can for spraying into spots which are difficult to reach. Spray this lubricant every few months onto fuel filler door hinges, the hinges at the bottoms of the rear door supports, on hood and door hinges and hinge checks, and the auxiliary hood catch.

Spray a lock cylinder lubricant such as Ford part number D8AZ-19587-A or equivalent into door and ignition lock cylinders; then, insert the key and work the cylinder back and forth several times.

Apply a silicone lubricant to all weatherstrips occasionally to prolong their life by preventing them from sticking to doors and hood.

Chassis Lubrication

The chassis of the Fiesta is lubricated for life, including the front wheel bearings. The wheel bearings are repacked only as an integral part of repair procedures; for information on this procedure, see Chapter 9.

PUSHING, TOWING AND JUMP STARTING

Push Starting

Pushing the car to start it is feasible with the Fiesta, but must be accomplished with great care, as damage to bumpers, etc. frequently occurs. Make sure bumpers align exactly before attempting a push start.

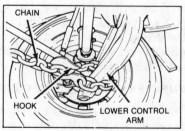

Location of tow chains

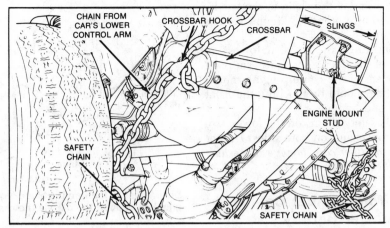

The crossbar should rest on the elbow of the center engine support, below and clear of the mounting stud

Turn the ignition on in the car to be started. Accelerate steadily with the push car in order to maintain bumper contact—avoid shifting gears. At about 15 miles per hour, depress the clutch and pull the transmission into second gear. Depress the accelerator once and then release if the engine is cold, and then *gently* release the clutch until it

becomes fully engaged. As soon as the engine starts, signal the driver of the push car to back off.

Towing

Tow by running tow chains around the lower control arm on both sides as shown. Then, at-

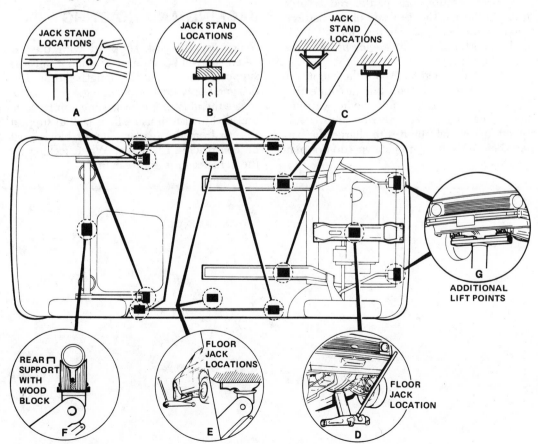

Jack, jackstand, and additional lift point locations. Lift the vehicle *only* where shown

tach the other end of the chain to the truck's cross bar as shown. Finally, lift the vehicle about one foot.

This should cause the crossbar to rest on the elbow of the center engine support, below and clear of the center engine mount stud. The sling should be touching the front lower panel and bumper.

Now, hook safety chains on the lower arm next to the tow chains on both sides. *Do not use J hooks as they can damage driveshaft boots. Do not tow from the rear.*

Starting With Jumper Cables and a Booster Battery

1. Start the engine in the vehicle with the booster battery and allow it to run for a few minutes. Park the vehicles near each other, but far enough apart so their bumpers are not touching.

2. Lay a heavy rag over the vent caps of both batteries. Turn on the heater or air conditioner blower motor. Everything else should be off.

3. Connect the ends of the red colored cable to the Positive (+) side of the battery. Connect the black cable to the minus (−) side of the booster and to the *engine block* of the car to be started.

4. Start the engine. Allow the engine to run at normal idle speed while disconnecting the cables (this may require some warming up). Then, make sure it runs above idle speed for several minutes to charge the battery before shutting it off, if you do not plan to drive.

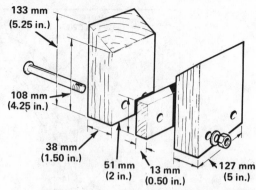

133 mm (5.25 in.)

108 mm (4.25 in.)

38 mm (1.50 in.)

51 mm (2 in.)

13 mm (0.50 in.)

127 mm (5 in.)

Dimensions of the wooden block required in using a jack to support the car via the rear axle

5. Disconnect the cables in exact reverse order, beginning with the removal of the negative cable from the engine block of the car being started.

6. Remove and dispose of the rags used to collect possible spillover from the batteries. Be careful in handling them.

JACKING AND HOISTING

Never use the jack supplied with the car when you will be under it or when it must be supported for a significant length of time. It is designed only for tire changing.

See the illustration for jacking points. Note that if you wish to use a floor jack to support the car from the rear, a support block must be constructed as shown. When jacking up the vehicle, raise the rear first.

Tune-Up

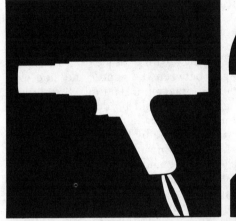

TUNE-UP PROCEDURES

The procedures described in this chapter are performed periodically to replace worn parts or to restore optimum operating clearances or adjustments where engine wear effects them. Optimum economy, performance, cold/damp weather starting, and emission control are all affected considerably by these adjustments and parts replacement procedures. Careful replacement of them at the specified intervals and using high quality replacement parts will amply reward you with a smooth running and reliable engine.

A general section describing more detailed tune-up procedures and ways in which your tune-up work can help to locate trouble in the engine can be found in Chapter 11.

Spark Plugs

While spark plugs require much less maintenance on cars using unleaded fuel and electronic ignition systems, they still must be changed periodically and, if the vehicle is driven under adverse conditions, cleaned periodically. See the vehicle maintenance chart in Chapter 1 for the definition of adverse conditions. When driven under these conditions, the plugs should be removed and cleaned and gapped every 6,000 miles. Plugs should be replaced every 15,000 miles on some vehicles, and every 30,000 miles on others, depending upon the designation shown on the engine compartment sticker. See the vehicle maintenance chart in Chapter 1.

The type of plug used in the Fiesta is

Tune-Up Specifications

When analyzing compression test results, look for uniformity among cylinders, rather than specific pressures.

Year	Engine Displace (cc)	SPARK PLUGS Type	Gap (in.)	DISTRIBUTOR Point Dwell (deg)	Point Gap (in.)	IGNITION TIMING (deg) MT	AT	Intake Valve Opens (deg)	Fuel Pump Pressure (psi)	Idle Speed (rpm)	VALVE CLEAR (in.) In	Ex
1978–80	1598	AWRF-32	.050	Electronic		12B	—	29B	3.5–6	*	.010	.021

B Before Top Dead Center
* See engine compartment sticker
Part numbers in this chart are not recommendations by Chilton for any product by brand name.

shown in the tune-up specifications chart above. This designation refers to the original equipment brand (Motorcraft). You may also use plugs made by other manufacturers if they are cross referenced to replace this particular type of Motorcraft plug.

Spark Plug Replacement or Cleaning

1. Remove the air cleaner housing as follows:

A. Remove the two nuts and flat washers from the air cleaner cover.

B. Remove the screw clamp from the fresh air hose at the air cleaner and pull the hose off the air cleaner spout.

C. Loosen the PCV hose clamp and disconnect the hose.

D. Disconnect the fuel evaporative hose, and the vacuum hoses at the rear and left side of the housing.

E. Remove the three housing bolts from the brackets.

F. Disconnect Nos 3 and 4 spark plug wires from the bottom of the air cleaner spout.

G. Lift the housing slightly at the rear and loosen the clamp bolt and disconnect the thermactor pump hose at the bottom of the housing. Disconnect the vacuum hose from the Tee at the rear of the carburetor.

H. Lift the housing out of the engine compartment.

2. Remove the plug wires from the spark plugs by grasping the rubber boot at the spark plug end with your fingers or a plug wire removal tool, and twisting the wire while pulling it off the plug. Make sure to pull the boot and not the wire to avoid damaging conducting material. The original equipment plug wires are numbered, so you can pull them all off without marking them. If replacement wires which are not marked are used, mark them by wrapping a piece of tape around each and writing the cylinder number (1 through 4 starting on the right side) on the tape.

3. Clean the area around each spark plug to prevent dirt from getting into the engine when the plugs are removed. This may be done with compressed air or a clean rag.

4. With a ⅝ in. (16mm) deep well socket, remove the plugs. You can reinstall the plugs in any order—they need not go back into the same cylinder. However, it is a good idea to keep track of the cylinder each came out of in

order to locate any sign of trouble in the engine.

5. Analyze the appearance of the plugs and, if they are not normal, take appropriate action as described in the chart. If the maintenance chart calls for spark plug replacement, replace them even if their appearance is nearly normal.

6. If you will reuse the plugs, clean them thoroughly with a wire brush to remove all deposits.

7. Using a wire type feeler gauge, check the gap between the center and side electrodes by dragging a .050 in. wire through the gap. This should be done both on new and used plugs. If the gap is incorrect, bend the *side* electrode by hooking the slot in the spark plug tool near the bent portion of the side electrode, and bend it so the gap increases or decreases. Recheck the gap and readjust the gap until it is correct.

8. Reinstall the plugs, torquing to 10–15 ft-lbs.

9. Using a small screwdriver (make sure it is clean), apply a thin layer of silicone dielectric compound (such as Ford Part D7AZ-19A331-A or equivalent) to the entire interior surface of each spark plug boot. Then, reconnect each wire to the proper plug.

10. Reinstall the air cleaner as follows:

A. Position the housing over the carburetor, and connect the vacuum hose to the Tee at the rear of the carburetor.

B. Reconnect the air pump hose on the underside of the housing and tighten the clamp.

C. Position the air cleaner spout under the accelerator cable and make sure the heat riser tube is in position over the heat shroud.

D. Reconnect plug wires for Nos. 3 and 4 cylinders to the clip on the underside of the housing.

E. Press the housing onto the carburetor so the housing seats in the gasket without crimping it.

F. Install the bolts securing the housing to the brackets and tighten them (if you have a torque wrench and wish to use it, torque to 5–7 ft-lbs).

G. Reconnect PCV, fuel evaporative, and vacuum hoses to the housing, making sure they are routed smoothly and without kinks or stretch.

H. Install the two nuts and flat washers that go onto the air cleaner cover.

Spark Plug Analysis

GAP BRIDGED

Identified by deposit build-up closing gap between electrodes.

Caused by oil or carbon fouling. Replace plug, or, if deposits are not excessive, the plug can be cleaned

OIL FOULED

Identified by wet black deposits on the insulator shell or electrodes caused by excessive oil entering combustion chamber through worn rings and pistons, excessive clearance between valve guides and stems, or worn or loose bearings. Replace the plug. If engine is not repaired, use a hotter plug

CARBON FOULED

Identified by black dry fluffy carbon deposits on insulator tips, exposed shell surfaces and electrodes.

Caused by too cold a plug, weak ignition, dirty air cleaner, defective fuel pump, too rich a fuel mixture, improperly operating heat riser or excessive idling. Can be cleaned

NORMAL

Identified by severely eroded or worn electrodes.
Caused by normal wear. Should be replaced

WORN

Identified by light tan or gray deposits on the firing tip

PRE-IGNITION

Identified by melted electrodes and possibly blistered insulator. Metallic deposits on insulator indicate engine damage.

Caused by wrong type of fuel, incorrect ignition timing or advance, too hot a plug, burnt valves or engine overheating. Replace the plug

OVERHEATING

Identified by a white or light gray insulator with small black or gray brown spots and with bluish-burnt appearance of electrodes. Caused by engine overheating, wrong type of fuel, loose spark plugs, too hot a plug, low fuel pump pressure or incorrect ignition timing. Replace the plug

FUSED SPOT DEPOSIT

Identified by melted or spotty deposits resembling bubbles or blisters.

Caused by sudden acceleration. Can be cleaned if not excessive. Otherwise replace plug

Magnetic Pickup Assembly
REMOVAL AND INSTALLATION

1. Remove the distributor cap, adapter, and rotor and disconnect the distributor wiring connector.

2. With a small gear puller or two small screwdrivers, lift or pry the armature up off the advance plate sleeve. Remove the roll pin.

3. Remove the snap ring, flat washer, and wavy washer that secure the pickup coil to the lower plate.

4. Remove the magnetic pickup ground screw and lift the assembly from the distributor.

5. To install, position the pickup assembly over the fixed baseplate and insert the pickup assembly post into the hole in the vacuum advance arm.

6. Slide the wiring grommet into the slot at the edge of the lower plate. Install the ground screw. Install the washers and snap ring which secure the pickup coil to the lower plate.

7. Install the armature on the advance plate sleeve.

8. Make sure the roll pin engages the matching slots.

9. Install the distributor rotor, and cap, and connect the wiring connector.

Ignition Timing
ADJUSTMENT

1. Clean the timing marks with a rag. These are located on the surface of the front cover (right side of the engine). Paint a white mark on the line for 12 degrees on the front cover. Also paint the notch in the crankshaft pulley.

2. Disconnect all vacuum line(s) going to the distributor and plug them with a golf tee or something similar.

3. Connect a timing light to No. 1 cylinder. The light may also have to be hooked up to the battery—see manufacturer's instructions. Ford recommends an inductive type light which does not require disconnecting the spark plug wire. Also, connect a tachometer between the coil minus terminal and ground.

4. Operate the engine until it is warm. Check idle speed and compare it to the speed specified for setting ignition timing on the engine compartment sticker. If necessary, adjust the idle speed (see the section of Idle Speed and Mixture Adjustment later in this chapter).

NOTE: *Be careful not to allow any of the timing light or tachometer wires, or parts of your clothing, to become entangled in moving belts, fan, etc.*

5. Aim the timing light at the timing marks. If they do not align, loosen the distributor hold-down bolt and rotate the distributor very slowly while watching the marks until the marks align. Tighten the hold-down bolt and recheck timing. Reset if necessary.

6. Unplug and reconnect distributor vacuum lines. Check the idle speed, and reset to normal idle (as specified on the engine compartment sticker) if necessary.

7. Stop the engine and remove instruments. If the plug wire to No. 1 cylinder had to be disconnected, make sure to coat the inside of the rubber boot with silicone grease as described in the Spark Plug Removal and Installation procedure above.

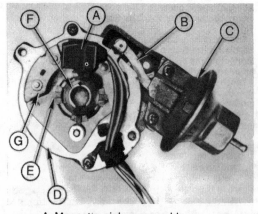

A Magnetic pickup assembly
B Vacuum advance link
C Vacuum advance-retard assembly
D Fixed base plate
E Armature
F Advance plate sleeve
G Stator

Distributor components

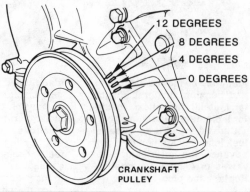

12 DEGREES
8 DEGREES
4 DEGREES
0 DEGREES

CRANKSHAFT PULLEY

Timing marks

Valve Lash

ADJUSTMENT

1. Run the engine until it is hot, and shut off. Remove the air cleaner housing as described above under Spark Plug Replacement. Disconnect and move other hoses or wires after marking them, as necessary. Then, remove the engine valve cover.

2. The rocker shaft mounting bolts (there are three) are located at about the height of the valve adjusting nuts (which are at the ends of the rockers), between adjacent rocker levers. Torque these bolts to 25–30 ft-lbs.

3. The valves are numbered from 1 through 8 starting on the right or thermostat housing end of the engine. Install a remote starter switch to the starter solenoid according to manufacturer's instructions. Then, bump the engine over with the switch a little bit at a time until valves 1 and 6 are fully open—that is, down all the way. Now, check clearance of valves 3 and 8.

   NOTE: *Clearances differ for different valves, depending on whether they are intake or exhaust valves.*
   Use these clearances:

Valve No.	Type	Clearance
1	Exhaust	.021
2	Intake	.010
3	Intake	.010
4	Exhaust	.021
5	Exhaust	.021
6	Intake	.010
7	Intake	.010
8	Exhaust	.021

For example, adjust valve No. 3 to .010 in., and valve No. 8 to .021 in. (use that size gauge). To check the clearance, insert the gauge between the tip of the valve and the rocker lever from the front or rear edge of the valve tip; that is, along the crankshaft centerline, not from one side of the engine to the other. If the valve is adjusted too tightly, the gauge will not pass between the two parts or will pass through only with great difficulty. If the gauge passes through without any resistance at all (there should be a slight pull required) the valve is too loose. To adjust, put a $7/16$ in. socket wrench or box wrench on the nut at the opposite end of the rocker arm. Turn the nut clockwise to tighten the adjustment or counterclockwise to loosen it. Remove the wrench from the nut and recheck the adjustment. Repeat the procedure until there is just a slight pull.

4. Repeat the adjustment procedure described in Step 3 for valves 5 & 7, 1 & 6, and 2 & 4. See the chart and rotate the crankshaft with the remote starter switch to open the valves listed in the top half of the chart before adjusting each set of valves.

5. Clean all gasket material from the cylinder head and valve cover. Then, reinstall the cover with a new gasket. Torque attaching screws to 2.5–3.5 ft lbs.

6. Reinstall or reconnect all the components that were moved to gain clearance. If plug wires have been disturbed, be sure to apply silicone lubricant when reconnecting them as described in the Spark Plug Replacement procedure above.

7. Start the engine and check for oil or vacuum leaks.

Idle Speed Adjustment

1. Connect a tachometer, bring the engine to normal operating temperature, and shut it off.

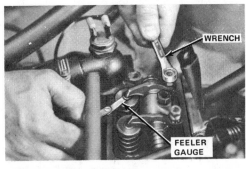

Adjusting valve clearances

Fully open these valve numbers	1&6	2&4	3&8	5&7
Check valve clearances of these valves	3&8	5&7	1&6	2&4

Table showing valves open and the valves to be adjusted at each of four crankshaft positions

2. Disconnect the leads from the radiator fan temperature switch located in the thermostat housing, and connect the two leads with a jumper wire so the fan runs all the time.

3. Remove the air cleaner as described in the Spark Plug Replacement procedure above.

4. If there is a spark delay valve in the distributor vacuum advance line, remove this valve and connect a jumper hose to the two open ends.

5. *If* there is a PVS valve between the EGR valve and the carburetor vacuum port, disconnect the vacuum hose at the EGR valve and plug it.

6. Turn off all accessories.

7. Start the engine and run it at about 2,500 rpm for 15 seconds; then allow it to stabilize at idle speed.

8. Check the curb idle speed figure on the engine compartment sticker and compare it with the reading on the tachometer. If necessary, adjust the idle solenoid or idle speed screw to get the proper idle speed. If the idle speed is changed, loosen the locknut on the dashpot (which controls how fast the throttle closes when it is released) and rotate the dashpot in or out to restore the clearance between the dashpot stem and throttle linkage. Then, tighten the dashpot locknut.

9. When speed is right, turn off the engine. Reinstall the air cleaner as described above under Spark Plug Replacement. Reconnect the radiator fan switch leads, the spark delay valve, and EGR valve, as necessary. Remove the tachometer.

Idle Mixture Adjustment

The procedure is performed only if all tune-up adjustments are correct, there are no vacuum leaks and engine idle is very poor or the engine cannot be made to deliver required carbon-dioxide levels. It is not required in normal service or maintenance. A special removal tool such as Ford Part number T75L-9500-A and a replacement tamperproof mixture adjustment plug are required.

1. Start the engine, bring it to operating temperature, and then shut it off. Install a tachometer. If the fuel evaporative system has a purge valve vacuum hose (running from the intake manifold to the evaporative canister), trace the line back from the canister to the first connection, disconnect the line and plug both ends. Then, disconnect the evaporative emission purge hose at the air cleaner and plug the nipple. Finally, disconnect the crankcase ventilation closure hose from the air cleaner and plug the nipple.

2. Using the special tool, remove the idle mixture tamperproof plug. Adjust the idle speed as described in the procedure above (Step 8). Back out the mixture adjustment screw to give the highest possible rpm.

3. Readjust the idle speed to the speed specified under "alternate idle speed change rpm" on the engine compartment sticker. Then, adjust the mixture screw back and forth to gain the highest possible rpm. Readjust the idle speed screw to the "alternate idle speed change rpm". Repeat the mixture and speed adjustments very carefully until the specified speed occurs when the mixture screw is adjusted to give the best possible mixture. In other words, turning the mixture screw in either direction from the optimum point should cause the rpm to fall below the "alternate idle speed change rpm", but at the optimum point, rpm should be as specified.

4. Very carefully turn the mixture screw in just until the rpm drops by the amount specified in under "alternate idle speed change rpm" on the sticker.

5. Turn the engine off, and install a new tamperproof plug in the carburetor.

6. Reconnect the vacuum hoses disconnected in Step 1.

Engine and Engine Rebuilding

ENGINE ELECTRICAL

Understanding the Engine Electrical System

The engine electrical system can be broken down into three separate and distinct systems: (1) the starting system (2) the charging system (3) the ignition system.

BATTERY AND STARTING SYSTEM

Basic Operating Principles

The battery is the first link in the chain of mechanisms which work together to provide cranking of the automobile engine. In most modern cars, the battery is a lead-acid electrochemical device consisting of six two-volt (2 V) subsections connected in series so the unit is capable of producing approximately 12 V of electrical pressure. Each subsection, or cell, consists of a series of positive and negative plates held a short distance apart in a solution of sulfuric acid and water. The two types of plates are of dissimilar metals. This causes a chemical reaction to be set up, and it is this reaction which produces current flow from the battery when its positive and negative terminals are connected to an electrical appliance such as a lamp or motor. The continued transfer of electrons would eventually convert the sulfuric acid in the electrolyte to water, and make the two plates identical in chemical composition. As electrical energy is removed from the battery, its voltage output tends to drop. Thus, measuring battery voltage and battery electrolyte composition are two ways of checking the ability of the unit to supply power. During the starting of the engine, electrical energy is removed from the battery. However, if the charging circuit is in good condition and the operating conditions are normal, the power removed from the battery will be replaced by the generator (or alternator) which will force electrons back through the battery, reversing the normal flow, and restoring the battery to its original chemical state.

The battery and starting motor are linked by very heavy electrical cables designed to minimize resistance to the flow of current. Generally, the major power supply cable that leaves the battery goes directly to the starter, while other electrical system needs are supplied by a smaller cable. During starter operation, power flows from the battery to the starter and is grounded through the car's frame and the battery's negative ground strap.

The starting motor is a specially designed, direct current electric motor capable of producing a very great amount of power for its size. One thing that allows the motor to produce a great deal of power is its tremendous rotating speed. It drives the engine through a tiny pinion gear (attached to the starter's armature), which drives the very large flywheel ring gear at a greatly reduced speed. Another factor allowing it to produce so much power is that only intermittent operation is required of it. Thus, little allowance for air circulation is required, and the windings can be built into a very small space.

The starter solenoid is a magnetic device which employs the small current supplied by the starting switch circuit of the ignition switch. This magnetic action moves a plunger which mechanically engages the starter and electrically closes the heavy switch which connects it to the battery. The starting switch circuit consists of the starting switch contained within the ignition switch, a transmission neutral safety switch or clutch pedal switch, and the wiring necessary to connect these in series with the starter solenoid or relay.

A pinion, which is a small gear, is mounted to a one-way drive clutch. This clutch is splined to the starter armature shaft. When the ignition switch is moved to the "start" position, the solenoid plunger slides the pinion toward the flywheel ring gear via a collar and spring. If the teeth on the pinion and flywheel match properly, the pinion will engage the flywheel immediately. If the gear teeth butt one another, the spring will be compressed and will force the gears to mesh as soon as the starter turns far enough to allow them to do so. As the solenoid plunger reaches the end of its travel, it closes the contacts that connect the battery and starter and then the engine is cranked.

As soon as the engine starts, the flywheel ring gear begins turning fast enough to drive the pinion at an extremely high rate of speed. At this point, the one-way clutch begins allowing the pinion to spin faster than the starter shaft so that the starter will not operate at excessive speed. When the ignition switch is released from the starter position, the solenoid is de-energized, and a spring contained within the solenoid assembly pulls the gear out of mesh and interrupts the current flow to the starter.

Some starters employ a separate relay, mounted away from the starter, to switch the motor and solenoid current on and off. The relay thus replaces the solenoid electrical switch, but does not elminate the need for a solenoid mounted on the starter used to mechanically engage the starter drive gears. The relay is used to reduce the amount of current the starting switch must carry.

THE CHARGING SYSTEM
Basic Operating Principles

The automobile charging system provides electrical power for operation of the vehicle's ignition and starting systems and all the electrical accessories. The battery serves as an electrical surge or storage tank, storing (in chemical form) the energy originally produced by the engine-driven generator. The system also provides a means of regulating generator output to protect the battery from being overcharged and to avoid excessive voltage to the accessories.

The storage battery is a chemical device incorporating parallel lead plates in a tank containing a sulfuric acid-water solution. Adjacent plates are slightly dissimilar, and the chemical reaction of the two dissimilar plates produces electrical energy when the battery is connected to a load such as the starter motor. The chemical reaction is reversible, so that when the generator is producing a voltage (electrical pressure) greater than that produced by the battery, electricity is forced into the battery, and the battery is returned to its fully charged state.

The vehicle's generator is driven mechanically, through V belts, by the engine crankshaft. It consists of two coils of fine wire, one stationary (the "stator"), and one movable (the "rotor"). The rotor may also be known as the "armature," and consists of fine wire wrapped around an iron core which is mounted on a shaft. The electricity which flows through the two coils of wire (provided initially by the battery in some cases) creates an intense magnetic field around both rotor and stator, and the interaction between the two fields creates voltage, allowing the generator to power the accessories and charge the battery.

There are two types of generators; the earlier is the direct current (DC) type. The current produced by the DC generator is generated in the armature and carried off the spinning armature by stationary brushes contacting the commutator. The commutator is a series of smooth metal contact plates on the end of the armature. The commutator plates, which are separated from one another by a very short gap, are connected to the armature circuits so that current will flow in one direction only in the wires carrying the generator output. The generator stator consists of two stationary coils of wire which draw some of the output current of the generator to form a powerful magnetic field and create the interaction of fields which generates the voltage. The generator field is wired in series with the regulator.

Newer automobiles use alternating current generators or "alternators," because they are more efficient, can be rotated at higher speeds, and have fewer brush problems. In an alternator, the field rotates while all the current produced passes only through the stator windings. The brushes bear against continuous slip rings rather than a commutator. This causes the current produced to periodically reverse the direction of its flow. Diodes (electrical one-way switches) block the flow of current from traveling in the wrong direction. A series of diodes is wired together to permit the alternating flow of the stator to be converted to a pulsating, but unidirectional flow at the alternator output. The alternator's field is wired in series with the voltage regulator.

The regulator consists of several circuits. Each circuit has a core, or magnetic coil of wire, which operates a switch. Each switch is connected to ground through one or more resistors. The coil of wire responds directly to system voltage. When the voltage reaches the required level, the magnetic field created by the winding of wire closes the switch and inserts a resistance into the generator field circuit, thus reducing the output. The contacts of the switch cycle open and close many times each second to precisely control voltage.

While alternators are self-limiting as far as maximum current is concerned, DC generators employ a current regulating circuit which responds directly to the total amount of current flowing through the generator circuit rather than to the output voltage. The current regulator is similar to the voltage regulator except that all system current must flow through the energizing coil on its way to the various accessories.

SAFETY PRECAUTIONS

Observing these precautions will ensure safe handling of the electrical system components, and will avoid damage to the vehicle's electrical system:

A. Be *absolutely* sure of the polarity of a booster battery before making connections. Connect the cables positive to positive, and negative to negative. Connect positive cables first and then make the last connection to a ground on the body of the booster vehicle so that arcing cannot ignite hydrogen gas that may have accumulated near the battery. Even momentary connection of a booster battery with the polarity reversed will damage alternator diodes.

B. Disconnect both vehicle battery cables before attempting to charge a battery.

C. Never ground the alternator or generator output or battery terminal. Be cautious when using metal tools around a battery to avoid creating a short circuit between the terminals.

D. Never ground the field circuit between the alternator and regulator.

E. Never run an alternator or generator without load unless the field circuit is disconnected.

F. Never attempt to polarize an alternator.

G. Keep the regulator cover in place when taking voltage and current limiter readings.

H. Use insulated tools when adjusting the regulator.

I. Whenever DC generator-to-regulator wires have been disconnected, the generator *must* be repolarized. To do this with an externally grounded, light duty generator, momentarily place a jumper wire between the battery terminal and the generator terminal of the regulator. With an internally grounded heavy duty unit, disconnect the wire to the regulator field terminal and touch the regulator battery terminal with it.

ELECTRONIC IGNITION SYSTEMS
Basic Operating Principles

Electronic Ignition systems are not as complicated as they may first appear. In actual fact, they differ only slightly from conventional ignition systems. Like conventional ignition systems, electronic systems have two circuits: a primary circuit, and a secondary circuit. *The entire secondary circuit is exactly the same as the secondary circuit in a conventional ignition system. Also, the section of the primary circuit from the battery to the BAT terminal at the coil is exactly the same as a conventional ignition system.*

Electronic ignition systems differ from conventional ignition systems in the distributor component area. Instead of a distributor cam, breaker plate, points, and condenser, an electronic ignition system has an armature (called variously a trigger wheel, reluctor, etc.), a pickup coil (stator, sensor, etc.), and an electronic control module. Essentially, all electronic ignition systems operate in the following manner:

With the ignition switch turned on, primary (battery) current flows from the battery through the ignition switch to the coil primary windings. Primary current is turned on and off by the action of the armature as it revolves.

As the armature nears the pickup coil, it induces a voltage which signals the electronic module to turn off the coil primary current. A timing circuit in the module will turn the current on again after the coil field has collapsed. When the current is off, however, the magnetic field built up in the coil is allowed to collapse, inducing a high voltage in the secondary windings of the coil. It is now operating on the secondary ignition circuit, which, as noted, is exactly the same as a conventional ignition system.

Troubleshooting electronic ignition systems ordinarily requires the use of a voltmeter and/or an ohmmeter. Sometimes the use of an ammeter is required also. Because of differences in design and construction, troubleshooting is specific to each system.

Troubleshooting the Dura-Spark II Electronic Ignition System

1. First, pull the lead from the plus (+) side of the coil, and turn the ignition switch to the on position. Connect an ohmmeter between the plus (+) side of the battery and the metal inside the coil connector. The resistance should be 1.05–1.15 ohms. If the ohmmeter does not respond, or if resistance is too high, check for excessive resistance or an open circuit in the resistance wire between the ignition switch and the coil, the ignition switch itself, or in the wiring to the ignition switch.

2. Pull the wire off the negative (−) side of the coil too, and connect the ohmmeter between the two coil primary terminals; it should read 1.13–1.23 ohms. Otherwise, replace the coil. Pull the high tension lead out of the coil tower.

3. Connect the ohmmeter between the

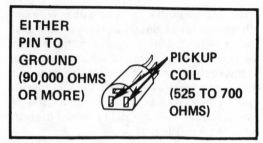

EITHER PIN TO GROUND (90,000 OHMS OR MORE)

PICKUP COIL (525 TO 700 OHMS)

Performing the Pickup Coil test

coil tower and the minus (−) primary terminal. The resistance should be 7,700–9,300 ohms; otherwise, replace the coil.

4. Pull the distributor connector apart and, working with the *distributor* side, connect the ohmmeter between each of the parallel connections and a good ground. Resistance must be 90,000 ohms or more on both sides. Finally, connect the ohmmeter between the two parallel connections (as shown in the illustration). Resistance must be 525–700 ohms. If the pickup coil fails either of the tests in this step, it should be replaced.

Testing of the electronic module requires special test equipment and training and should be left to a qualified professional. See also the Tune-Up and Troubleshooting section above for tests which reveal whether or not there is a simple mechanical problem in the distributor.

Distributor
REMOVAL AND INSTALLATION

1. Remove the air cleaner assembly as described in the Spark Plug Replacement procedure in Chapter 2. Note the position of No. 1 spark plug wire on the distributor cap. Then, remove the cap and position it to one side.

2. Rotate the engine with a remote starter switch until the groove on the front pulley lines up with the 12 degree (or earliest) mark on the front cover. Check to see if the distributor rotor is pointing toward the location of the No. 1 cylinder ignition wire. If it points 180 degrees away (to No. 4), turn the engine over one full turn and align the marks as described above. Otherwise, leave the engine in position.

NOTE: *Do not disturb the position of the engine throughout the remaining portions of this procedure.*

3. Disconnect the distributor wiring connector and the vacuum advance hose.

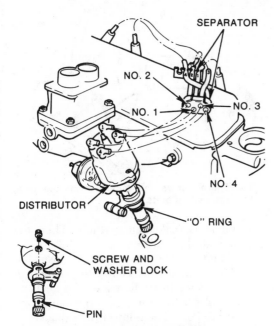

NO. 2
NO. 1
NO. 3
NO. 4
SEPARATOR
DISTRIBUTOR
"O" RING
SCREW AND
WASHER LOCK
PIN

Firing order and distributor installation

4. Remove the mounting bolt and lock-washer from the retaining clamp.

5. Pull the distributor straight up and out of the engine. Remove the old O-ring and replace it before reinstalling the distributor.

6. To install the distributor, first align the side of the gear securing pin which protrudes with the center of the mounting bolt hole. If the engine is still in the position established in Step 2, proceed with Step 7. If the engine has been turned over, connect a remote starter switch and remove the No. 1 spark plug (see "Spark Plug Replacement" in Chapter 2). Then, place your finger over the open spark plug hole and feel for air pressure while bumping the engine over. As the engine approaches the 12 degrees (or earliest) timing mark, you should feel air under

pressure coming out of the spark plug hole. If there is no pressure, continue cranking the engine one more full turn and align the notch on the pulley with the 12 degree mark. Replace the spark plug.

7. With the distributor aligned as described above, insert it into its mounting hole until the gear engages the camshaft and the distributor can be inserted to the point where the retaining clamp sits right against the block. The rotor will rotate due to the pitch of the drive gear teeth for the last inch or so of travel. If the unit cannot be inserted fully, press downward lightly while rotating the rotor very slightly either way to get the gear teeth to mesh, and then push the distributor into position.

8. Install the retaining bolt and washer and torque to 4.6–6.9 ft-lbs.

9. Reconnect the wiring connector and vacuum advance hoses. Reinstall the distributor cap and air cleaner.

Alternator
REMOVAL AND INSTALLATION

1. Disconnect the battery Negative (−) cable. On Bosch alternators, disconnect the wiring plug connector retaining clip at the rear of the unit and pull the connector out. On Motorcraft units, disconnect both stator and field connectors by pulling *straight off.*

2. Disconnect the heater hose bracket at the alternator.

3. On the Bosch units, loosen the three mounting bolts and tilt the unit toward the engine. Then disengage and remove the drive belt. On the Motorcraft units, loosen the mounting bolts and remove the adjusting arm-to-alternator attaching bolt. Then, push

Alternator and Regulator Specifications

| | | ALTERNATOR | | | REGULATOR | | | | | | |
| | | | | | | Field Relay | | | Regulator | | |
Year	Model	Part No. or Manufacturer	Field Current @ 12 v	Output (amps)	Part No. or Manufacturer	Air Gap (in.)	Point Gap (in.)	Volts to Close	Air Gap (in.)	Point Gap (in.)	Volts @ 75°
1978–80	All	Bosch K-1	—	55	Integral	N/A	N/A	—	N/A	N/A	13.7–14.4
1979–80	All*	D7AF-AA	29	40	D4AF-AA	—	—	2.5–4.0	—	—	13.7–14.4
1979–80	All*	D7AF-CA	29	60	D4AF-AA	—	—	2.5–4.0	—	—	13.7–14.4

* Without A/C only
N/A—Not applicable

the unit in toward the engine and disengage and remove the belt.

4. Completely remove the mounting bolts, and remove the unit.

5. Position the unit on the engine and install the three mounting bolts (Bosch), or the mounting bolts and spacer (Motorcraft), but do not tighten bolts all the way.

6. Install the alternator drive belt. Then, on Motorcraft units, install the adjusting arm-to-alternator bolt, but do not tighten fully. Adjust the belt as described in Chapter One. *When tightening the belt, apply pressure only on the alternator front housing.*

7. Connect the heater hose bracket to the alternator front housing.

8. On the Bosch unit, install the wiring connector into the socket on back of the unit, and install the retaining clip. On Motorcraft units, install the connectors, being sure to seat the stator and field push-on connectors on the terminal studs.

9. Reconnect the battery.

Regulator

REMOVAL AND INSTALLATION

To remove the regulator, simply disconnect the battery Negative (−) terminal, disconnect the plug at the regulator, and remove the two mounting bolts. Replace the unit in reverse. See the precautions above—do not try to polarize the unit.

Starter

REMOVAL AND INSTALLATION

1. Disconnect the battery Negative (−) cable at the battery. Support the front of the vehicle on jack stands.

2. The starter wires are marked with various color tracers. Note which wire goes

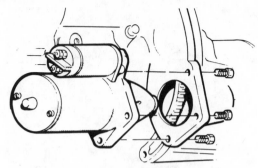

This figure shows the locations of the three starter mounting bolts

to which terminal and mark them. Then, disconnect all three wires.

3. Remove the two rubber insulators which hold the exhaust connector to the body and crossmember. Remove the exhaust clamp bolts (A) which hold the exhaust pipe to the manifold. Then, lower the exhaust system and allow it to rest far enough below the starter to provide clearance for its removal. Support the exhaust system so that no strain is placed on hangers.

4. Remove the three securing bolts, and guide the assembly straight out of the bell housing.

5. Installation is the reverse of removal. Be especially careful in making the wiring connections that wires are routed away from any metal surfaces, especially the hot exhaust pipe.

STARTER OVERHAUL

Brush Replacement

1. Clamp the starter motor in a soft-jawed vise with the solenoid at the top. Remove the nut and washer which secure the

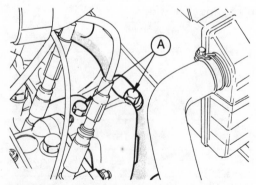

Remove the exhaust clamp bolts ("A") to lower the exhaust pipe

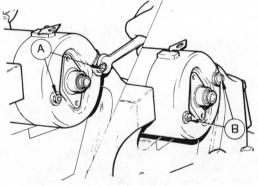

A—Starter with nuts and washers
B—Starter with through bolts

Removing nuts/removing through bolts

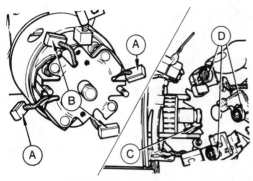

A Field brushes
B Bround brushes
C Brush plate
D Brush retaining springs

Removing the brushes

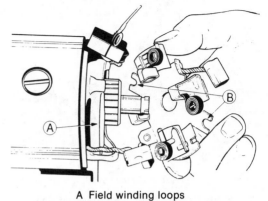

A Field winding loops
B Cutouts

Aligning the cutouts with field winding loops

field connection to the solenoid main terminal, and pull the connector off the terminal.

2. Remove the two screws which retain the armature shaft cap and remove the cap and rubber seal.

3. Wipe the grease off the armature shaft end with a clean rag. Remove the C-clip and shims from the end of the shaft.

4. Remove the nuts and washers from the studs that retain the commutator end housing, or if through bolts are used, remove the through-bolts. Then, remove the housing.

5. Pry the brush retaining and tensioning springs clear, and then slide the brushes out of the brush holder. Then, slide the brush holder plate off the two studs and armature shaft.

NOTE: *Do not attempt to remove the plate without first releasing the brushes.*

6. Check the brushes for sticking. If they do not move in and out freely, clean the brushes and brush channels with a non-volatile solvent. Also, measure the brushes for wear. If they are worn to a length of .39 in., replace them. To replace brushes, cut the leads midway between the brush and connection, and then solder the leads of the new brushes to the old leads. Make sure soldered connections are good.

7. On starter motors with through-bolts, slide the brush plate over the end of the armature shaft with the cutout portions of the brush plate sliding over the through bolts. On starters with screws, slide the plate over the end of the armature shaft and align the cutouts in the brush plate with the loops in the field windings. With the plate properly aligned, the screws will pass through the cutouts when they are installed.

8. Install the brushes in the holders, and then install the brush springs. Make sure the field winding leads do not touch the yoke.

9. Slide the commutator end housing into position so that the insulator around the field winding lead fits onto the cutout in the housing. Install nuts and washers or screws. Be sure the commutator end housing bearing is onto the armature shaft as far as possible, and install the shims at the commutator end to eliminate end play.

10. Install the bearing cap seal onto the commutator end housing. Smear a small amount of lithium grease on the end of the armature shaft, and then install the bearing cap and the two bearing cap screws.

Drive Replacement

1. Clamp the starter motor in a soft jawed vise. Remove the nut and washer securing the field connector to the main terminal on the solenoid, and pull the connector off the solenoid.

2. Remove the two screws securing the housing cap for the rear bearing, and remove the cap. Wipe grease from the armature shaft.

3. Remove the C-clip and shims from the rear end of the armature. Remove the nuts and washers from the ends of the through bolts or remove screws that run through the starter assembly.

4. Remove the commutator housing. Remove the brushes from the brush plate assembly by carefully prying brush retaining and tension springs clear and then sliding the brushes out. *Do not attempt to remove the brush plate without first pulling out brushes.*

5. Gently tap the yoke assembly and pull the drive end housing forward to separate the

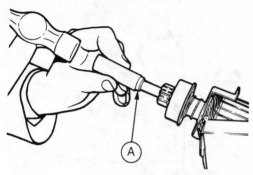

A Thrust washer

Driving the thrust washer over the snap ring

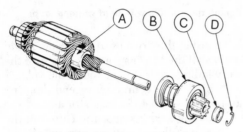

A Clutch stop
B Drive pinion and clutch
C Thrust washer
D Snap ring

Armature assembly parts

two parts. Pull the yoke backward and separate it from the drive end housing and armature shaft.

6. Pull the armature shaft out of the bearing at the front of the drive end housing, and then guide it downward and away from engagement with the actuating arm and then out of the drive end housing.

7. Slide an appropriate tool (a cylinder which fits snugly around the starter shaft) onto the shaft and use it to tap the thrust washer back toward the drive pinion to expose the snap ring. Pry the snap ring out of the groove and then slide it off the shaft. Fi-

nally, slide the thrust washer and drive pinion and clutch off the shaft.

8. Slide the new drive pinion and clutch onto the shaft. Slide the thrust washer onto the shaft, small inside diameter first. Work the snap ring onto the shaft and seat it in its groove. Then, pull the thrust washer up over the snap ring.

9. Slide the armature shaft into the drive end housing and engage the shift fork and pinion flange. Insert the front end of the shaft carefully on into the front bearing.

10. Guide the yoke assembly over the armature shaft, aligning the notch in the yoke with the rubber insert. Then, tap the yoke into full contact with the drive end housing.

11. Follow steps 7–10 of the Brush Replacement procedure above. Then reconnect the solenoid field connection.

SOLENOID REPLACEMENT

1. Clamp the starter motor in a soft jawed vise. Remove the nut and washer securing the field connector to the main terminal on the solenoid, and pull the connector off the solenoid.

2. Then, remove the three screws from the front end of the solenoid. Guide the solenoid body away from the drive end housing and plunger. Replace the solenoid in reverse of the above.

Battery

REMOVAL AND INSTALLATION

1. Using a 10 mm wrench, disconnect the battery cable connections from the battery. *Always disconnect the Negative (−) terminal first.*

2. Remove the battery clamp bolt with a 13 mm wrench. Remove the clamp.

3. Remove the battery.

4. Install in reverse order, *connecting the*

Battery and Starter Specifications

All cars use 12 volt, negative ground electrical systems

									Starter		
		Battery Amp Hour Capacity	Lock Test			No Load Test			Brush Spring Tension (oz)	Min. Brush Length (in.)
Year	Model		Amps	Volts	Torque (ft/lbs)	Amps	Volts	RPM		
1978–80	All	35*	350	12	6.9	Not used			2.0–2.7	.39

* 43 with A/C

positive terminal first. Cover the connections with petroleum jelly.

NOTE: *Be very carefuul about polarity. If you do not connect cables Positive (+) to Positive and Negative (−) to Negative, the alternator may be damaged.*

ENGINE MECHANICAL

Understanding the Engine

The basic piston engine is a metal block containing a series of chambers. The upper engine block is usually an iron or aluminum alloy casting, consisting of outer walls, which form hollow jackets around the cylinder walls. The lower block provides a number of rigid mounting points for the bearings which hold the crankshaft in place, and is known as the crankcase. The hollow jackets of the upper block add to the rigidity of the engine and contain the liquid coolant which carries the heat away from the cylinders and other engine parts. The block of an air cooled engine consists of a crankcase which provides for the rigid mounting of the crankshaft and for studs which hold the cylinders in place. The cylinders are individual, single-wall castings, finned for cooling, and are usually bolted to the crankcase, rather than cast integrally with the block. In a watercooled engine, only the cylinder head is bolted to the top of the block. The water pump is mounted directly to the block.

The crankshaft is a long, iron or steel shaft mounted rigidly in the bottom of the crankcase, at a number of points (usually 4–7). The crankshaft is free to turn and contains a number of counterweighted crankpins (one for each cylinder) that are offset several inches from the center of the crankshaft and turn in a circle as the crankshaft turns. The crankpins are centered under each cylinder. Pistons with circular rings to seal the small space between the pistons and wall of the cylinders are connected to the crankpins by steel connecting rods. The rods connect the pistons at their upper ends with the crankpins at their lower ends.

When the crankshaft spins, the pistons move up and down in the cylinders, varying the volume of each cylinder, depending on the position of the piston. Two openings in each cylinder head (above the cylinders) allow the intake of the air/fuel mixture and the exhaust of burned gasses. The volume of

the combustion chamber must be variable for the engine to compress the fuel charge before combustion, to make use of the expansion of the burning gasses and to exhaust the burned gasses and take in a fresh fuel mixture. As the pistons are forced downward by the expansion of burning fuel, the connecting rods convert the reciprocating (up and down) motion of the pistons into rotary (turning) motion of the crankshaft. A round flywheel at the rear of the crankshaft provides a large, stable mass to smooth out the rotation.

The cylinder heads form tight covers for the tops of the cylinders and contain machined chambers into which the fuel mixture is forced as it is compressed by the pistons reaching the upper limit of their travel. Each combustion chamber contains one intake valve, one exhaust valve and one spark plug per cylinder. The spark plugs are screwed into holes in the cylinder head so that the tips protrude into the combustion chambers. The valve in each opening in the cylinder head is opened and closed by the action of the camshaft. The camshaft is driven by the crankshaft through a chain or belt at ½ crankshaft speed (the camshaft gear is twice the size of the crankshaft gear). The valves are operated either through rocker arms and pushrods (overhead valve engine) or directly by the camshaft (overhead cam engine).

Lubricating oil is stored in a pan at the bottom of the engine and is force fed to all parts of the engine by a gear type pump, driven from the crankshaft. The oil lubricates the entire engine and also seals the piston rings, giving good compression.

Design

The Fiesta engine employs a cast iron cylinder block which is cast integrally with the upper half of the crankcase. The cylinder bores are machined directly into the block. The combustion chambers are formed by a bowl shaped depression in the piston for lower emissions.

The cylinder head is a cross-flow type so that the carburetor and intake manifold are mounted on one side and the exhaust manifold on the other. The camshaft is located on one side of the block and is driven by a roller chain, which uses a special tensioner to maintain exact timing. The overhead valves are operated through conventional lifters, pushrods and rockers.

The engine is mounted transversely in the

General Engine Specifications

Year	Engine Displacement Cu In. (cc)	Carburetor Type	Horsepower (@ rpm)	Torque @ rpm (ft lbs)	Bore x Stroke (in.)	Compression Ratio	Oil Pressure @ rpm (psi)
1978–80	97.5(1598)	2V	N/A*	N/A*	3.18 x 3.05	8.6	24–45 @ 2000

*N/A—Not available

Ring Gap
All measurements are given in inches

Year	Engine No. Cyl Displacement (cu in.)	Top Compression	Bottom Compression	Oil Control
1978–80	4(97.5)	.009–.017	.009–.014①	.009–.014

① Applies to 1978; 1979–80—.009–.017

Ring Side Clearance
All measurements are given in inches

Year	Engine	Top Compression	Bottom Compression	Oil Control
1978–80	All	.0016–.0036	.0016–.0036	.0018–.0038

Piston Clearance

Year	Engine No. Cyl Displacement (cu in.)	Piston to Bore Clearance (in.)
1978–80	All	.0009–.0017

Torque Specifications
All readings in ft lbs

Year	Engine Displacement Cu in. (cc)	Cylinder Head Bolts	Rod Bearing Bolts	Main Bearing Bolts	Crankshaft Pulley Bolt	Flywheel-to-Crankshaft Bolts	MANIFOLDS Intake	MANIFOLDS Exhaust
1978–80	97.5(1598)	①	30–35	55–60	40–44	50–55	12–13	15–18

① Step 1—5   Step 3—50–55
   Step 2—20–30   Step 4—65–70

Valve Specifications

Year	Engine Displacement Cu In. (cc)	Seat Angle (deg)	Face Angle (deg)	Spring Test Pressure (lbs @ in.)	Spring Installed Height (in.)	STEM TO GUIDE CLEARANCE (in.)		STEM DIAMETER (in.)	
						Intake	Exhaust	Intake	Exhaust
1978–80	97.5(1598)	45	45	42 @ 1.263①	1¼–1⁹⁄₃₂	.0008–.0027②	.0017–.0036②	.3098–.3105③	.3089–.3096③

① Also—104 @ .952
② Wear Limit—.0055 in.
③ Also available in .015 in. oversize

Crankshaft and Connecting Rod Specifications

All measurements are given in inches

Year	Engine Displacement Cu in. (cc)	CRANKSHAFT				CONNECTING ROD		
		Main Brg Journal Dia	Main Brg Oil Clearance	Shaft End-Play	Thrust on No.	Journal Diameter	Oil Clearance	Side Clearance
1978–80	97.5(1598)	2.1253–2.1261①	.0005–.0016②	.003–.030	3	1.9368–1.9376①	.0004–.0024③	—

① Out of round maximum—.0004 in.
② Applies to 1978; 1979–80—.0004–.0023
③ Applies to 1978; 1979–80—.0002–.0024

front compartment, driving the front wheels through a four speed transaxle assembly. A two stage, two venturi carburetor is used with an air cleaner which is mounted to the valve cover rather than the carburetor. The cooling system fan is electrical and controlled thermostatically to save fuel.

Emissions are controlled by an unusual Crankcase Ventilation System built into the oil filler cap; Exhaust Gas Recirculation; a Thermactor Air Injection System, which forces air into the exhaust manifold to improve further burning of hydrocarbons and carbon monoxide there and within the catalytic converter, and various Spark Control Systems.

Engine Removal and Installation

1. Disconnect the battery cables and remove the battery. Shift the transmission to fourth gear.

NOTE: *Transmission must be in fourth gear position to permit proper readjustment of shift linkage upon reinstallation.*

2. Drain the oil pan and cooling system. Disconnect the lower radiator hose at the radiator, and the upper hose at the thermostat housing. Remove the heater hoses from the side water pipe and the intake manifold connector.

3. Remove the air cleaner mounting bolts and disconnect the breather hose below the air cleaner.

4. Remove the clip which retains the accelerator cable to the lever on the carburetor. Then, remove the complete cable and bracket from the manifold.

5. Disconnect the inlet line at the fuel pump and then remove the pump. Disconnect the fuel vent hoses at the carburetor.

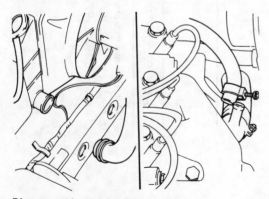

Disconnect heater hoses as shown

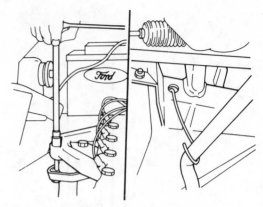

Disconnect the inlet pipe as shown

6. Disconnect and remove emission and servo vacuum hoses.

7. Disconnect electrical leads from the temperature sending unit, oil pressure switch, distributor, choke, ignition coil, and fan switch (if equipped). Disconnect and remove the ground strap from the engine.

8. Disconnect the speedometer cable at the transaxle.

9. Briefly depress the clutch cable and then release it. Then, unhook it from the release lever.

10. Remove the exhaust manifold heat stove.

11. Remove the two connecting bolts and disconnect the inlet pipe at the exhaust manifold. Support the disconnected pipe with wire.

12. Disconnect the ground wire at the air pump. Then, raise the vehicle on a hoist.

13. Release the gear selector rod clamp bolt and remove the selector rod. Unhook the spring that runs between the rod and the longitudinal member.

14. Back off the mounting nuts on the rubber insulators on the stabilizers and the engine mounts. Loosen the locknut on the stud and remove the stud from the transmission using an Allen wrench.

NOTE: *You will need an assistant to remove the exhaust system in the next step.*

15. Remove the complete exhaust system as an assembly, disconnecting it at the mounting rubbers.

16. Remove the shift tower from the floor pan by removing the four mounting nuts from the floor pan and pulling it off. Rotate the gear selector rod with the stabilizer half a turn and suspend it with wire.

17. Disconnect all starter motor and alternator leads.

The left panel shows the engine mounts. The right panel shows the transmission stud locknut being loosened

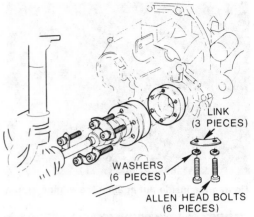

LINK
(3 PIECES)

WASHERS
(6 PIECES)

ALLEN HEAD BOLTS
(6 PIECES)

Arrangement of the bolts, washers, and links

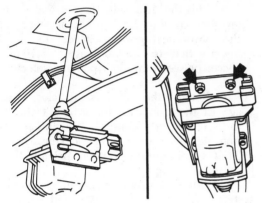

The left panel shows the shift tower, while the right panel shows the floor pan bolts

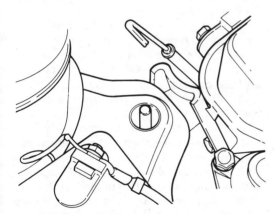

Engage the engine insulator stud in the apron bracket

18. Remove the right tie bar and bracket from the crossmember.

19. Disconnect the left axle driveshaft with stubshaft by removing the six Allen head bolts. Separate the coupling and remove links and washers with the bolts.

20. Disconnect the right side driveshaft at the inner constant velocity joint by removing the six Allen head bolts.

21. Securely support the engine-transmission assembly on a floor jack or lowboy transmission jack. Spread the weight by supporting on a wooden beam and blocks.

22. Disconnect engine mountings as follows:

a. Remove the right, front upper engine mounting rubber insulator nut (from inside the engine compartment) and remove the insulator.

b. Remove the engine-to-body bracket from inside the engine compartment.

c. Remove the left engine mounting nut and bolt and remove the mounting.

d. Remove the lower engine mounting strap retaining bolts (there are four) and remove the strap.

23. Raise the hoist so the vehicle is pulled upward and away from the engine and transmission assembly. Then, lower the jack and withdraw the assembly from underneath.

24. To install, position the engine-transmission assembly on a jack underneath the vehicle. Carefully lower the vehicle and raise the jack until the engine is in position.

25. Engage the engine front insulator stud with the right apron bracket, and then install the nut to the insulator stud finger tight.

NOTE: *Be sure the front mount rubber insulators are parallel to the front of the engine and that they do not distort when the nut is tightened.*

26. Install the left engine mount and retaining bolt and nut. Install the engine-to-body bracket from inside the engine compartment.

27. Install the lower engine mounting bracket and its four mounting bolts and

Tighten the inside nut against the engine mount

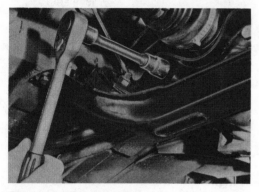

Tighten the stabilizer jam nut

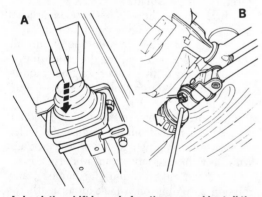

A. Lock the shift lever in fourth gear and install the spacer
B. Rotate the shift shaft until it is against the stop

torque the bolts. Torque nuts on right and left engine mounts *without* distorting insulators; torque to 35 ft lbs.

28. Install the right front axle driveshaft by installing the six Allen head bolts at the inner constant velocity joint coupling. Install the left front driveshaft by connecting it in the same way to the stubshaft. Note the arrangement of bolts, washers, and links.

29. Connect all starter motor and alternator leads.

30. Install the right tie bar and brackets onto the front crossmember.

31. Position the shift tower with the linkage onto the floor pan and install the four mounting bolts from underneath.

32. Carefully install the Allen setscrew until it hits the shift tower and then lock it with the stabilizer rubber insulator nut. Tighten the inside nut against the engine mount and tighten the jam nut. Then, tighten shift tower retaining nuts.

33. Install the gear selector rod on the shift shaft and adjust as follows:

a. Be sure the transmission is still in fourth gear and then slide the selector rod into the shaft.

b. Pull the gear selector rod and shift lever downward. Lock the shift lever in the fourth gear position inside the shift tower with a .16 in. arbor. Insert a 2.76 in. spacer between the floor pan and selector rod.

c. Rotate the shift shaft clockwise against the stop with the arbor. Tighten the selector rod locating bolt in this position. Remove the spacer and locking arbor.

34. Connect the selector rod spring to the longitudinal member.

35. With an assistant, install the exhaust system assembly to the chassis and tighten retaining nuts.

36. Check the transmission oil level and fill if required.

37. Lower the vehicle to the floor. Connect the ground wire at the air pump.

38. Connect the inlet pipe to the manifold and torque bolts. Install the heat stove and air hose bracket.

39. Connect the clutch cable to the release lever.

40. Connect the speedometer cable.

41. Connect the leads to the temperature sending unit, oil pressure switch, ignition coil, electric choke (if equipped), and fan switch. Connect the engine ground strap.

42. Connect the vacuum hose to the intake manifold. Install the fuel pump and connect the inlet line.

43. Connect emission system vacuum hoses, including the fuel vent hoses running from the carburetor to the canister.

44. Connect the accelerator cable and bracket to the intake manifold. Adjust the cable with the accelerator pedal depressed all the way. Clearance between the carburetor lever and its stop is .015 inches or less.

45. Connect the ground cable at the accel-

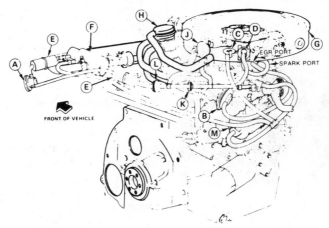

FRONT OF VEHICLE

EGR PORT
SPARK PORT

A—Thermactor Idle Vacuum Valve (TIV)
B—Exhaust Gas Recirculation (EGR) Valve
C—Bimetal Sensor
D—TVS Switch (Normally Open)
E—Vacuum Reservoir
F—Valve Assembly (Air Bypass)

G—Air Cleaner Assembly
H—Oil Filler Cap Assembly
J—Valve Assembly (Vacuum Vent)
K—Check Valve
L—Delay Valve
M—Distributor

Reconnect all emission controls

erator cable mounting bracket on the intake manifold.

46. Connect the heater hoses at the side pipe and intake manifold. Install the upper and lower heater hoses and secure them with clamps.

47. Install the battery and reconnect cables.

48. Fill the radiator and crankcase, install the air cleaner. Make sure the accelerator cable is routed *over* the air cleaner spout, or cable damage or ignition system grounding may occur.

48. Reconnect emission controls, as shown.

Cylinder Head
REMOVAL AND INSTALLATION

1. Remove the air cleaner assembly.

2. Remove the fuel line from the fuel pump to the carburetor.

3. Drain the coolant from the radiator and the engine block.

4. Disconnect the spark plug wires and tie them out of the way. Disconnect the fan switch wires and the temperature sending switch wire.

5. Remove the heater and vacuum hoses at the intake manifold. Disconnect the hoses at the choke housing.

6. Disconnect the exhaust inlet pipe and cover the pipe opening to avoid loss of nuts or bolts.

7. Disconnect the throttle linkage and vacuum hoses at the carburetor.

8. Disconnect and remove the air pump and brackets from the cylinder head.

9. Remove the thermostat and housing.

10. Remove the rocker arm cover and the rocker arm assembly.

11. Lift the push rods out of the head, while keeping them in proper order.

12. Remove the cylinder head bolts and lift the cylinder head off the engine block.

13. Installation is the reverse order of removal. Note the following during installation:

a. Clean the gasket sealing area and check head for warpage with a straight-edge. Warpage should not exceed 0.0015 in. in a twelve inch span.

b. Tighten the cylinder head bolts in sequence in the increments listed in the specifications.

c. Lubricate both ends of the pushrods with Lubriplate® or equivalent before installation.

d. When installing rocker shaft assembly, remember to engage pushrods with rockers before installing the mounting bolts. Torque the mounting bolts to 35 ft-lbs evenly and in several increments.

e. Adjust the valves.

Torque sequences

OVERHAUL

See the Engine Overhaul Section which follows this chapter. The Fiesta cylinder head is conventional in design and is overhauled as described in detail in that section.

Rocker Shafts

REMOVAL AND INSTALLATION

1. Remove the air cleaner. Mark (if necessary) and then disconnect the spark plug secondary cables. Pull cables out of the clips on the rocker cover, and then tie them out of the way.

2. Remove the rocker cover attaching screws, pull the cover off, and discard the gasket.

3. Remove the rocker shaft attaching bolts, and remove the rocker shaft assembly.

4. If it is necessary to remove rockers from the shaft, remove the cotter pin from one end of the shaft, and slip the flat washer, crimped washer, and second flat washer off the shaft. Note order of disassembly and remove rockers, supports and springs as necessary.

5. When reassembling rocker shaft assembly note the following points:

a. Bolt holes in the shaft supports must face the side on which the rocker adjusting screws are located.

b. There are right hand and left hand type rockers. They must be installed with the pads inclined toward the support.

c. When springs, rockers, and supports are assembled, install washers and then insert the cotter pins with the heads upward and the legs bent over.

6. Lubricate valve stem tips, rocker arm

pads, and push rod ends with Lubriplate® or equivalent.

7. Install the assembly, engaging the push rods with the adjusting screws before installing bolts. Install bolts and torque evenly in several stages to 25–30 ft-lbs.

8. Adjust valve clearances as described in the Tune-Up chapter.

9. Clean all old gasket material off the valve and cylinder head cover, and install a new gasket. Install the valve cover and tighten screws evenly.

10. Reverse the remaining removal procedures.

Intake Manifold

REMOVAL AND INSTALLATION

1. Remove the carburetor air cleaner assembly.

2. Drain the cooling system.

3. Disconnect the accelerator cable from the carburetor throttle lever. Remove the accelerator cable mounting bracket from the intake manifold by removing the two mounting bolts.

4. Disconnect the fuel line and the vacuum line at the carburetor.

5. Disconnect the fan switch wires; remove the thermostat and housing.

6. Disconnect the water outlet hose and the crankcase ventilation hose from the manifold.

7. Remove the decel valve to carburetor pipe, if equipped, from the carburetor.

8. Remove the manifold attaching bolts and nuts and remove the manifold from the cylinder head.

9. Installation of the intake manifold is the reverse of removal and the following recommendations should be observed.

a. Clean the gasket surface of all old material.

b. Apply waterproof sealer to both sides of a new manifold gasket at the water ports.

c. Tighten all nuts and bolts to the proper torque specifications. Torque evenly and in several stages.

d. If using a new manifold, transfer all components. When installing the decel valve, place the valve over the adapter, install the adapter, and torque mounting bolts. Then, hold the valve against the face of the adapter and engage and tighten the nut.

Exhaust Manifold
REMOVAL AND INSTALLATION

1. If it is necessary to remove the air pump and its mounting bracket to gain access to the inlet pipe, remove them. Then, support the inlet pipe and remove the two nuts which attach the manifold to the inlet pipe flange, and separate the pipe from the manifold.

2. Disconnect the hot air pipe from the air cleaner at the exhaust manifold.

3. Remove the nuts and bolts which attach the manifold to the head, and remove the assembly. Remove and discard all gaskets.

4. Clean gasket material from both mounting surfaces. If a new manifold is to be installed, transfer the choke heat stove to the new manifold.

5. To install, position the center gasket on the studs, making sure the gasket is right side up. Then, put the manifold into position on the studs. Slide the remaining gaskets into position between the manifold flanges and the head. Then, install nuts and bolts and torque to specifications evenly and in several stages.

6. Connect the manifold and head pipe flanges and install the nuts.

7. Connect the hot air pipe at the manifold. Run the engine and check for leaks.

Timing Gear Cover
REMOVAL AND INSTALLATION

1. Remove the engine from the car as described above.

2. Remove the air pump, alternator, and water pump drive belts.

3. Remove the water pump (see appropriate sections of the procedure below).

4. Remove the crankshaft pulley with a puller.

5. Remove the front cover.

6. To install, position the front cover gasket, portions of the oil pan gasket if necessary, and the end seal on the front cover. Apply an oil resistant sealer at all seal ends. Then, position the cover on the block—the centralizing lug and pulley will ensure proper location.

7. Tighten attaching bolts evenly.

8. Position the crankshaft pulley on the crankshaft with the key and keyway aligned. Install the bolt and torque to 40–44 ft-lbs.

9. Install the water pump. Reconnect belts and adjust their tension.

10. Reinstall the engine. Run the engine and check for leaks.

TIMING COVER OIL SEAL REPLACEMENT

The oil seal can be replaced while the cover is on the car provided special tools, a seal remover and a seal installer, are used.

1. Loosen the alternator and remove the drive belt.

2. Raise the vehicle on a hoist. Remove the crankshaft damper retaining bolt and washer and remove the damper with a puller.

3. Use a seal remover to remove the seal.

4. Install the new seal with a seal installer.

5. Reverse the remaining removal procedures to install, torquing pulley and damper bolt to 40–55 ft lbs.

Timing Chain and Tensioner
REMOVAL AND INSTALLATION

1. Remove the front cover as described above.

2. Remove the crankshaft oil slinger. Then, remove the camshaft sprocket retainer and bolts.

3. Remove the oil pan. See the procedure below.

4. Remove the two attaching bolts and remove the timing chain tensioner and arm.

5. Unbolt the camshaft sprocket and remove it and the timing chain.

6. To install, locate the timing chain over the camshaft sprockets so the timing marks are aligned as shown when the sprocket is in-

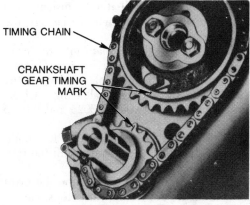

TIMING CHAIN

CRANKSHAFT
GEAR TIMING
MARK

Align valve timing marks as shown

stalled. Torque the mounting bolts and bend over the locking tabs.

7. Install the crankshaft oil slinger, camshaft sprocket retainer and bolts. Install the timing chain tensioner. Follow Steps 6–10 of the Front Cover Removal and Installation procedure above to reinstall the front cover.

Camshaft
REMOVAL AND INSTALLATION

1. Remove the engine from the vehicle as described above.

2. Remove the fuel line at the fuel pump and remove the air pump drive belt, air pump, and brackets.

3. Remove the alternator drive belt and water pump pulley.

4. Remove the oil pump and the fuel pump.

5. Remove the rocker arm cover from the head.

6. Remove the distributor from the engine.

7. Remove the rocker arm retaining bolts and lift out the rocker arm assembly.

8. Lift the pushrods from the engine and keep them in order.

9. Invert the engine. Remove the oil pan and gasket, dipstick and with a puller, the crankshaft pulley. See the appropriate procedure below for oil pan removal.

10. Remove the front cover, crankshaft oil slinger, and the timing chain tensioner assembly.

11. Remove the timing chain and the camshaft sprocket.

12. Remove the camshaft thrust plate and remove the camshaft from the engine block, being careful not to damage the cam bearings.

13. Carefully install the camshaft into the engine block so as not to damage the camshaft bearings.

14. Install the thrust plate into the camshaft groove and install the retaining bolts.

15. Measure the free play between the thrust plate and the camshaft flange. Clearance should be between 0.0025 and 0.0075 in.

16. Align the timing marks on the crankshaft and camshaft gears and install the timing chain.

17. Install the tensioner arm on the pivot pin and install the timing chain tensioner.

18. Install the crankshaft oil slinger and the front cover, using new gaskets.

19. Install the oil pan, using new gaskets and oil resistant sealer at all joints.

20. Install the dipstick.

21. Install the crankshaft pulley and tighten to specifications.

22. Install and time the distributor.

23. Install the oil pump, using a new gasket. Install a new oil filter.

24. Install the fuel pump to the engine block, using a new gasket.

25. Install the pushrods into their original positions.

26. Install the rocker arm shaft assembly.

27. Adjust the valve clearance to specifications, following the chart in the tune-up section.

28. Install the water pump pulley, vacuum lines, fuel lines, and drive belts. Adjust as necessary.

29. Install the engine into the vehicle.

30. Start the engine and check for any oil or water leaks.

31. Readjust the valves to normal operating temperature specifications. Install the rocker arm cover.

Pistons and Connecting Rods
REMOVAL

1. Remove the engine from the car as described above.

2. Remove the cylinder head from the engine as described above.

3. Remove the oil pan from the engine as described below.

4. Remove the oil inlet tube and screen, and return tube. Clean the oil pan and block faces and remove the end seals.

5. Inspect the connecting rods to make sure that all rods have been numbered correctly. The numbers should be stamped on the camshaft side of the big end.

6. Remove the ring ridge at the top of each cylinder bore with a ridge reamer (see the Engine Rebuilding Section).

7. Partially remove the bearing cap bolts and then tap the bolt ends to release the caps. Completely remove the bearing bolts and remove caps, keeping them in the same order. Push the piston and rod upward and out of each bore.

PISTON SELECTION

Cylinder bores and pistons are graded according to size. This piston grade number is marked on the piston crown and stamped on

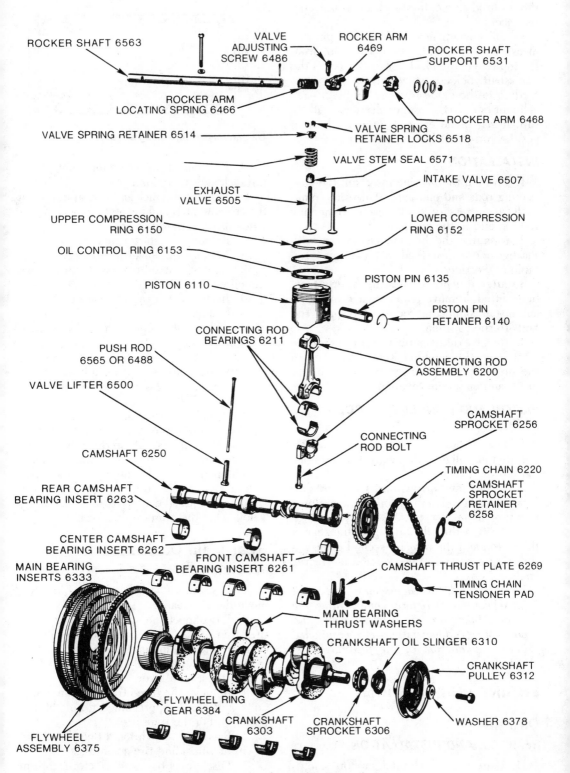

Exploded view of major engine internal parts

the pushrod side of the block adjacent to the top face.

When selecting new standard size pistons, measure each cylinder bore $2^{11}/_{32}$ in. from the top face of the block across the axis of the crankshaft. Select a standard size piston according to the grade number found on each cylinder bore so the proper clearance will result. It may be necessary to hone the bore to get the correct fit.

INSTALLATION

1. Position the bearing inserts in the connecting rods and end caps. Turn the crankshaft as necessary to fit each connecting rod big end to the crankpin.

2. Measure the bearing clearances with Plastigage® as described in the Engine Rebuilding Section.

3. After the proper bearing inserts have been fitted, remove all Plastigage material, and install connecting rod caps, torquing rod bolts to specifications.

4. Reverse disassembly procedures for the remaining disassembled items, referring to the proper procedures for oil pan, cylinder head, and engine installation.

PISTON AND CONNECTING ROD POSITIONING

1. The "Front" markings on the connecting rod must align with the arrow on the piston crown.

2. "Front" and arrow markings must face forward when rods and pistons are assembled into the engine.

3. Position the oil ring gap to the rear of the piston and the top and second compression ring gaps at 180 degree and 90 degree angles.

NOTE: *Dip the piston assembly into an oil filled container before compressing the rings. Make sure the cylinder walls and connecting rod journals are clean and oiled before installation of the piston/rod assembly.*

ENGINE LUBRICATION

Oil Pan

REMOVAL AND INSTALLATION

1. Raise the vehicle and support safely.

2. Drain the oil pan and remove the dipstick.

3. Disconnect the battery ground cable.

4. Disconnect the throttle linkage from the carburetor.

Oil pan gasket tightening sequence

5. Disconnect the steering cable from the rack and pinion unit.

6. Remove the rack and pinion unit from the crossmember and move it forward to provide oil pan removal clearance.

7. Remove the starter motor.

8. Remove the lower flywheel cover.

9. Remove the oil pan bolts and remove the oil pan assembly.

10. Installation is the reverse of removal. Note the following:

   a. Clean the inlet screen and tube asembly.

   b. Clean the seal retainer grooves in the front cover and the rear main bearing cap.

   c. Install the gasket to the engine block with an oil resistant sealer.

   d. Apply oil resistant sealer to the end joints of the gasket and end seals.

   e. First, finger tighten the corner bolts. Then, following the illustration exactly, tighten the bolts in the alphabetical pattern just enough to clamp the gasket. Finally, torque the bolts to 5.9–8.1 ft lbs following the numerical pattern.

Rear Main Oil Seal

REPLACEMENT

1. Disconnect both batttery cables. Remove the air cleaner.

2. Disconnect the speedometer cable at the transmission. Disconnect the clutch cable by first pulling on the exposed portion to loosen the adjustment and then unhooking it from the clutch lever.

3. Remove the three transmission flange bolts and the support bracket bolt at the upper end of the transaxle.

4. Raise the vehicle on a hoist. Remove the front wheel and tire assemblies.

5. Disconnect the gear selector rod from the gear selector shaft.

6. Remove the stabilizer shift mechanism from the transmission.

7. Remove the cotter pin and the castellated nut from the left tie rod ball joint.

8. Remove the left lower arm from the body. Disconnect the ball joint from the spindle carrier and disconnect the arm.

9. Remove the left front axle shaft and CV joint.

10. Remove the center support bearing cover and driveshaft.

11. Remove the starter motor as described above.

12. Disconnect the backup light switch wires.

13. Remove the bolt from the engine-to-transaxle bracket. If the vehicle has air conditioning, support the compressor.

14. Remove the stabilizer bar left/front nut.

15. Remove the bolt and nut at the upper A frame and swing the spindle carrier up and out of the way.

16. Securely support the transaxle with a jack. Remove the three bolts holding the engine intermediate support bracket to the transaxle.

17. Support the oil pan with a jack. Raise the engine enough to extract the bolts.

18. Remove the four bolts holding the intermediate engine support bracket and remove the bracket.

19. Remove the three bolts holding the upper support bracket to the transaxle.

20. Support the transaxle with a jack and remove the two engine-to-transaxle bolts. Remove the transaxle.

NOTE: *You will need an assistant to remove the transaxle.*

21. Remove the six retaining bolts from the clutch pressure plate and disc.

22. Remove the six bolts and remove the flywheel and/or adapter plate spacer.

23. Remove rear oil seal carrier. Then, install two metal screws above the center line of the seal, *being careful not to let them bottom against the crankshaft or block.* Then, pry against the two seals and pry the seal out. Remove burrs from oil seal surfaces.

24. Install a new rear oil seal in the carrier using the Ford tool shown in the illustration or an equivalent type tool of another brand. Apply oil resistant sealer at both ends of the seal.

25. Install the rear oil seal carrier onto the block face, using a new gasket, and align the carrier with the Ford tool shown in the illustration or the equivalent. Torque retaining bolts to 12–15 ft lbs.

26. Position the adapter plate on the dowels, and then install the flywheel. Apply sealer to the six flywheel bolts, and install them, torquing to 50–55 ft lbs.

27. Check flywheel runout using a dial indicator. Clutch face runout must not exceed .005 in., and lateral (ring gear) runout must not exceed .025 in. If the specifications are not met, flywheel may need machining or replacement.

28. Install the clutch disc and pressure plate, and torque bolts to 12–15 ft lbs.

29. Perform the remaining steps in reverse of the removal procedure. When installing bolts in the rear engine mount, make sure to connect the catalyst hanger. Check transaxle fluid level and refill as necessary.

Oil Pump

REMOVAL AND INSTALLATION

1. The oil pump is located outside the block, below the distributor. Place a drain pan under the pump to collect oil which will drain out when mounting bolts are loosened.

2. Remove the three mounting bolts, and remove the assembly. Separate the filter from the pump.

3. To install, clean all gasket surfaces thoroughly, and apply an oil resistant sealer to both sides of a new gasket. Torque mounting bolts to 12–15 ft lbs.

4. Run the engine at slow idle until oil pressure is built up. Then, stop and refill the crankcase to the proper level.

ENGINE COOLING

Radiator

REMOVAL AND INSTALLATION

1. Disconnect the battery cables and position a drain pan of adequate size under the radiator.

2. Remove the radiator cap. Loosen the

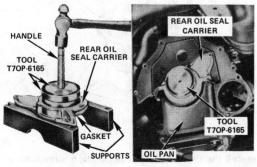

Installing a new rear crankshaft oil seal

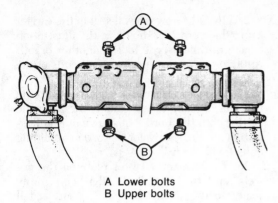

A Lower bolts
B Upper bolts

Radiator retaining bolts

hose clamp connecting the lower hose to the radiator, and then pull the hose off the connection.

3. Loosen the clamp for the top hose, and pull it off the radiator connection.

4. Pull the expansion tank tube off the radiator filler neck. Disconnect the wiring connector from the back of the fan motor and unclip the wire where it attaches to the back of the fan shroud.

5. Remove the two lower radiator retaining bolts from the front of the vehicle. Then, remove the two upper mounting bolts from inside the engine compartment.

6. Remove the mounting clips and remove the radiator.

7. Remove the four shroud bolts and remove the shroud.

8. To install the radiator, first install the shroud. Then, position the two upper mounting clips, position the radiator, and install the two upper retaining bolts.

9. Install the lower mounting clips and the bolts.

10. Reverse the remaining removal procedures.

11. Refill the system with the specified mix of antifreeze and water. When the radiator is full, start the engine and idle it while refilling to keep the radiator water level up as air is expelled from the system. When the system remains full, replace the cap, and, while the engine is still running, check for any leaks.

Water Pump
REMOVAL AND INSTALLATION

1. Perform the first three steps of the radiator removal procedure to drain coolant.

2. Loosen the three pump pulley bolts before removing belt tension.

3. Remove the air pump belt and the pump bracket.

4. Loosen the three alternator mounting bolts and the alternator adjusting arm, and swing the alternator towards the engine. Remove the drive belt.

5. Loosen the hose clamp, and pull the hose leading to the water pump off the hose connection.

6. Remove the three pump pulley bolts and the washers and remove the pulley.

7. Remove the three pump retaining bolts and remove the pump.

8. To install, reverse the above procedure, bearing the following points in mind:

   a. Clean the pump and block mating surfaces thoroughly and use a new gasket.

   b. Install the hose which connects to the water pump before mounting the pump on the block.

   c. Install the pump mounting bolts and tighten evenly in several stages to 5–7 ft lbs.

   d. Refill the cooling system as described in the last step of the radiator removal procedure above.

Thermostat
REMOVAL AND INSTALLATION

1. Disconnect the two battery cables, and the electrical connector at the thermostat housing.

2. Remove the radiator cap. Put a drain pan under the radiator, loosen the lower hose clamp at the radiator, and pull off the hose to drain about half the coolant from the system.

3. Loosen the upper hose clamp at the radiator. Remove the two thermostat housing

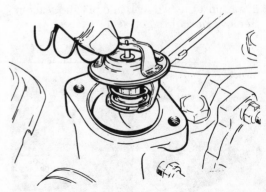

Install the thermostat in the position shown here

mounting bolts, pull the housing clean, and remove the thermostat.

4. To install, reverse the removal procedure, bearing the following points in mind:

    a. *The thermostat must be installed with the pellet and spring downward as shown, or overheating may occur.*

    b. Clean the mounting surfaces and install a new gasket. Torque housing bolts to 12–15 ft lbs.

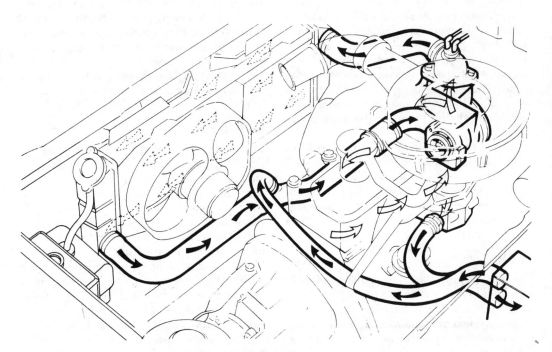

Coolant flow

ENGINE REBUILDING

Most procedures involved in rebuilding an engine are fairly standard, regardless of the type of engine involved. This section is a guide accepted rebuilding procedures. Examples of standard rebuilding practices are illustrated and should be used along with specific details concerning your particular engine, found earlier in this chapter.

The procedures given here are those used by any competent rebuilder. Obviously some of the procedures cannot be performed by the do-it-yourself mechanic, but are provided so that you will be familiar with the services that should be offered by rebuilding or machine shops. As an example, in most instances, it is more profitable for the home mechanic to remove the cylinder heads, buy the necessary parts (new valves, seals, keepers, keys, etc.) and deliver these to a machine shop for the necessary work. In this way you will save the money to remove and install the cylinder head and the mark-up on parts.

On the other hand, most of the work involved in rebuilding the lower end is well within the scope of the do-it-yourself mechanic. Only work such as hot-tanking, actually boring the block or Magnafluxing (invisible crack detection) need be sent to a machine shop.

Tools

The tools required for basic engine rebuilding should, with a few exceptions, be those included in a mechanic's tool kit. An accurate torque wrench, and a dial indicator (reading in thousandths) mounted on a universal base should be available. Special tools, where required, are available from the major tool suppliers. The services of a competent automotive machine shop must also be readily available.

Precautions

Aluminum has become increasingly popular for use in engines, due to its low weight and excellent heat transfer characteristics. The following precautions must be observed when handling aluminum (or any other) engine parts:
—Never hot-tank aluminum parts.
—Remove all aluminum parts (identification tags, etc.) from engine parts before hot-tanking (otherwise they will be removed during the process).

—Always coat threads lightly with engine oil or anti-seize compounds before installation, to prevent seizure.
—Never over-torque bolts or spark plugs in aluminum threads. Should stripping occur, threads can be restored using any of a number of thread repair kits available (see next section).

Inspection Techniques

Magnaflux and Zyglo are inspection techniques used to locate material flaws, such as stress cracks. Magnaflux is a magnetic process, applicable only to ferrous materials. The Zyglo process coats the matrial with a fluorescent dye penetrant, and any material may be tested using Zyglo. Specific checks of suspected surface cracks may be made at lower cost and more readily using spot check dye. The dye is sprayed onto the suspected area, wiped off, and the area is then sprayed with a developer. Cracks then will show up brightly.

Overhaul

The section is divided into two parts. The first, Cylinder Head Reconditioning, assumes that the cylinder head is removed from the engine, all manifolds are removed, and the cylinder head is on a workbench. The camshaft should be removed from overhead cam cylinder heads. The second section, Cylinder Block Reconditioning, covers the block, pistons, connecting rods and crankshaft. It is assumed that the engine is mounted on a work stand, and the cylinder head and all accessories are removed.

Procedures are identified as follows:

Unmarked—Basic procedures that must be performed in order to successfully complete the rebuilding process.

Starred (*)—Procedures that should be performed to ensure maximum performance and engine life.

Double starred (**)—Procedures that may be performed to increase engine performance and reliability.

When assembling the engine, any parts that will be in frictional contact must be pre-lubricated, to provide protection on initial start-up. Any product specifically formulated for this purpose may be used. NOTE: *Do not use engine oil.* Where semi-permanent (locked but removable) installation of bolts or nuts is desired, threads should be cleaned and located with Loctite® or a similar product (non-hardening).

Repairing Damaged Threads

Several methods of repairing damaged threads are available. Heli-Coil® (shown here), Keenserts® and Microdot® are among the most widely used. All involve basically the same principle—drilling out stripped threads, tapping the hole and installing a prewound insert—making welding, plugging and oversize fasteners unnecessary.

Two types of thread repair inserts are usually supplied—a standard type for most Inch Coarse, Inch Fine, Metric Coarse and Metric Fine thread sizes and a spark plug type to fit most spark plug port sizes. Consult the individual manufacturer's catalog to determine exact applications. Typical thread repair kits will contain a selection of prewound threaded inserts, a tap (corresponding to the outside diameter threads of the insert) and an installation tool. Spark plug inserts usually differ because they require a tap equipped with pilot threads and a combined reamer/tap section. Most manufacturers also supply blister-packed thread repair inserts separately in addition to a master kit containing a variety of taps and inserts plus installation tools.

Before effecting a repair to a threaded hole, remove any snapped, broken or damaged bolts or studs. Penetrating oil can be used to free frozen threads; the offending item can be removed with locking pliers or with a screw or stud extractor. After the hole is clear, the thread can be repaired, as follows:

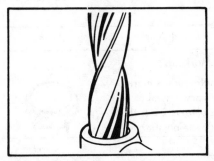
Drill out the damaged threads with specified drill. Drill completely through the hole or to the bottom of a blind hole

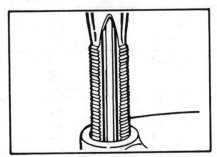
With the tap supplied, tap the hole to receive the thread insert. Keep the tap well oiled and back it out frequently to avoid clogging the threads

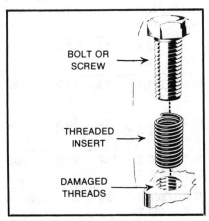

BOLT OR SCREW →

THREADED INSERT →

DAMAGED THREADS →

Damaged bolt holes can be repaired with thread repair inserts

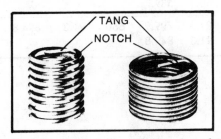
TANG
NOTCH

Standard thread repair insert (left) and spark plug thread insert (right)

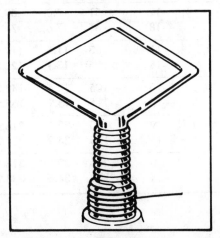
Screw the threaded insert onto the installation tool until the tang engages the slot. Screw the insert into the tapped hole until it is ¼–½ turn below the top surface. After installation break off the tang with a hammer and punch

Standard Torque Specifications and Fastener Markings

The Newton-metre has been designated the world standard for measuring torque and will gradually replace the foot-pound and kilogram-meter. In the absence of specific torques, the following chart can be used as a guide to the maximum safe torque of a particular size/grade of fastener.

- There is no torque difference for fine or coarse threads.
- Torque values are based on clean, dry threads. Reduce the value by 10% if threads are oiled prior to assembly.
- The torque required for aluminum components or fasteners is considerably less.

U. S. BOLTS

SAE Grade Number	1 or 2			5			6 or 7		

Bolt Markings

Manufacturer's marks may vary—number of lines always 2 less than the grade number.

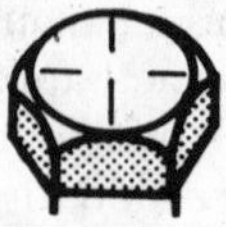

Usage	Frequent			Frequent			Infrequent		
Bolt Size (inches)—(Thread)	Maximum Torque			Maximum Torque			Maximum Torque		
	Ft-Lb	kgm	Nm	Ft-Lb	kgm	Nm	Ft-Lb	kgm	Nm
¼—20	5	0.7	6.8	8	1.1	10.8	10	1.4	13.5
—28	6	0.8	8.1	10	1.4	13.6			
5⁄16—18	11	1.5	14.9	17	2.3	23.0	19	2.6	25.8
—24	13	1.8	17.6	19	2.6	25.7			
⅜—16	18	2.5	24.4	31	4.3	42.0	34	4.7	46.0
—24	20	2.75	27.1	35	4.8	47.5			
7⁄16—14	28	3.8	37.0	49	6.8	66.4	55	7.6	74.5
—20	30	4.2	40.7	55	7.6	74.5			
½—13	39	5.4	52.8	75	10.4	101.7	85	11.75	115.2
—20	41	5.7	55.6	85	11.7	115.2			
9⁄16—12	51	7.0	69.2	110	15.2	149.1	120	16.6	162.7
—18	55	7.6	74.5	120	16.6	162.7			
⅝—11	83	11.5	112.5	150	20.7	203.3	167	23.0	226.5
—18	95	13.1	128.8	170	23.5	230.5			
¾—10	105	14.5	142.3	270	37.3	366.0	280	38.7	379.6
—16	115	15.9	155.9	295	40.8	400.0			
⅞— 9	160	22.1	216.9	395	54.6	535.5	440	60.9	596.5
—14	175	24.2	237.2	435	60.1	589.7			
1— 8	236	32.5	318.6	590	81.6	799.9	660	91.3	894.8
—14	250	34.6	338.9	660	91.3	849.8			

METRIC BOLTS

NOTE: *Metric bolts are marked with a number indicating the relative strength of the bolt. These numbers have nothing to do with size.*

Description	Torque ft-lbs (Nm)			
Thread size x pitch (mm)	Head mark—4		Head mark—7	
6 x 1.0	2.2–2.9	(3.0–3.9)	3.6–5.8	(4.9–7.8)
8 x 1.25	5.8–8.7	(7.9–12)	9.4–14	(13–19)
10 x 1.25	12–17	(16–23)	20–29	(27–39)
12 x 1.25	21–32	(29–43)	35–53	(47–72)
14 x 1.5	35–52	(48–70)	57–85	(77–110)
16 x 1.5	51–77	(67–100)	90–120	(130–160)
18 x 1.5	74–110	(100–150)	130–170	(180–230)
20 x 1.5	110–140	(150–190)	190–240	(160–320)
22 x 1.5	150–190	(200–260)	250–320	(340–430)
24 x 1.5	190–240	(260–320)	310–410	(420–550)

NOTE: *This engine rebuilding section is a guide to accepted rebuilding procedures. Typical examples of standard rebuilding procedures are illustrated. Use these procedures along with the detailed instructions earlier in this chapter, concerning your particular engine.*

Cylinder Head Reconditioning

Procedure	Method
Remove the cylinder head:	See the engine service procedures earlier in this chapter for details concerning specific engines.
Identify the valves:	Invert the cylinder head, and number the valve faces front to rear, using a permanent felt-tip marker.
Remove the rocker arms:	Remove the rocker arms with shaft(s) or balls and nuts. Wire the sets of rockers, balls and nuts together, and identify according to the corresponding valve.
Remove the valves and springs:	Using an appropriate valve spring compressor (depending on the configuration of the cylinder head), compress the valve springs. Lift out the keepers with needlenose pliers, release the compressor, and remove the valve, spring, and spring retainer. See the engine service procedures earlier in this chapter for details concerning specific engines.
Check the valve stem-to-guide clearance: 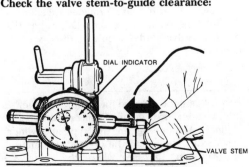 DIAL INDICATOR — VALVE STEM **Check the valve stem-to-guide clearance**	Clean the valve stem with lacquer thinner or a similar solvent to remove all gum and varnish. Clean the valve guides using solvent and an expanding wire-type valve guide cleaner. Mount a dial indicator so that the stem is at 90° to the valve stem, as close to the valve guide as possible. Move the valve off its seat, and measure the valve guide-to-stem clearance by rocking the stem back and forth to actuate the dial indicator. Measure the valve stems using a micrometer, and compare to specifications, to determine whether stem or guide wear is responsible for excessive clearance. **NOTE:** *Consult the Specifications tables earlier in this chapter.*

Cylinder Head Reconditioning

Procedure	Method

De-carbon the cylinder head and valves:

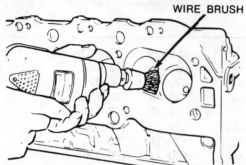
WIRE BRUSH

Remove the carbon from the cylinder head with a wire brush and electric drill

Chip carbon away from the valve heads, combustion chambers, and ports, using a chisel made of hardwood. Remove the remaining deposits with a stiff wire brush.
NOTE: *Be sure that the deposits are actually removed, rather than burnished.*

Hot-tank the cylinder head (cast iron heads only):
CAUTION: *Do not hot-tank aluminum parts.*

Have the cylinder head hot-tanked to remove grease, corrosion, and scale from the water passages.
NOTE: *In the case of overhead cam cylinder heads, consult the operator to determine whether the camshaft bearings will be damaged by the caustic solution.*

Degrease the remaining cylinder head parts:

Clean the remaining cylinder head parts in an engine cleaning solvent. Do not remove the protective coating from the springs.

Check the cylinder head for warpage:

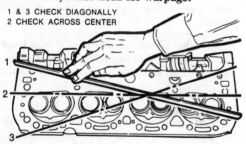
1 & 3 CHECK DIAGONALLY
2 CHECK ACROSS CENTER

Check the cylinder head for warpage

Place a straight-edge across the gasket surface of the cylinder head. Using feeler gauges, determine the clearance at the center of the straight-edge. If warpage exceeds .003″ in a 6″ span, or .006″ over the total length, the cylinder head must be resurfaced.
NOTE: *If warpage exceeds the manufacturer's maximum tolerance for material removal, the cylinder head must be replaced.*
   When milling the cylinder heads of V-type engines, the intake manifold mounting position is altered, and must be corrected by milling the manifold flange a proportionate amount.

---

*Knurl the valve guides:

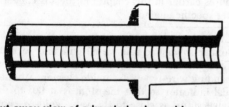

Cut-away view of a knurled valve guide

*Valve guides which are not excessively worn or distorted may, in some cases, be knurled rather than replaced. Knurling is a process in which metal is displaced and raised, thereby reducing clearance. Knurling also provides excellent oil control. The possibility of knurling rather than replacing valve guides should be discussed with a machinist.

Replace the valve guides:
NOTE: *Valve guides should only be replaced if damaged or if an oversize valve stem is not available.*

See the engine service procedures earlier in this chapter for details concerning specific engines. Depending on the type of cylinder head, valve guides may be pressed, hammered, or shrunk in. In cases where the guides are shrunk into the head, replacement should be left to an equipped machine shop. In other

Cylinder Head Reconditioning

Procedure	Method

A—VALVE GUIDE I.D.   B—LARGER THAN THE VALVE GUIDE O.D.

WASHERS

B—A—

A—VALVE GUIDE I.D.   B—LARGER THAN THE VALVE GUIDE O.D.

Valve guide installation tool using washers for installation

cases, the guides are replaced using a stepped drift (see illustration). Determine the height above the boss that the guide must extend, and obtain a stack of washers, their I.D. similar to the guide's O.D., of that height. Place the stack of washers on the guide, and insert the guide into the boss.

NOTE: *Valve guides are often tapered or beveled for installation.* Using the stepped installation tool (see illustration), press or tap the guides into position. Ream the guides according to the size of the valve stem.

Replace valve seat inserts:

Replacement of valve seat inserts which are worn beyond resurfacing or broken, if feasible, must be done by a machine shop.

Resurface (grind) the valve face:

FOR DIMENSIONS, REFER TO SPECIFICATIONS

CHECK FOR BENT STEM

DIAMETER

VALVE FACE ANGLE

1/32″ MINIMUM   THIS LINE PARALLEL WITH VALVE HEAD

Critical valve dimensions

Using a valve grinder, resurface the valves according to specifications given earlier in this chapter.

CAUTION: *Valve face angle is not always identical to valve seat angle.* A minimum margin of 1/32″ should remain after grinding the valve. The valve stem top should also be squared and resurfaced, by placing the stem in the V-block of the grinder, and turning it while pressing lightly against the grinding wheel.

NOTE: *Do not grind sodium filled exhaust valves on a machine. These should be hand lapped.*

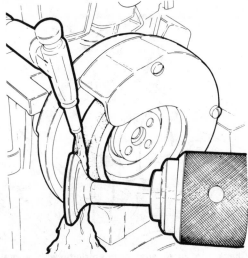

Valve grinding by machine

Cylinder Head Reconditioning

Procedure	Method

Resurface the valve seats using reamers of grinder:

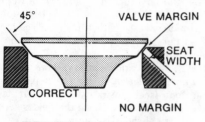

Valve seat width and centering

Reaming the valve seat with a hand reamer

Select a reamer of the correct seat angle, slightly larger than the diameter of the valve seat, and assemble it with a pilot of the correct size. Install the pilot into the valve guide, and using steady pressure, turn the reamer clockwise.
CAUTION: *Do not turn the reamer counterclockwise.* Remove only as much material as necessary to clean the seat. Check the concentricity of the seat (following). If the dye method is not used, coat the valve face with Prussian blue dye, install and rotate it on the valve seat. Using the dye marked area as a centering guide, center and narrow the valve seat to specifications with correction cutters.
NOTE: *When no specifications are available, minimum seat width for exhaust valves should be 5/64", intake valves 1/16".*
After making correction cuts, check the position of the valve seat on the valve face using Prussian blue dye.

To resurface the seat with a power grinder, select a pilot of the correct size and coarse stone of the proper angle. Lubricate the pilot and move the stone on and off the valve seat at 2 cycles per second, until all flaws are gone. Finish the seat with a fine stone. If necessary the seat can be corrected or narrowed using correction stones.

Check the valve seat concentricity:

Check the valve seat concentricity with a dial gauge

Coat the valve face with Prussian blue dye, install the valve, and rotate it on the valve seat. If the entire seat becomes coated, and the valve is known to be concentric, the seat is concentric.

*Install the dial gauge pilot into the guide, and rest of the arm on the valve seat. Zero the gauge, and rotate the arm around the seat. Run-out should not exceed .002".

Cylinder Head Reconditioning

Procedure	Method

*Lap the valves:
NOTE: *Valve lapping is done to ensure efficient sealing of resurfaced valves and seats.*

Invert the cylinder head, lightly lubricate the valve stems, and install the valves in the head as numbered. Coat valve seats with fine grinding compound, and attach the lapping tool suction cup to a valve head.
NOTE: *Moisten the suction cup.* Rotate the tool between the palms, changing position and lifting the tool often to prevent grooving. Lap the valve until a smooth, polished seat is evident. Remove the valve and tool, and rinse away all traces of grinding compound.

**Fasten a suction cup to a piece of drill rod, and mount the rod in a hand drill. Proceed as above, using the hand drill as a lapping tool.
CAUTION: *Due to the higher speeds involved when using the hand drill, care must be exercised to avoid grooving the seat.* Lift the tool and change direction of rotation often.

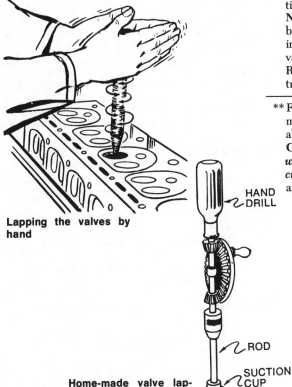

Lapping the valves by hand

HAND DRILL

ROD

SUCTION CUP

Home-made valve lapping tool

Check the valve springs:

Place the spring on a flat surface next to a square. Measure the height of the spring, and rotate it against the edge of the square to measure distortion. If spring height varies (by comparison) by more than $1/16''$ or if distortion exceeds $1/16''$, replace the spring.

**In addition to evaluating the spring as above, test the spring pressure at the installed and compressed (installed height minus valve lift) height using a valve spring tester. Springs used on small displacement engines (up to 3 liters) should be $\mp$ 1 lb of all other springs in either position. A tolerance of $\mp$ 5 lbs is permissible on larger engines.

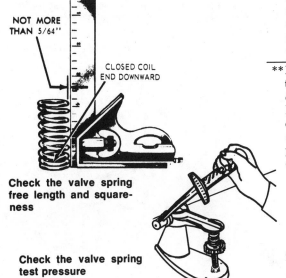

NOT MORE THAN 5/64''

CLOSED COIL END DOWNWARD

Check the valve spring free length and squareness

Check the valve spring test pressure

Cylinder Head Reconditioning

Procedure	Method
*Install valve stem seals: 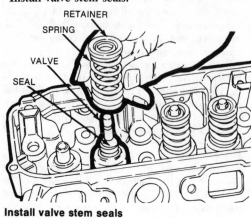 **Install valve stem seals**	*Due to the pressure differential that exists at the ends of the intake valve guides (atmospheric pressure above, manifold vacuum below), oil is drawn through the valve guides into the intake port. This has been alleviated somewhat since the addition of positive crankcase ventilation, which lowers the pressure above the guides. Several types of valve stem seals are available to reduce blow-by. Certain seals simply slip over the stem and guide boss, while others require that the boss be machined. Recently, Teflon guide seals have become popular. Consult a parts supplier or machinist concerning availability and suggested usages. NOTE: *When installing seals, ensure that a small amount of oil is able to pass the seal to lubricate the valve guides; otherwise, excessive wear may result.*
Install the valves:	See the engine service procedures earlier in this chapter for details concerning specific engines. Lubricate the valve stems, and install the valves in the cylinder head as numbered. Lubricate and position the seals (if used) and the valve springs. Install the spring retainers, compress the springs, and insert the keys using needlenose pliers or a tool designed for this purpose. NOTE: *Retain the keys with wheel bearing grease during installation.*
Check valve spring installed height: 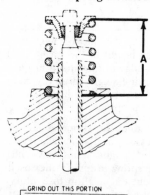 Valve spring installed height (A)  Measure the valve spring installed height (A) with a modified steel rule	Measure the distance between the spring pad the lower edge of the spring retainer, and compare to specifications. If the installed height is incorrect, add shim washers between the spring pad and the spring. CAUTION: *Use only washers designed for this purpose.*

Cylinder Head Reconditioning

Procedure	Method

Inspect the rocker arms, balls, studs, and nuts:

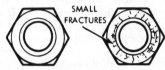

Stress cracks in the rocker nuts

Visually inspect the rocker arms, balls, studs, and nuts for cracks, galling, burning, scoring, or wear. If all parts are intact, liberally lubricate the rocker arms and balls, and install them on the cylinder head. If wear is noted on a rocker arm at the point of valve contact, grind it smooth and square, removing as little material as possible. Replace the rocker arm if excessively worn. If a rocker stud shows signs of wear, it must be replaced (see below). If a rocker nut shows stress cracks, replace it. If an exhaust ball is galled or burned, substitute the intake ball from the same cylinder (if it is intact), and install a new intake ball.

NOTE: *Avoid using new rocker balls on exhaust valves.*

Replace rocker studs:

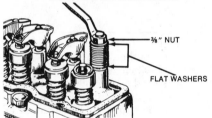

Extracting a pressed-in rocker stud

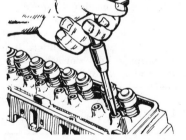

Ream the stud bore for oversize rocker studs

In order to remove a threaded stud, lock two nuts on the stud, and unscrew the stud using the lower nut. Coat the lower threads of the new stud with Loctite, and install.

Two alternative methods are available for replacing pressed in studs. Remove the damaged stud using a stack of washers and a nut (see ilustration). In the first, the boss is reamed .005–.006″ oversize, and an oversize stud pressed in. Control the stud extension over the boss using washers, in the same manner as valve guides. Before installing the stud, coat it with white lead and grease. To retain the stud more positively drill a hole through the stud and boss, and install a roll pin. In the second method, the boss is tapped, and a threaded stud installed.

Inspect the rocker shaft(s) and rocker arms:

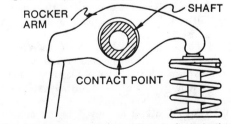

Check the rocker arm-to-rocker shaft contact area

Remove the rocker arms, springs and washers from rocker shaft.

NOTE: *Lay out parts in the order as they are removed.* Inspect rocker arms for pitting or wear on the valve contact point, or excessive bushing wear. Bushings need only be replaced if wear is excessive, because the rocker arm normally contacts the shaft at one point only. Grind the valve contact point of rocker arm smooth if necessary, removing as little material as possible. If excessive material must be removed to smooth and square the arm, it should be replaced. Clean out all oil holes and passages in rocker shaft. If shaft is grooved or worn, replace it. Lubricate and assemble the rocker shaft.

Cylinder Head Reconditioning

Procedure	Method
Inspect the pushrods:	Remove the pushrods, and, if hollow, clean out the oil passages using fine wire. Roll each pushrod over a piece of clean glass. If a distinct clicking sound is heard as the pushrod rolls, the rod is bent, and must be replaced.
	*The length of all pushrods must be equal. Measure the length of the pushrods, compare to specifications, and replace as necessary.
*Inspect the valve lifters: 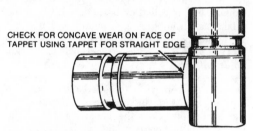 CHECK FOR CONCAVE WEAR ON FACE OF TAPPET USING TAPPET FOR STRAIGHT EDGE **Check the lifter face for squareness**	Remove lifters from their bores, and remove gum and varnish, using solvent. Clean walls of lifter bores. Check lifters for concave wear as illustrated. If face is worn concave, replace lifter, and carefully inspect the camshaft. Lightly lubricate lifter and insert it into its bore. If play is excessive, an oversize lifter must be installed (where possible). Consult a machinist concerning feasibility. If play is satisfactory, remove, lubricate, and reinstall the lifter.
*Testing hydraulic lifter leak down:	Submerge lifter in a container of kerosene. Chuck a used pushrod or its equivalent into a drill press. Position container of kerosene so pushrod acts on the lifter plunger. Pump lifter with the drill press, until resistance increases. Pump several more times to bleed any air out of lifter. Apply very firm, constant pressure to the lifter, and observe rate at which fluid bleeds out of lifter. If the fluid bleeds very quickly (less than 15 seconds), lifter is defective. If the time exceeds 60 seconds, lifter is sticking. In either case, recondition or replace lifter. If lifter is operating properly (leak down time 15–60 seconds), lubricate and install it.

Cylinder Block Reconditioning

Procedure	Method
Checking the main bearing clearance: 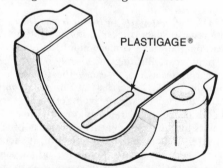 PLASTIGAGE® **Plastigage® installed on the lower bearing shell**	Invert engine, and remove cap from the bearing to be checked. Using a clean, dry rag, thoroughly clean all oil from crankshaft journal and bearing insert. NOTE: *Plastigage® is soluble in oil; therefore, oil on the journal or bearing could result in erroneous readings.* Place a piece of Plastigage along the full length of journal, reinstall cap, and torque to specifications. NOTE: **Specifications are given in the engine specifications earlier in this chapter.** Remove bearing cap, and determine bearing clearance by comparing width of Plastigage to the scale on Plastigage envelope. Journal taper is determined by comparing width of the Plas-

Cylinder Block Reconditioning

Procedure	Method

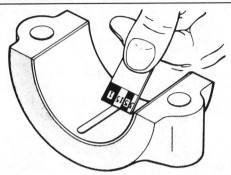

Measure Plastigage® to determine main bearing clearance

tigage strip near its ends. Rotate crankshaft 90° and retest, to determine journal eccentricity. **NOTE:** *Do not rotate crankshaft with Plastigage installed.* If bearing insert and journal appear intact, and are within tolerances, no further main bearing service is required. If bearing or journal appear defective, cause of failure should be determined before replacement.

*Remove crankshaft from block (see below). Measure the main bearing journals at each end twice (90° apart) using a micrometer, to determine diameter, journal taper and eccentricity. If journals are within tolerances, reinstall bearing caps at their specified torque. Using a telescope gauge and micrometer, measure bearing I.D. parallel to piston axis and at 30° on each side of piston axis. Subtract journal O.D. for bearing I.D. to determine oil clearance. If crankshaft journals appear defective, or do not meet tolerances, there is no need to measure bearings; for the crankshaft will require grinding and/or undersize bearings will be required. If bearing appears defective, cause for failure should be determined prior to replacement.

Check the connecting rod bearing clearance:

Connecting rod bearing clearance is checked in the same manner as main bearing clearance, using Plastigage. Before removing the crankshaft, connecting rod side clearance also should be measured and recorded.

*Checking connecting rod bearing clearance, using a micrometer, is identical to checking main bearing clearance. If no other service is required, the piston and rod assemblies need not be removed.

Remove the crankshaft:

Using a punch, mark the corresponding main bearing caps and saddles according to position (i.e., one punch on the front main cap and saddle, two on the second, three on the third, etc.). Using number stamps, identify the corresponding connecting rods and caps, according to cylinder (if no numbers are present). Remove the main and connecting rod caps, and place

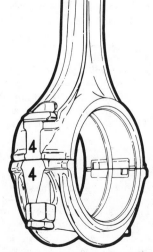

Match the connecting rod to the cylinder with a number stamp

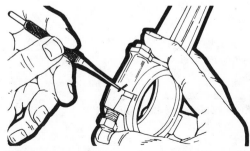

Match the connecting rod and cap with scribe marks

Cylinder Block Reconditioning

Procedure	Method
	sleeves of plastic tubing or vacuum hose over the connecting rod bolts, to protect the journals as the crankshaft is removed. Lift the crankshaft out of the block.
Remove the ridge from the top of the cylinder: RIDGE CAUSED BY CYLINDER WEAR CYLINDER WALL TOP OF PISTON **Cylinder bore ridge**	In order to facilitate removal of the piston and connecting rod, the ridge at the top of the cylinder (unworn area; see illustration) must be removed. Place the piston at the bottom of the bore, and cover it with a rag. Cut the ridge away using a ridge reamer, exercising extreme care to avoid cutting too deeply. Remove the rag, and remove cuttings that remain on the piston. **CAUTION:** *If the ridge is not removed, and new rings are installed, damage to rings will result.*
Remove the piston and connecting rod: **Push the piston out with a hammer handle**	Invert the engine, and push the pistons and connecting rods out of the cylinders. If necessary, tap the connecting rod boss with a wooden hammer handle, to force the piston out. **CAUTION:** *Do not attempt to force the piston past the cylinder ridge* (see above).
Service the crankshaft:	Ensure that all oil holes and passages in the crankshaft are open and free of sludge. If necessary, have the crankshaft ground to the largest possible undersize.
	** Have the crankshaft Magnafluxed, to locate stress cracks. Consult a machinist concerning additional service procedures, such as surface hardening (e.g., nitriding, Tuftriding) to improve wear characteristics, cross drilling and chamfering the oil holes to improve lubrication, and balancing.
Removing freeze plugs:	Drill a small hole in the middle of the freeze plugs. Thread a large sheet metal screw into the hole and remove the plug with a slide hammer.
Remove the oil gallery plugs:	Threaded plugs should be removed using an appropriate (usually square) wrench. To remove soft, pressed in plugs, drill a hole in the plug, and thread in a sheet metal screw. Pull the plug out by the screw using pliers.

Cylinder Block Reconditioning

Procedure	Method
Hot-tank the block: NOTE: *Do not hot-tank aluminum parts.*	Have the block hot-tanked to remove grease, corrosion, and scale from the water jackets. NOTE: *Consult the operator to determine whether the camshaft bearings will be damaged during the hot-tank process.*
Check the block for cracks:	Visually inspect the block for cracks or chips. The most common locations are as follows: Adjacent to freeze plugs. Between the cylinders and water jackets. Adjacent to the main bearing saddles. At the extreme bottom of the cylinders. Check only suspected cracks using spot check dye (see introduction). If a crack is located, consult a machinist concerning possible repairs.
	** Magnaflux the block to locate hidden cracks. If cracks are located, consult a machinist about feasibility of repair.
Install the oil gallery plugs and freeze plugs:	Coat freeze plugs with sealer and tap into position using a piece of pipe, slightly smaller than the plug, as a driver. To ensure retention, stake the edges of the plugs. Coat threaded oil gallery plugs with sealer and install. Drive replacement soft plugs into block using a large drift as a driver.
	* Rather than reinstalling lead plugs, drill and tap the holes, and install threaded plugs.
Check the bore diameter and surface: 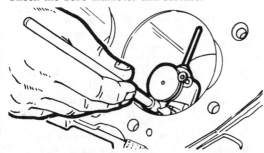 **Measure the cylinder bore with a dial gauge**	Visually inspect the cylinder bores for roughness, scoring, or scuffing. If evident, the cylinder bore must be bored or honed oversize to eliminate imperfections, and the smallest possible oversize piston used. The new pistons should be given to the machinist with the block, so that the cylinders can be bored or honed exactly to the piston size (plus clearance). If no flaws are evident, measure the bore diameter using a telescope gauge and micrometer, or dial gauge, parallel and perpendicular to the engine centerline, at the top (below the ridge) and bottom of the bore. Subtract the bottom measurements from the top to determine taper, and the parallel to

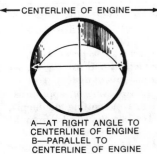

Cylinder bore measuring points

A—AT RIGHT ANGLE TO CENTERLINE OF ENGINE
B—PARALLEL TO CENTERLINE OF ENGINE

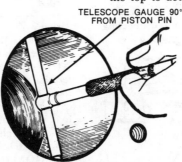

Measure the cylinder bore with a telescope gauge

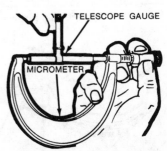

Measure the telescope gauge with a micrometer to determine the cylinder bore

Cylinder Block Reconditioning

Procedure	Method
	the centerline measurements from the perpendicular measurements to determine eccentricity. If the measurements are not within specifications, the cylinder must be bored or honed, and an oversize piston installed. If the measurements are within specifications the cylinder may be used as is, with only finish honing (see below). **NOTE:** *Prior to submitting the block for boring, perform the following operation(s).*
Check the cylinder block bearing alignment: 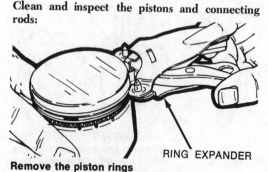 **Check the main bearing saddle alignment**	Remove the upper bearing inserts. Place a straightedge in the bearing saddles along the centerline of the crankshaft. If clearance exists between the straightedge and the center saddle, the block must be alignbored.
***Check the deck height:**	The deck height is the distance from the crankshaft centerline to the block deck. To measure, invert the engine, and install the crankshaft, retaining it with the center main cap. Measure the distance from the crankshaft journal to the block deck, parallel to the cylinder centerline. Measure the diameter of the end (front and rear) main journals, parallel to the centerline of the cylinders, divide the diameter in half, and subtract it from the previous measurement. The results of the front and rear measurements should be identical. If the difference exceeds .005″, the deck height should be corrected. **NOTE:** *Block deck height and warpage should be corrected at the same time.*
Check the block deck for warpage:	Using a straightedge and feeler gauges, check the block deck for warpage in the same manner that the cylinder head is checked (see Cylinder Head Reconditioning). If warpage exceeds specifications, have the deck resurfaced. **NOTE:** *In certain cases a specification for total material removal (cylinder head and block deck) is provided. This specification must not be exceeded.*
Clean and inspect the pistons and connecting rods: **RING EXPANDER** **Remove the piston rings**	Using a ring expander, remove the rings from the piston. Remove the retaining rings (if so equipped) and remove piston pin. **NOTE:** *If the piston pin must be pressed out, determine the proper method and use the proper tools; otherwise the piston will distort.* Clean the ring grooves using an appropriate tool, exercising care to avoid cutting too deeply. Thoroughly clean all carbon and varnish from the piston with solvent. **CAUTION:** *Do not use a wire brush or caustic solvent on pistons.* Inspect the pistons for scuffing, scoring, cracks, pitting, or excessive ring

Cylinder Block Reconditioning

Procedure	Method

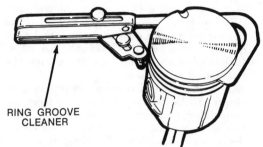

RING GROOVE
CLEANER

Clean the piston ring grooves

groove wear. If wear is evident, the piston must be replaced. Check the connecting rod length by measuring the rod from the inside of the large end to the inside of the small end using calipers (see illustration). All connecting rods should be equal length. Replace any rod that differs from the others in the engine.

* Have the connecting rod alignment checked in an alignment fixture by a machinist. Replace any twisted or bent rods.

* Magnaflux the connecting rods to locate stress cracks. If cracks are found, replace the connecting rod.

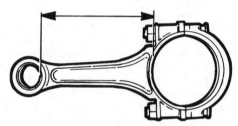

Check the connecting rod length (arrow)

Fit the pistons to the cylinders:

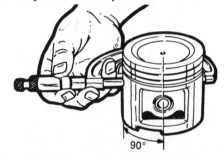

90°

Measure the piston prior to fitting

Using a telescope gauge and micrometer, or a dial gauge, measure the cylinder bore diameter perpendicular to the piston pin, 2½″ below the deck. Measure the piston perpendicular to its pin on the skirt. The difference between the two measurements is the piston clearance. If the clearance is within specifications or slightly below (after boring or honing), finish honing is all that is required. If the clearance is excessive, try to obtain a slightly larger piston to bring clearance within specifications. Where this is not possible, obtain the first oversize piston, and hone (or if necessary, bore) the cylinder to size.

Assemble the pistons and connecting rods:

Install the piston pin lock-rings (if used)

Inspect piston pin, connecting rod small end bushing, and piston bore for galling, scoring, or excessive wear. If evident, replace defective part(s). Measure the I.D. of the piston boss and connecting rod small end, and the O.D. of the piston pin. If within specifications, assemble piston pin and rod.
CAUTION: *If piston pin must be pressed in, determine the proper method and use the proper tools; otherwise the piston will distort.*
    Install the lock rings; ensure that they seat properly. If the parts are not within specifications, determine the service method for the type of engine. In some cases, piston and pin are serviced as an assembly when either is defective. Others specify reaming the piston and connecting rods for an oversize pin. If the connecting rod bushing is worn, it may in many cases be replaced. Reaming the piston and replacing the rod bushing are machine shop operations.

Cylinder Block Reconditioning

Procedure	Method

Clean and inspect the camshaft:

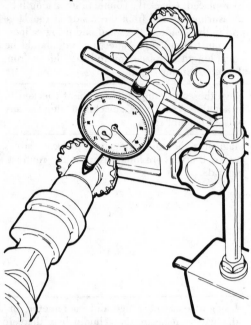

Check the camshaft for straightness

Degrease the camshaft, using solvent, and clean out all oil holes. Visually inspect cam lobes and bearing journals for excessive wear. If a lobe is questionable, check all lobes as indicated below. If a journal or lobe is worn, the camshaft must be regrounded or replaced.

NOTE: *If a journal is worn, there is a good chance that the bushings are worn.* If lobes and journals appear intact, place the front and rear journals in V-blocks, and rest a dial indicator on the center journal. Rotate the camshaft to check straightness. If deviation exceeds .001", replace the camshaft.

* Check the camshaft lobes with a micrometer, by measuring the lobes from the nose to base and again at 90° (see illustration). The lift is determined by subtracting the second measurement from the first. If all exhaust lobes and all intake lobes are not identical, the camshaft must be reground or replaced.

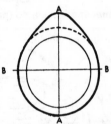

Camshaft lobe measurement

Replace the camshaft bearings:

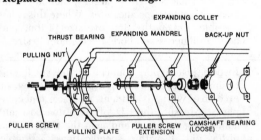

Camshaft bearing removal and installation tool (OHV engines only)

If excessive wear is indicated, or if the engine is being completely rebuilt, camshaft bearings should be replaced as follows: Drive the camshaft rear plug from the block. Assemble the removal puller with its shoulder on the bearing to be removed. Gradually tighten the puller nut until bearing is removed. Remove remaining bearings, leaving the front and rear for last. To remove front and rear bearings, reverse position of the tool, so as to pull the bearings in toward the center of the block. Leave the tool in this position, pilot the new front and rear bearings on the installer, and pull them into position: Return the tool to its original position and pull remaining bearings into position.

NOTE: *Ensure that oil holes align when installing bearings.* Replace camshaft rear plug, and stake it into position to aid retention.

Finish hone the cylinders:

Chuck a flexible drive hone into a power drill, and insert it into the cylinder. Start the hone, and remove it up and down in the cylinder at a rate which will produce approximately a 60° cross-hatch pattern.

NOTE: *Do not extend the hone below the cylinder bore.* After developing the pattern, remove

Cylinder Block Reconditioning

Procedure	Method

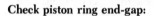

CROSS HATCH
PATTERN

50°-60°

Cylinder bore after honing

the hone and recheck piston fit. Wash the cylinders with a detergent and water solution to remove abrasive dust, dry, and wipe several times with a rag soaked in engine oil.

Check piston ring end-gap:

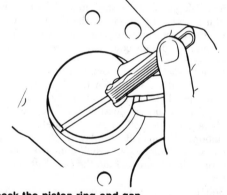

Check the piston ring end gap

Compress the piston rings to be used in a cylinder, one at a time, into that cylinder, and press them approximately 1″ below the deck with an inverted piston. Using feeler gauges, measure the ring end-gap, and compare to specifications. Pull the ring out of the cylinder and file the ends with a fine file to obtain proper clearance.

CAUTION: *If inadequate ring end-gap is utilized, ring breakage will result.*

Install the piston rings:

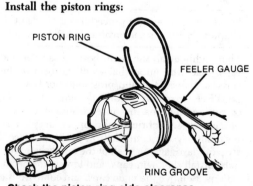

PISTON RING

FEELER GAUGE

RING GROOVE

Check the piston ring side clearance

Inspect the ring grooves in the piston for excessive wear or taper. If necessary, recut the groove(s) for use with an overwidth ring or a standard ring and spacer. If the groove is worn uniformly, overwidth rings, or standard rings and spacers may be installed without recutting. Roll the outside of the ring around the groove to check for burrs or deposits. If any are found, remove with a fine file. Hold the ring in the groove, and measure side clearance. If necessary, correct as indicated above.

NOTE: *Always install any additional spacers above the piston ring.*

The ring groove must be deep enough to allow the ring to seat below the lands (see illustration). In many cases, a "go-no-go" depth gauge will be provided with the piston rings. Shallow grooves may be corrected by recutting, while deep grooves require some type of filler or expander

Cylinder Block Reconditioning

Procedure	Method
	behind the piston. Consult the piston ring supplier concerning the suggested method. Install the rings on the piston, lowest ring first, using a ring expander. NOTE: *Position the rings as specified by the manufacturer.* Consult the engine service procedures earlier in this chapter for details concerning specific engines.
Install the camshaft:	Liberally lubricate the camshaft lobes and journals, and install the camshaft. CAUTION: *Exercise extreme care to avoid damaging the bearings when inserting the camshaft.* Install and tighten the camshaft thrust plate retaining bolts.
	See the engine service procedures earlier in this chapter for details concerning specific engines.
Check camshaft end-play (OHV engines only):	Using feeler gauges, determine whether the clearance between the camshaft boss (or gear) and backing plate is within specifications. Install shims behind the thrust plate, or reposition the camshaft gear and retest endplay. In some cases, adjustment is by replacing the thrust plate. See the engine service procedures earlier in this chapter for details concerning specific engines.

Check the camshaft end-play with a feeler gauge

Check the camshaft end-play with a dial indicator

*Mount a dial indicator stand so that the stem of the dial indicator rests on the nose of the camshaft, parallel to the camshaft axis. Push the camshaft as far in as possible and zero the gauge. Move the camshaft outward to determine the amount of camshaft endplay. If the endplay is not within tolerance, install shims behind the thrust plate, or reposition the camshaft gear and retest.
See the engine service procedures earlier in this chapter for details concerning specific engines.

Install the rear main seal:	See the engine service procedures earlier in this chapter for details concerning specific engines.
Install the crankshaft:	Thoroughly clean the main bearing saddles and caps. Place the upper halves of the bearing inserts on the saddles and press into position. NOTE: *Ensure that the oil holes align.* Press the corresponding bearing inserts into the main bearing caps. Lubricate the upper main bearings, and lay the crankshaft in position. Place a strip of Plastigage on each of the crankshaft journals, install the main caps, and torque to specifications. Remove the main caps, and compare the Plastigage to the scale on the Plastigage envelope. If clearances are within tolerances, remove the Plastigage, turn the crankshaft 90°, wipe off all oil and retest. If all clearances are correct,

Remove or install the upper bearing insert using a roll-out pin

Cylinder Block Reconditioning

Procedure	Method

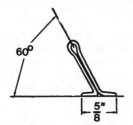

Home-made bearing roll-out pin

remove all Plastigage, thoroughly lubricate the main caps and bearing journals, and install the main caps. If clearances are not within tolerance, the upper bearing inserts may be removed, without removing the crankshaft, using a bearing roll out pin (see illustration). Roll in a bearing that will provide proper clearance, and retest. Torque all main caps, excluding the thrust bearing cap, to specifications. Tighten the thrust bearing cap finger tight. To properly align the thrust bearing, pry the crankshaft the extent of its axial travel several times, the last movement held toward the front of the engine, and torque the thrust bearing cap to specifications. Determine the crankshaft end-play (see below), and bring within tolerance with thrust washers.

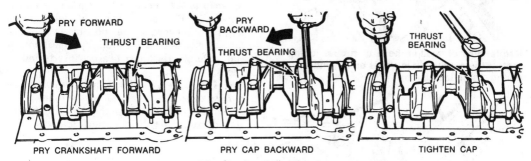

Aligning the thrust bearing

Measure crankshaft end-play:

Mount a dial indicator stand on the front of the block, with the dial indicator stem resting on the nose of the crankshaft, parallel to the crankshaft axis. Pry the crankshaft the extent of its travel rearward, and zero the indicator. Pry the crankshaft forward and record crankshaft end-play.
NOTE: *Crankshaft end-play also may be measured at the thrust bearing, using feeler gauges (see illustration).*

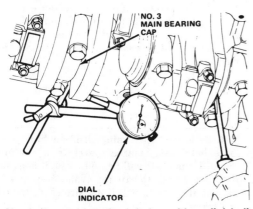

Check the crankshaft end-play with a dial indicator

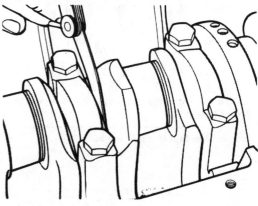

Check the crankshaft end-play with a feeler gauge

Cylinder Block Reconditioning

Procedure	Method

Install the pistons:

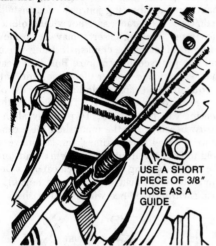

USE A SHORT PIECE OF 3/8" HOSE AS A GUIDE

Use lengths of vacuum hose or rubber tubing to protect the crankshaft journals and cylinder walls during piston installation

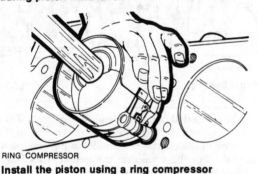

RING COMPRESSOR

Install the piston using a ring compressor

Press the upper connecting rod bearing halves into the connecting rods, and the lower halves into the connecting rod caps. Position the piston ring gaps according to specifications (see car section), and lubricate the pistons. Install a ring compresser on a piston, and press two long (8") pieces of plastic tubing over the rod bolts. Using the tubes as a guide, press the pistons into the bores and onto the crankshaft with a wooden hammer handle. After seating the rod on the crankshaft journal, remove the tubes and install the cap finger tight. Install the remaining pistons in the same manner. Invert the engine and check the bearing clearance at two points (90° apart) on each journal with Plastigage. **NOTE: *Do not turn the crankshaft with Plastigage installed.*** If clearance is within tolerances, remove *all* Plastigage, thoroughly lubricate the journals, and torque the rod caps to specifications. If clearance is not within specifications, install different thickness bearing inserts and recheck.

CAUTION: *Never shim or file the connecting rods or caps.* Always install plastic tube sleeves over the rod bolts when the caps are not installed, to protect the crankshaft journals.

Check connecting rod side clearance:

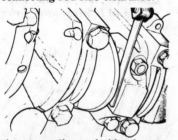

Check the connecting rod side clearance with a feeler gauge

Determine the clearance between the sides of the connecting rods and the crankshaft using feeler gauges. If clearance is below the minimum tolerance, the rod may be machined to provide adequate clearance. If clearance is excessive, substitute an unworn rod, and recheck. If clearance is still outside specifications, the crankshaft must be welded and reground, or replaced.

Inspect the timing chain (or belt):

Visually inspect the timing chain for broken or loose links, and replace the chain if any are found. If the chain will flex sideways, it must be replaced. Install the timing chain as specified. Be sure the timing belt is not stretched, frayed or broken.

NOTE: *If the original timing chain is to be reused, install it in its original position.*

Cylinder Block Reconditioning

Procedure	Method
Check timing gear backlash and runout (OHV engines):  **Check the camshaft gear backlash**	Mount a dial indicator with its stem resting on a tooth of the camshaft gear (as illustrated). Rotate the gear until all slack is removed, and zero the indicator. Rotate the gear in the opposite direction until slack is removed, and record gear backlash. Mount the indicator with its stem resting on the edge of the camshaft gear, parallel to the axis of the camshaft. Zero the indicator, and turn the camshaft gear one full turn, recording the runout. If either backlash or runout exceed specifications, replace the worn gear(s). 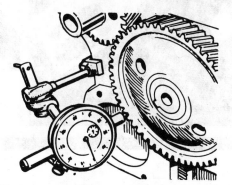 **Check the camshaft gear run-out**

Completing the Rebuilding Process

Follow the above procedures, complete the rebuilding process as follows:

Fill the oil pump with oil, to prevent cavitating (sucking air) on initial engine start up. Install the oil pump and the pickup tube on the engine. Coat the oil pan gasket as necessary, and install the gasket and the oil pan. Mount the flywheel and the crankshaft vibration damper or pulley on the crankshaft. NOTE: *Always use new bolts when installing the flywheel.* Inspect the clutch shaft pilot bushing in the crankshaft. If the bushing is excessively worn, remove it with an expanding puller and a slide hammer, and tap a new bushing into place.

Position the engine, cylinder head side up. Lubricate the lifters, and install them into their bores. Install the cylinder head, and torque it as specified. Insert the pushrods and install the rocker shaft(s) or position the rocker arms on the pushrods. Adjust the valves.

Install the intake and exhaust manifolds, the carburetor(s), the distributor and spark plugs. Adjust the point gap and the static ignition timing. Mount all accessories and install the engine in the car. Fill the radiator with coolant, and the crankcase with high quality engine oil.

Break-in Procedure

Start the engine, and allow it to run at low speed for a few minutes, while checking for leaks. Stop the engine, check the oil level, and fill as necessary. Restart the engine, and fill the cooling system to capacity. Check the point dwell angle and adjust the ignition timing and the valves. Run the engine at low to medium speed (800–2500 rpm) for approximately ½ hour, and retorque the cylinder head bolts. Road test the car, and check again for leaks.

Follow the manufacturer's recommended engine break-in procedure and maintenance schedule for new engines.

Emission Controls and Fuel System

EMISSION CONTROLS

Crankcase Ventilation

SYSTEM OPERATION

A small amount of the fuel/air mixture in each cylinder escapes from the combustion chamber around the piston rings and enters the engine's crankcase, above the oil level. Since this material has been cooled by the lubricating oil and metal parts well below burning temperature, it is only partially burned and constitutes a large source of pollution. The PCV system allows outside air to

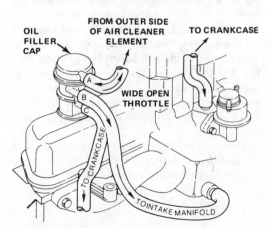

The PCV System

be drawn in to the crankcase and to sweep this material back into the intake passages of the engine to be reburned before it either dirties the oil or escapes to the outside air. A PCV valve is employed to keep the amount of air drawn in at a fairly constant level in spite of the fact that the amount of vacuum produced by the engine's intake system varies, depending on operating conditions.

As shown in the illustration, outside air is drawn in; filtered to remove potentially damaging dirt particles; allowed to enter the crankcase through the valve cover and the oil drains for the valve system; and finally drawn back out of the crankcase; throttled by the PCV valve; and routed to the intake manifold. The throttle is an ingeniously designed movable plunger that is sprung toward the open end of its travel. When the manifold vacuum is high, the vacuum itself compresses the spring and pulls the plunger toward the smaller end of a passage. This keeps the volume of air drawn through the system small enough so that lean carburetor mixtures and consequent rough running or stalling are prevented.

TESTING

1. Disconnect the crankcase inlet air hose at the air cleaner. Run the engine at normal idle speed.

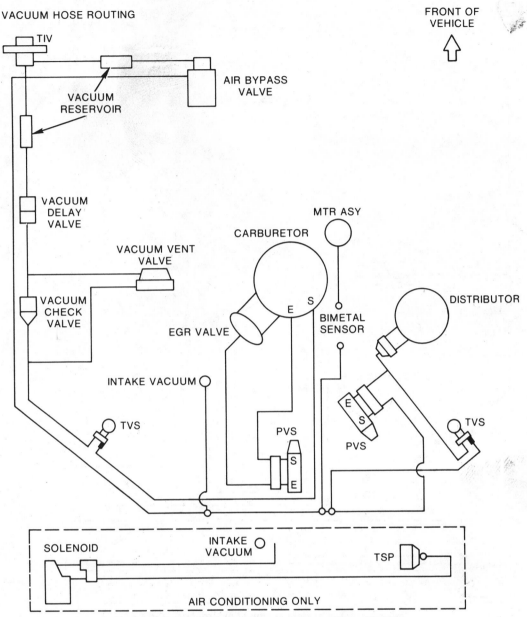

VACUUM HOSE ROUTING

FRONT OF VEHICLE

TIV

VACUUM RESERVOIR

AIR BYPASS VALVE

VACUUM DELAY VALVE

VACUUM VENT VALVE

MTR ASY

CARBURETOR

VACUUM CHECK VALVE

DISTRIBUTOR

EGR VALVE

BIMETAL SENSOR

INTAKE VACUUM

TVS

PVS

TVS

PVS

SOLENOID

INTAKE VACUUM

TSP

AIR CONDITIONING ONLY

Emission control system vacuum hose routing—49 states

2. Allow a stiff piece of paper such as a 3 x 5 card to be drawn against the open end of the hose and release the paper. If the vacuum holds the paper in position, the system is o.k.

CLEANING

1. If the system does not pass this test, first clean the valve and orifice as described in Chapter 1. If the system will not pass the test after this routine service is performed, proceed with the following steps to further clean the system.

2. Carefully noting the location of each part, remove the hoses, fittings, and attachments from the engine.

3. Clean the rubber hoses with an appropriate brush. Then, wash them in a low volatility solvent and allow them to dry.

4. Clean the remaining tubes and fittings and allow them to dry in the same way.

5. Inspect all tubes and fittings for cracks, brittleness, or stretched condition which prevents a tight seal at a joint. Replace parts as necessary.

6. Reassemble the parts in their proper locations.

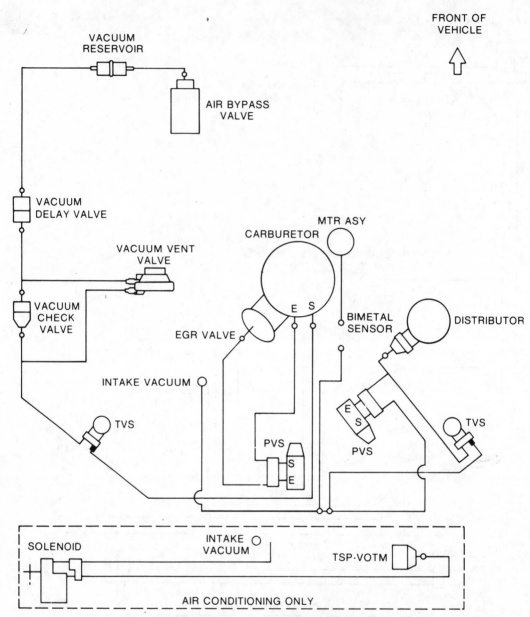

Emission control system vacuum hose routing—California

Thermactor Emission Control System

OPERATION

This system supports the further combustion of carbon monoxide and hydrocarbons in the exhaust manifold and catalytic converter by pumping in extra air. A belt driven air pump is used to pressurize the air and force it through nozzles (one at each exhaust port) to force it into the manifold and mix it completely with the exhaust gases. The system permits richer and more responsive carbu-retor settings while enabling the engine to meet stringent emission standards.

The air pump system incorporates an Air Bypass Valve which closes off the air pump discharge to the exhaust manifold and permits the air to be blown off to the atmosphere. This action occurs for a short time when the throttle is suddenly released, in order to prevent backfire, and, after a time delay, during prolonged idling. This latter action occurs to prevent excessive temperatures in the engine compartment during prolonged idling. When the throttle reaches idle

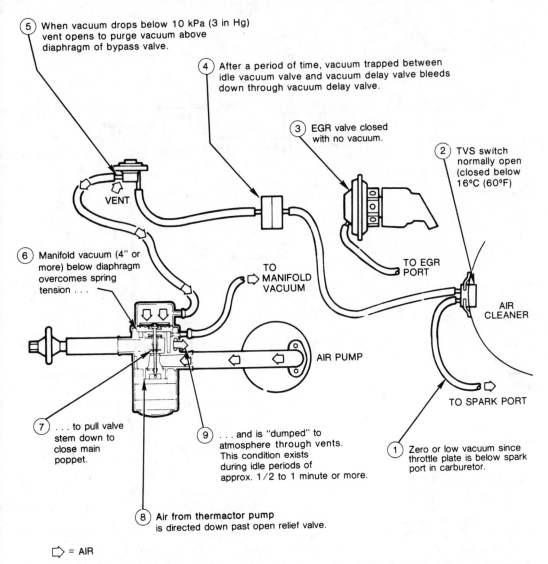

(5) When vacuum drops below 10 kPa (3 in Hg) vent opens to purge vacuum above diaphragm of bypass valve.

(4) After a period of time, vacuum trapped between idle vacuum valve and vacuum delay valve bleeds down through vacuum delay valve.

(3) EGR valve closed with no vacuum.

(2) TVS switch normally open (closed below 16°C (60°F)

VENT

(6) Manifold vacuum (4" or more) below diaphragm overcomes spring tension . . .

TO MANIFOLD VACUUM

TO EGR PORT

AIR CLEANER

AIR PUMP

(7) . . . to pull valve stem down to close main poppet.

(9) . . . and is "dumped" to atmosphere through vents. This condition exists during idle periods of approx. 1/2 to 1 minute or more.

TO SPARK PORT

(1) Zero or low vacuum since throttle plate is below spark port in carburetor.

(8) Air from thermactor pump is directed down past open relief valve.

= AIR

The sequence of events which leads to Thermactor Air Pump bypass during prolonged idle

position, the Spark Port no longer applies vacuum to the system—it is above the throttle plate at that time. At this point, the Vacuum Delay Valve allows pressure to gradually bleed through its orifice until, after 30 seconds to a minute, the pressure is sufficient to activate the Vacuum Vent Valve. This valve bleeds vacuum off the Air bypass Valve, and the air discharged from the pump is sent back to the atmosphere.

Since the Vacuum Delay Valve may be subject to clogging, and its function is critical to vehicle operation under some conditions, periodic testing of the valve is required as a part of normal maintenance. See the maintenance charts in Chapter 1 for required inter-

vals. The testing procedure is provided below.

TESTING THE VACUUM DELAY VALVE

1. Disconnect both inlet and outlet hoses from the valve. Connect a vacuum gauge on the white side of the valve and a measured source of vacuum on the other side. The vacuum gauge hose must be 24 inches long.

2. Apply 10 inches of Mercury vacuum to the system with the vacuum source and maintain it while watching the vacuum gauge and a watch with a second hand. On 1979–80 cars, the vacuum must reach 8 inches of Mercury in 14–47 seconds. For 1978 cars with a white and brown VDR this must occur in 2–5

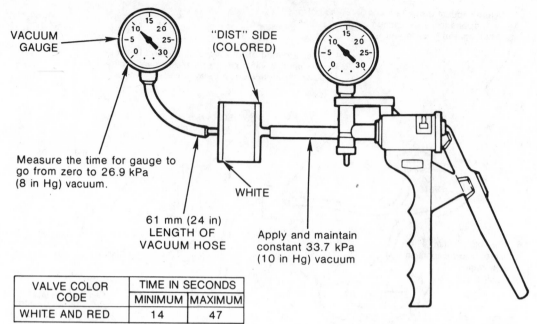

VACUUM GAUGE

"DIST" SIDE (COLORED)

Measure the time for gauge to go from zero to 26.9 kPa (8 in Hg) vacuum.

WHITE

61 mm (24 in) LENGTH OF VACUUM HOSE

Apply and maintain constant 33.7 kPa (10 in Hg) vacuum

VALVE COLOR CODE	TIME IN SECONDS	
	MINIMUM	MAXIMUM
WHITE AND RED	14	47

Vacuum Delay Valve test. Time figures apply to 1979 and 1980 vehicles only; see text for 1978 figures

seconds. For 1978 cars with a white and green valve, the figure is 9 to 20 seconds.

FUEL SYSTEM

Mechanical Fuel Pump
REMOVAL AND INSTALLATION

1. Allow the engine to cool so that if fuel is spilled, it will not ignite. Use a screwdriver or a pair of pliers to spread the crimped portion of the clamps. Just pry under the band where it wraps around the connection to pry it away from the hose—new clamps will be installed anyway. Then, disconnect the inlet and outlet hoses from the connections on the body of the pump.

Fuel pump and hose connections

2. Remove the two 13 mm mounting bolts, and remove the pump from the block.

3. Clean the gasket surfaces on the pump and block with a rag soaked in a non-voltaile solvent.

4. Position a new gasket against the pump mounting surface on the pump, and then position the assembly against the block with the holes in the pump, gasket, and block aligned. Install and tighten the mounting bolts evenly.

5. Inspect the rubber hose connections; if they are brittle or cracked, they should be replaced. Install two hose clamps of the screw tightened type onto each rubber connection. Force the connections over the pump connectors and fuel lines as far as possible. Then move the clamps to a position right near the ends of each rubber connector and tighten snugly.

6. Start the engine and check for leaks: repair any leakage as necessary.

Carburetor
REMOVAL AND INSTALLATION

1. Disconnect the two spark plug wires at the retaining clip running under the air cleaner duct. Then, without loosening the support bracket bolts at the EGR valve or intake manifold, remove the (three) bracket bolts at the air cleaner tray and remove the air cleaner assembly.

Carburetor Operating Principles

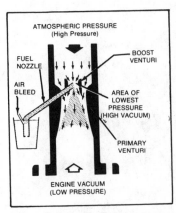

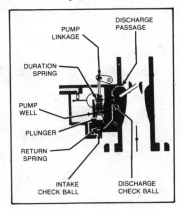

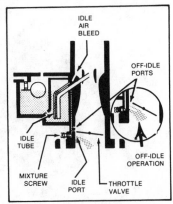

The venturi principle in operation. The pumping action of the pistons creates a vacuum which is amplified by the venturi in the carburetor. This pressure drop will pull fuel from the float bowl through the fuel nozzle. Unfortunately, there is not enough suction present at idle or low speed to make this system work, which is why the carburetor is equipped with an idle and low speed circuit

Accelerator pump system. When the throttle is opened, the air flowing through the venturi starts flowing faster almost immediately, but there is a lag in the flow of fuel out of the main nozzle. The result is that the engine runs lean and stumbles. It needs an extra shot of fuel just when the throttle is opened. This shot is provided by the accelerator pump, which is nothing more than a little pump operated by the throttle linkage that shoots a squirt of fuel through a separate nozzle into the throat of the carburetor

Idle and low-speed system. The vacuum in the intake manifold at idle is high because the throttle is almost completely closed. This vacuum is used to draw fuel into the engine through the idle system and keep it running. Vacuum acts on the idle jet (usually a calibrated tube that sticks down into the main well, below the fuel level) and sucks the fuel into the engine. The idle mixture screw is there to limit the amount of fuel that can go into the engine

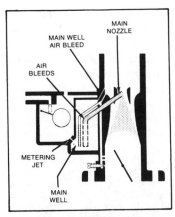

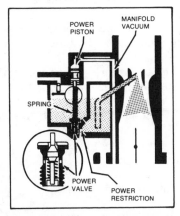

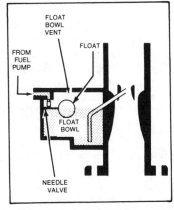

The main metering system may be the simplest system of all, since it is simply the venturi principle in operation. At cruising speeds, the engine sucks enough air to constantly draw fuel through the main fuel nozzle. The main fuel nozzle or jet is calibrated to provide a metering system. The metering system is necessary to prevent an excess amount of fuel flowing into the intake manifold, creating an overly rich mixture

Power circuit. The main metering system works very well at normal engine loads, but when the throttle is in the wide-open position, the engine needs more fuel to prevent detonation and give it full power. The power system provides additional fuel by opening up another passage that leads to the main nozzle. This passageway is controlled by a power valve

Float circuit. When the fuel pump pushes fuel into the carburetor, it flows through a seat and past a needle which is a kind of shutoff valve. The fuel flows into the float bowl and raises a hinged float so that the float arm pushes the needle into the seat and shuts off the fuel. When the fuel level drops, the float drops and more fuel enters the bowl. In this way, a constant fuel supply is maintained

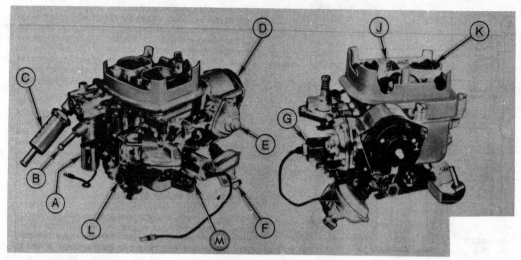

A Vent solenoid
B Vent connection (external)
C Fuel filter
D Electric choke

E Choke pulldown diaphragm
F Dashpot
G Fuel shutoff solenoid
J Primary venturi

K Secondary venturi
L Accelerator pump
M Limiter cap

Carburetor   **omponents**

2. Disconnect the following:

a. The bowl vent hose at the carburetor bowl vent.

b. Fuel vent solenoid, fuel shutoff solenoid, and electric choke wiring connectors.

c. With pliers, pry open the crimp type clamp at the outer end of the fuel filter. Discard the clamp and replace it later with a screw type hose clamp. If the carburetor is to be rebuilt, unscrew the fuel filter with a wrench and discard it.

d. Disconnect the throttle cable at the carburetor linkage.

3. Remove the four carburetor mounting bolts, and remove the carburetor.

4. To install, reverse the above procedures, bearing the following points in mind:

a. Reinstall the carburetor with a new mounting gasket, and torque the bolts evenly and in several stages to 10–15 ft lbs.

b. Install a new fuel filter if the carburetor has been rebuilt. Inspect the rubber connector and replace it if it is cracked or brittle. Install two new hose clamps onto the connector, install it, and tighten hose clamps carefully.

c. After all connections have been made, and the air cleaner is in place, run the engine and check for leaks. Repair leaks as necessary.

FLOAT LEVEL ADJUSTMENT

1. Remove the air cleaner and disconnect the fuel line as described in the procedure above. Disconnect the electric choke wiring connector.

2. Remove the attaching screws from the carburetor cover, and remove the cover from the top of the carburetor.

3. Follow the instructions shown on the illustration. Make sure to hold the carburetor at exactly the angle shown so the needle valve will be just closed.

4. If the clearance is incorrect, bend the tang on the float bracket near where it

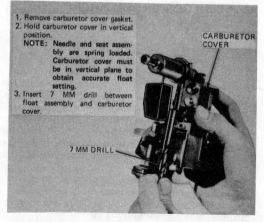

1. Remove carburetor cover gasket.
2. Hold carburetor cover in vertical position.
   NOTE: Needle and seat assembly are spring loaded. Carburetor cover must be in vertical plane to obtain accurate float setting.
3. Insert 7 MM drill between float assembly and carburetor cover.

CARBURETOR COVER

7 MM DRILL

Checking the float level

operates the needle valve in the appropriate direction to correct the setting.

5. Clean the bowl cover mounting surfaces and install a new gasket in the proper position. Open the throttle to clear the fast idle cam, and install the bolt cover and tighten screws alternately and evenly in several stages.

6. Reconnect the fuel filter, using a new screw type clamp and, if necessary, a new rubber connector. Reconnect the choke wiring connector and install the air cleaner in reverse of the above.

FAST IDLE ADJUSTMENT

1. Connect a tachometer. Idle the engine until it is hot and shut it off.

2. Disconnect the fan switch leads located on the thermostat housing and connect the two leads with a jumper wire. Tape the connections to prevent a ground.

3. Disconnect:

a. The two spark plug wires from the air cleaner duct.

b. Vacuum, evaporative, and air pump hoses from the air cleaner.

c. Electrical connectors from the air cleaner. Then, remove the three mounting bolts at the air cleaner tray and remove the assembly.

4. If the vacuum distributor advance line has a spark delay (small cylindrical) valve in it, remove the valve and use a jumper hose to reconnect the two hoses.

5. If the EGR valve vacuum line incorporates a PVS valve, disconnect the EGR valve at the valve and plug the open vacuum line.

6. Turn off all accessories.

7. Open the throttle slightly and close the choke plates until the fast idle screw is on the step of the fast idle cam which is specified on the engine compartment sticker. The step will be visible through the hole in the choke housing. When the throttle is released with the choke mechanism in the right position, the fast idle screw will remain in the proper position.

8. Release the choke linkage and start the engine. Make sure the choke plates are wide open. When the rpm stabilizes, compare the reading to the specified reading on the engine compartment sticker. If the rpm is more than 100 rpm below or above the setting, loosen the fast idle screw locknut, turn the screw in to speed up the fast idle or out to slow it down until the specified speed is obtained, and then tighten the locknut.

9. Run the engine at 2,500 rpm for 15 seconds, and then repeat step 7 to set the fast idle screw on the proper step of the cam. Release the choke plates and reread the fast idle speed. Reset if necessary.

10. Accelerate the engine to release the fast idle cam and shut it off. Install the air cleaner, and reconnect the vacuum hoses and wiring as necessary.

AUTOMATIC CHOKE ADJUSTMENT

1. Remove the air cleaner as described in Step 3 of the procedure above.

2. Note the relationship between the ridged mark on the electric heating element ("A") and the marking on the choke housing (at the left in the illustration). The heating element mark should be in alignment with the "Index" or longest mark on the housing.

3. If the alignment is not correct, loosen the three screws which hold the heating element in place via the metal collar *very slightly* and rotate the element until the mark on it is in alignment with the index. Then, retighten the collar screws alternately. Replace the air cleaner.

CHOKE PLATE VACUUM PULLDOWN ADJUSTMENT

NOTE: *A controllable vacuum source with vacuum gauge is required for you to be able to perform this procedure. Get a replacement choke pulldown adjusting screw seal and have it on hand during the procedure.*

1. Remove the carburetor as described above.

2. Remove the three retaining screws, and

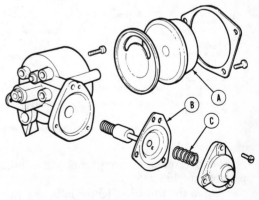

A Heating element
B Pulldown diaphragm
C Spring

Exploded view of the electric choke

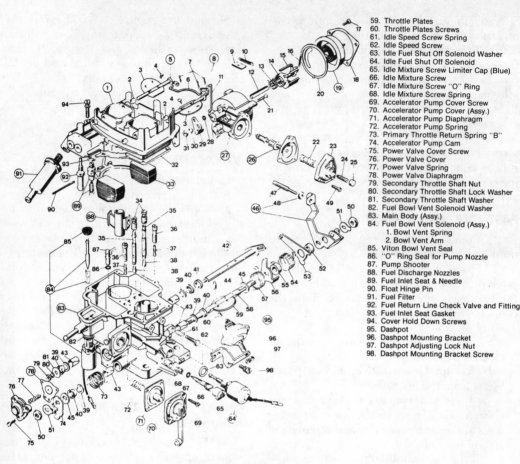

59. Throttle Plates
60. Throttle Plates Screws
61. Idle Speed Screw Spring
62. Idle Speed Screw
63. Idle Fuel Shut Off Solenoid Washer
64. Idle Fuel Shut Off Solenoid
65. Idle Mixture Screw Limiter Cap (Blue)
66. Idle Mixture Screw
67. Idle Mixture Screw "O" Ring
68. Idle Mixture Screw Spring
69. Accelerator Pump Cover Screw
70. Accelerator Pump Cover (Assy.)
71. Accelerator Pump Diaphragm
72. Accelerator Pump Spring
73. Primary Throttle Return Spring "B"
74. Accelerator Pump Cam
75. Power Valve Cover Screw
76. Power Valve Cover
77. Power Valve Spring
78. Power Valve Diaphragm
79. Secondary Throttle Shaft Nut
80. Secondary Throttle Shaft Lock Washer
81. Secondary Throttle Shaft Washer
82. Fuel Bowl Vent Solenoid Washer
83. Main Body (Assy.)
84. Fuel Bowl Vent Solenoid (Assy.)
   1. Bowl Vent Spring
   2. Bowl Vent Arm
85. Viton Bowl Vent Seal
86. "O" Ring Seal for Pump Nozzle
87. Pump Shooter
88. Fuel Discharge Nozzles
89. Fuel Inlet Seat & Needle
90. Float Hinge Pin
91. Fuel Filter
92. Fuel Return Line Check Valve and Fitting
93. Fuel Inlet Seat Gasket
94. Cover Hold Down Screws
95. Dashpot
96. Dashpot Mounting Bracket
97. Dashpot Adjusting Lock Nut
98. Dashpot Mounting Bracket Screw

1. Cover (Assy.)
2. Choke Shaft Bushings
3. Choke Plate
4. Choke Plate Screws
5. Secondary Choke Shaft
6. Secondary Choke Link
7. Choke Linkage Retaining Clips
8. Primary Choke Shaft
9. Primary Choke Link Dirt Seal
10. Dirt Seal Retainer
11. Primary Choke Link
12. Choke Bimetal Shaft Bushing
13. Fast Idle Cam Spring
14. Choke Bimetal Lever
15. Choke Bimetal Shaft
16. Choke Assist Spring
17. Electric Choke Retaining Screws
18. Electric Choke Retaining Ring
19. Electric Choke Unit
20. Choke Housing Dirt Shield
21. Choke Housing Screws
22. Choke Pulldown Spring
23. Cover
24. Choke Pulldown Adjusting Screw
25. Choke Pulldown Adjusting Screw Seal
26. Choke Pulldown Diaphragm Assembly
27. Choke Housing (Assy.)
28. Choke Housing Vacuum Seal (O Ring)
29. Choke Lever

30. Choke Bimetal Shaft Lock Washer
31. Choke Bimetal Shaft Nut
32. Cover Gasket
33. Fuel Bowl Float
34. High Speed Air Bleeds
35. Well Tubes
36. Idle Jet Holder
37. Idle Jet
38. Main Jet
39. Teflon Shaft Seal
40. Teflon Shaft Seal
41. Secondary Throttle Shaft Spacer
42. Secondary Throttle Shaft
43. Throttle Shaft Bushings
44. Secondary Throttle Stop Screw
45. Primary Shaft Locator Washers
46. Throttle Lever
47. Fast Idle Speed Adjusting Screw
48. Fast Idle Speed Adjusting Screw Lock Nut
49. Choke Pull Down Diaphragm Cover Screw
50. Primary Throttle Shaft Nut
51. Primary Throttle Shaft Nut Locking Tab
52. Secondary Throttle Operating Lever Bushing
53. Secondary Throttle Operating Lever
54. Secondary Throttle Return Spring
55. Secondary Throttle Return Spring Spacer
56. Primary Throttle Idle Stop Lever
57. Primary Throttle Return Spring "A"
58. Primary Throttle Shaft

Exploded view of the carburetor

remove the retaining ring, choke housing, and heat shield.

3. Open the throttle slightly and close the choke until the fast idle screw is aligned with the first step of the fast idle cam. Then, release the throttle and choke in that order.

4. Hook your vacuum source and gauge into the vacuum channel on the pump bore under the base of the carburetor. Then, apply exactly 17 in. Hg. (inches of mercury) vacuum.

5. Close the choke plates very gently until they just reach the limit set by the vacuum pulldown mechanism.

CHILTON'S
FUEL ECONOMY
& TUNE-UP TIPS

55 WAYS TO IMPROVE FUEL ECONOMY

Tune-up • Spark Plug Diagnosis • Emission Controls

Fuel System • Cooling System • Tires and Wheels

General Maintenance

CHILTON'S FUEL ECONOMY & TUNE-UP TIPS

Fuel economy is important to everyone, no matter what kind of vehicle you drive. The maintenance-minded motorist can save both money and fuel using these tips and the periodic maintenance and tune-up procedures in this Repair and Tune-Up Guide.

There are more than 130,000,000 cars and trucks registered for private use in the United States. Each travels an average of 10-12,000 miles per year, and, and in total they consume close to 70 billion gallons of fuel each year. This represents nearly ⅔ of the oil imported by the United States each year. The Federal government's goal is to reduce consumption 10% by 1985. A variety of methods are either already in use or under serious consideration, and they all affect you driving and the cars you will drive. In addition to "down-sizing", the auto industry is using or investigating the use of electronic fuel delivery, electronic engine controls and alternative engines for use in smaller and lighter vehicles, among other alternatives to meet the federally mandated Corporate Average Fuel Economy (CAFE) of 27.5 mpg by 1985. The government, for its part, is considering rationing, mandatory driving curtailments and tax increases on motor vehicle fuel in an effort to reduce consumption. The government's goal of a 10% reduction could be realized — and further government regulation avoided — if every private vehicle could use just 1 less gallon of fuel per week.

How Much Can You Save?

Tests have proven that almost anyone can make at least a 10% reduction in fuel consumption through regular maintenance and tune-ups. When a major manufacturer of spark plugs sur-

TUNE-UP

1. Check the cylinder compression to be sure the engine will really benefit from a tune-up and that it is capable of producing good fuel economy. A tune-up will be wasted on an engine in poor mechanical condition.

2. Replace spark plugs regularly. New spark plugs alone can increase fuel economy 3%.

3. Be sure the spark plugs are the correct type (heat range) for your vehicle. See the Tune-Up Specifications.

Heat range refers to the spark plug's ability to conduct heat away from the firing end. It must conduct the heat away in an even pattern to avoid becoming a source of pre-ignition, yet it must also operate hot enough to burn off conductive deposits that could cause misfiring.

The heat range is usually indicated by a number on the spark plug, part of the manufacturer's designation for each individual spark plug. The numbers in bold-face indicate the heat range in each manufacturer's identification system.

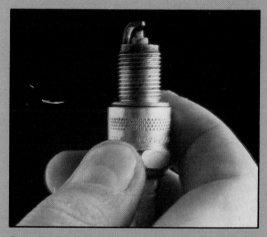

Periodically, check the spark plugs to be sure they are firing efficiently. They are excellent indicators of the internal condition of your engine.

Manufacturer	Typical Designation
AC	R **45** TS
Bosch (old)	WA **145** T30
Bosch (new)	HR **8** Y
Champion	RBL **15** Y
Fram/Autolite	4**15**
Mopar	P-**62** PR
Motorcraft	BRF-**42**
NGK	BP **5** ES-15
Nippondenso	W **16** EP
Prestolite	14GR **5** 2A

On AC, Bosch (new), Champion, Fram/Autolite, Mopar, Motorcraft and Prestolite, a higher number indicates a hotter plug. On Bosch (old), NGK and Nippondenso, a higher number indicates a colder plug.

4. Make sure the spark plugs are properly gapped. See the Tune-Up Specifications in this book.

5. Be sure the spark plugs are firing efficiently. The illustrations on the next 2 pages show you how to "read" the firing end of the spark plug.

6. Check the ignition timing and set it to specifications. Tests show that almost all cars have incorrect ignition timing by more than 2°.

veyed over 6,000 cars nationwide, they found that a tune-up, on cars that needed one, increased fuel economy over 11%. Replacing worn plugs alone, accounted for a 3% increase. The same test also revealed that 8 out of every 10 vehicles will have some maintenance deficiency that will directly affect fuel economy, emissions or performance. Most of this mileage-robbing neglect could be prevented with regular maintenance.

Modern engines require that all of the functioning systems operate properly for maximum efficiency. A malfunction anywhere wastes fuel. You can keep your vehicle running as efficiently and economically as possible, by being aware of your vehicle's operating and performance characteristics. If your vehicle suddenly develops performance or fuel economy problems it could be due to one or more of the following:

PROBLEM	POSSIBLE CAUSE
Engine Idles Rough	Ignition timing, idle mixture, vacuum leak or something amiss in the emission control system.
Hesitates on Acceleration	Dirty carburetor or fuel filter, improper accelerator pump setting, ignition timing or fouled spark plugs.
Starts Hard or Fails to Start	Worn spark plugs, improperly set automatic choke, ice (or water) in fuel system.
Stalls Frequently	Automatic choke improperly adjusted and possible dirty air filter or fuel filter.
Performs Sluggishly	Worn spark plugs, dirty fuel or air filter, ignition timing or automatic choke out of adjustment.

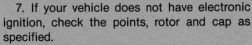

Check spark plug wires on conventional point type ignition for cracks by bending them in a loop around your finger.

Be sure that spark plug wires leading to adjacent cylinders do not run too close together. (Photo courtesy Champion Spark Plug Co.)

7. If your vehicle does not have electronic ignition, check the points, rotor and cap as specified.

8. Check the spark plug wires (used with conventional point-type ignitions) for cracks and burned or broken insulation by bending them in a loop around your finger. Cracked wires decrease fuel efficiency by failing to deliver full voltage to the spark plugs. One misfiring spark plug can cost you as much as 2 mpg.

9. Check the routing of the plug wires. Misfiring can be the result of spark plug leads to adjacent cylinders running parallel to each other and too close together. One wire tends to pick up voltage from the other causing it to fire "out of time".

10. Check all electrical and ignition circuits for voltage drop and resistance.

11. Check the distributor mechanical and/or vacuum advance mechanisms for proper functioning. The vacuum advance can be checked by twisting the distributor plate in the opposite direction of rotation. It should spring back when released.

12. Check and adjust the valve clearance on engines with mechanical lifters. The clearance should be slightly loose rather than too tight.

SPARK PLUG DIAGNOSIS

Normal

APPEARANCE: This plug is typical of one operating normally. The insulator nose varies from a light tan to grayish color with slight electrode wear. The presence of slight deposits is normal on used plugs and will have no adverse effect on engine performance. The spark plug heat range is correct for the engine and the engine is running normally.

CAUSE: Properly running engine.

RECOMMENDATION: Before reinstalling this plug, the electrodes should be cleaned and filed square. Set the gap to specifications. If the plug has been in service for more than 10-12,000 miles, the entire set should probably be replaced with a fresh set of the same heat range.

Oil Deposits

APPEARANCE: The firing end of the plug is covered with a wet, oily coating.

CAUSE: The problem is poor oil control. On high mileage engines, oil is leaking past the rings or valve guides into the combustion chamber. A common cause is also a plugged PCV valve, and a ruptured fuel pump diaphragm can also cause this condition. Oil fouled plugs such as these are often found in new or recently overhauled engines, before normal oil control is achieved, and can be cleaned and reinstalled.

RECOMMENDATION: A hotter spark plug may temporarily relieve the problem, but the engine is probably in need of work.

Incorrect Heat Range

APPEARANCE: The effects of high temperature on a spark plug are indicated by clean white, often blistered insulator. This can also be accompanied by excessive wear of the electrode, and the absence of deposits.

CAUSE: Check for the correct spark plug heat range. A plug which is too hot for the engine can result in overheating. A car operated mostly at high speeds can require a colder plug. Also check ignition timing, cooling system level, fuel mixture and leaking intake manifold.

RECOMMENDATION: If all ignition and engine adjustments are known to be correct, and no other malfunction exists, install spark plugs one heat range colder.

Photos Courtesy Fram Corporation

Carbon Deposits

APPEARANCE: Carbon fouling is easily identified by the presence of dry, soft, black, sooty deposits.

CAUSE: Changing the heat range can often lead to carbon fouling, as can prolonged slow, stop-and-start driving. If the heat range is correct, carbon fouling can be attributed to a rich fuel mixture, sticking choke, clogged air cleaner, worn breaker points, retarded timing or low compression. If only one or two plugs are carbon fouled, check for corroded or cracked wires on the affected plugs. Also look for cracks in the distributor cap between the towers of affected cylinders.

RECOMMENDATION: After the problem is corrected, these plugs can be cleaned and reinstalled if not worn severely.

MMT Fouled

APPEARANCE: Spark plugs fouled by MMT (Methycyclopentadienyl Maganese Tricarbonyl) have reddish, rusty appearance on the insulator and side electrode.

CAUSE: MMT is an anti-knock additive in gasoline used to replace lead. During the combustion process, the MMT leaves a reddish deposit on the insulator and side electrode.

RECOMMENDATION: No engine malfunction is indicated and the deposits will not affect plug performance any more than lead deposits (see Ash Deposits). MMT fouled plugs can be cleaned, regapped and reinstalled.

High Speed Glazing

APPEARANCE: Glazing appears as shiny coating on the plug, either yellow or tan in color.

CAUSE: During hard, fast acceleration, plug temperatures rise suddenly. Deposits from normal combustion have no chance to fluff-off; instead, they melt on the insulator forming an electrically conductive coating which causes misfiring.

RECOMMENDATION: Glazed plugs are not easily cleaned. They should be replaced with a fresh set of plugs of the correct heat range. If the condition recurs, using plugs with a heat range one step colder may cure the problem.

Ash (Lead) Deposits

APPEARANCE: Ash deposits are characterized by light brown or white colored deposits crusted on the side or center electrodes. In some cases it may give the plug a rusty appearance.

CAUSE: Ash deposits are normally derived from oil or fuel additives burned during normal combustion. Normally they are harmless, though excessive amounts can cause misfiring. If deposits are excessive in short mileage, the valve guides may be worn.

RECOMMENDATION: Ash-fouled plugs can be cleaned, gapped and reinstalled.

Detonation

APPEARANCE: Detonation is usually characterized by a broken plug insulator.

CAUSE: A portion of the fuel charge will begin to burn spontaneously, from the increased heat following ignition. The explosion that results applies extreme pressure to engine components, frequently damaging spark plugs and pistons.

Detonation can result by over-advanced ignition timing, inferior gasoline (low octane) lean air/fuel mixture, poor carburetion, engine lugging or an increase in compression ratio due to combustion chamber deposits or engine modification.

RECOMMENDATION: Replace the plugs after correcting the problem.

Photos Courtesy Champion Spark Plug Co.

EMISSION CONTROLS

13. Be aware of the general condition of the emission control system. It contributes to reduced pollution and should be serviced regularly to maintain efficient engine operation.

14. Check all vacuum lines for dried, cracked or brittle conditions. Something as simple as a leaking vacuum hose can cause poor performance and loss of economy.

15. Avoid tampering with the emission control system. Attempting to improve fuel econ-

FUEL SYSTEM

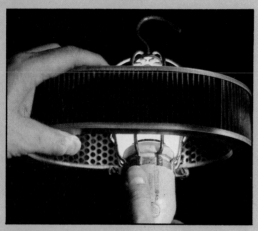

Check the air filter with a light behind it. If you can see light through the filter it can be reused.

Extremely clogged filters should be discarded and replaced with a new one.

18. Replace the air filter regularly. A dirty air filter richens the air/fuel mixture and can increase fuel consumption as much as 10%. Tests show that 1/3 of all vehicles have air filters in need of replacement.

19. Replace the fuel filter at least as often as recommended.

20. Set the idle speed and carburetor mixture to specifications.

21. Check the automatic choke. A sticking or malfunctioning choke wastes gas.

22. During the summer months, adjust the automatic choke for a leaner mixture which will produce faster engine warm-ups.

COOLING SYSTEM

29. Be sure all accessory drive belts are in good condition. Check for cracks or wear.

30. Adjust all accessory drive belts to proper tension.

31. Check all hoses for swollen areas, worn spots, or loose clamps.

32. Check coolant level in the radiator or expansion tank.

33. Be sure the thermostat is operating properly. A stuck thermostat delays engine warm-up and a cold engine uses nearly twice as much fuel as a warm engine.

34. Drain and replace the engine coolant at least as often as recommended. Rust and scale

TIRES & WHEELS

38. Check the tire pressure often with a pencil type gauge. Tests by a major tire manufacturer show that 90% of all vehicles have at least 1 tire improperly inflated. Better mileage can be achieved by over-inflating tires, but never exceed the maximum inflation pressure on the side of the tire.

39. If possible, install radial tires. Radial tires deliver as much as 1/2 mpg more than bias belted tires.

40. Avoid installing super-wide tires. They only create extra rolling resistance and decrease fuel mileage. Stick to the manufacturer's recommendations.

41. Have the wheels properly balanced.

omy by tampering with emission controls is more likely to worsen fuel economy than improve it. Emission control changes on modern engines are not readily reversible.

16. Clean (or replace) the EGR valve and lines as recommended.

17. Be sure that all vacuum lines and hoses are reconnected properly after working under the hood. An unconnected or misrouted vacuum line can wreak havoc with engine performance.

---

23. Check for fuel leaks at the carburetor, fuel pump, fuel lines and fuel tank. Be sure all lines and connections are tight.

24. Periodically check the tightness of the carburetor and intake manifold attaching nuts and bolts. These are a common place for vacuum leaks to occur.

25. Clean the carburetor periodically and lubricate the linkage.

26. The condition of the tailpipe can be an excellent indicator of proper engine combustion. After a long drive at highway speeds, the inside of the tailpipe should be a light grey in color. Black or soot on the insides indicates an overly rich mixture.

27. Check the fuel pump pressure. The fuel pump may be supplying more fuel than the engine needs.

28. Use the proper grade of gasoline for your engine. Don't try to compensate for knocking or "pinging" by advancing the ignition timing. This practice will only increase plug temperature and the chances of detonation or pre-ignition with relatively little performance gain.

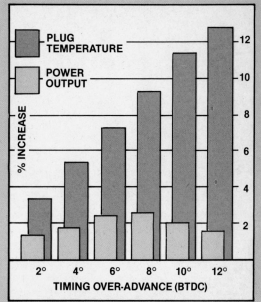

Increasing ignition timing past the specified setting results in a drastic increase in spark plug temperature with increased chance of detonation or preignition. Performance increase is considerably less. (Photo courtesy Champion Spark Plug Co.)

---

that form in the engine should be flushed out to allow the engine to operate at peak efficiency.

35. Clean the radiator of debris that can decrease cooling efficiency.

36. Install a flex-type or electric cooling fan, if you don't have a clutch type fan. Flex fans use curved plastic blades to push more air at low speeds when more cooling is needed; at high speeds the blades flatten out for less resistance. Electric fans only run when the engine temperature reaches a predetermined level.

37. Check the radiator cap for a worn or cracked gasket. If the cap does not seal properly, the cooling system will not function properly.

---

42. Be sure the front end is correctly aligned. A misaligned front end actually has wheels going in differed directions. The increased drag can reduce fuel economy by .3 mpg.

43. Correctly adjust the wheel bearings. Wheel bearings that are adjusted too tight increase rolling resistance.

Check tire pressures regularly with a reliable pocket type gauge. Be sure to check the pressure on a cold tire.

GENERAL MAINTENANCE

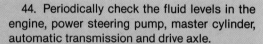

Check the fluid levels (particularly engine oil) on a regular basis. Be sure to check the oil for grit, water or other contamination.

A vacuum gauge is another excellent indicator of internal engine condition and can also be installed in the dash as a mileage indicator.

44. Periodically check the fluid levels in the engine, power steering pump, master cylinder, automatic transmission and drive axle.

45. Change the oil at the recommended interval and change the filter at every oil change. Dirty oil is thick and causes extra friction between moving parts, cutting efficiency and increasing wear. A worn engine requires more frequent tune-ups and gets progressively worse fuel economy. In general, use the lightest viscosity oil for the driving conditions you will encounter.

46. Use the recommended viscosity fluids in the transmission and axle.

47. Be sure the battery is fully charged for fast starts. A slow starting engine wastes fuel.

48. Be sure battery terminals are clean and tight.

49. Check the battery electrolyte level and add distilled water if necessary.

50. Check the exhaust system for crushed pipes, blockages and leaks.

51. Adjust the brakes. Dragging brakes or brakes that are not releasing create increased drag on the engine.

52. Install a vacuum gauge or miles-per-gallon gauge. These gauges visually indicate engine vacuum in the intake manifold. High vacuum = good mileage and low vacuum = poorer mileage. The gauge can also be an excellent indicator of internal engine conditions.

53. Be sure the clutch is properly adjusted. A slipping clutch wastes fuel.

54. Check and periodically lubricate the heat control valve in the exhaust manifold. A sticking or inoperative valve prevents engine warm-up and wastes gas.

55. Keep accurate records to check fuel economy over a period of time. A sudden drop in fuel economy may signal a need for tune-up or other maintenance.

© 1980 Chilton Book Company, Radnor, PA 19089

6. Insert at 6 mm drill between the choke plate and throttle bore on the lower side of the plate. If the clearance is incorrect, adjust the pulldown diaphragm adjusting screw in or out as required, and recheck.

7. Install the choke dirt shield, cap, retaining ring, and the three screws. Do not tighten the screws all the way until the choke is adjusted as described above. Then, tighten them evenly.

8. Reinstall the carburetor.

OVERHAUL

Purchase a complete overhaul kit from a reputable parts manufacturer. These kits will usually contain complete, step by step procedures for rebuilding the unit. All the carburetor metal parts should be thoroughly cleaned in a safe, low volatile solvent. Get a shallow pan of some sort to hold the solvent and permit you to soak the parts. It can also be helpful to use some sort of divided parts tray to keep the parts of the carburetor systems together.

Bear the following points in mind:

1. Replace *all* gaskets, O-rings, and diaphragms for which new parts are supplied in the kit. Make sure all gasket surfaces are absolutely clean. Tighten screws alternately and evenly.

2. Blow out jets with compressed air.

3. The general order of disassembly is: bowl cover; automatic choke; accelerator pump; main body.

4. During disassembly of the bowl cover and choke linkage, the throttle plates may have to be opened slightly to clear the fast idle screw.

5. The air bleeds, main well tubes, and main jets are installed by hand—they are a press fit.

6. Adjust the float level, choke, and choke pulldown as described above when assembling the bowl cover.

7. When completely assembled, install on

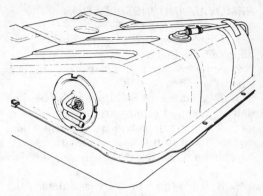

Fuel tank showing the sending unit on the forward side of the tank

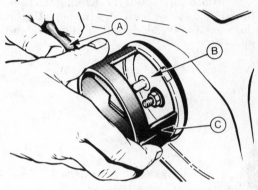

A Tool prybar
B Sending unit
C Special tool

Using Ford special tool T77F-9275-A to remove the sending unit

the car as described above. Run the engine and check for leaks. Then, adjust the mixture as described in Chapter 2 and the fast idle as described in this chapter.

Fuel Tank

NOTE: *This procedure requires Ford special tool No. T77F-9275-A or equivalent to unlock the sending unit as the fuel tank is removed.*

Carburetor Specifications

Carburetor Model	Part No.	Float Setting (mm)	Idle Jet Size (mm)	Main Jet Size (mm)	Main Well Tube No.	High Speed Bleed (mm)	Choke Pulldown (mm)	Choke Setting	Fast Idle RPM	Dechoke Setting (mm)
9510	771F9510HC	7	.60	1.05*	F22	2.50	6	INDEX	2000	7

* Applies to primary; secondary—1.00 mm

REMOVAL AND INSTALLATION

1. Disconnect both battery cables. Siphon out the fuel.

2. Support the rear of the car on jack stands.

3. Disconnect the fuel lines at the sending unit. If crimped clamps are used, pry them off by enlarging them with a screwdriver, and replace them during assembly with a screw type clamp. Disconnect the sending unit wiring.

4. Remove the four bolts, and detach the tank and remove the tank guard (if so equipped). Leave the filler pipe in place.

5. Attach the tool to the sending unit and turn it clockwise until it detaches. Unclip the vent pipe and detach it. Remove the tank.

6. Carefully pry out the filler pipe seal to avoid damaging it.

7. To install, reverse the removal procedures, bearing the following points in mind:

a. Use a new seal on the sending unit. Use the special tool to install the unit and turn it clockwise.

b. Lubricate the tank filler pipe exterior with engine oil before putting the tank into position. Be sure the filler pipe seats fully into the tank.

c. As the tank is installed, make sure the vent pipe is not kinked or trapped under the tank.

d. Make sure sending unit wiring is secure. If the tank is to be refilled immediately, do not connect the battery cables until after the tank filling operation is complete.

Chassis Electrical

HEATER

NOTE: *The Heater Blower Motor and Fan and Heater Core Removal and Installation procedures below apply to cars without air conditioning only. To perform these procedures on air conditioned models, highly specialized tools, equipment and training are required; therefore, those procedures are not included here.*

Blower Motor and Fan

REMOVAL AND INSTALLATION

Purchase additional retaining clamps from your dealer or parts supply house for the heater assembly before removing the unit.

1. Remove the heater assembly as described in the Heater Core Removal and Installation procedure below.

2. Cut the two foam gaskets on the joints of the heater assembly, as shown.

3. Unclip the two retaining clamps from the motor mounting. Then, position the assembly so the side containing the control valves is facing downward. Separate the halves, using a screwdriver to pry outward lightly on the flange so as to free the locking pins. Separate the clips with your fingers,

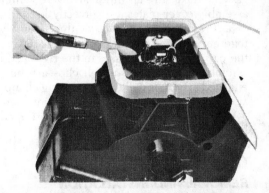

Cut the foam gasket at the joints of the heater assembly

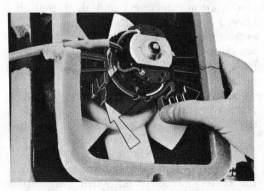

Unclip the two retaining clips from the motor mounting

Make sure all three (arrowed) assembly cover plates are correctly located

Heater assembly bracket screws

starting at the defrost outlet. Remove the blower motor.

4. Install the blower motor with the lead pointing to the rear. Fit the cable into the groove of the housing underneath the seal gasket. Make sure all three (arrowed) center assembly cover plates are correctly located.

5. Press the two halves of the assembly together, guiding the control valve shafts into the corresponding recesses in the right hand assembly half. Make sure all clips are fully engaged. Then, install extra retaining clamps at even intervals along the flange joint.

6. Install the assembly as described below.

Core

REMOVAL AND INSTALLATION

1. Disconnect the battery ground cable. Loosen the hose clamps on both hoses leading to the heater core from under the hood. Get a clean container, and then pull the lower hose off and drain off as much coolant as possible into the container. When coolant has drained, pull the upper hose off and tie both hoses together with the open ends facing upward.

2. Remove the two screws from the cover plate (which surrounds the two core connections) and gasket from the bulkhead. Seal the open tube ends with adhesive tape to prevent coolant from leaking out.

3. Remove the two screws and remove the right hand lower dash trim panel from under the dash. Do the same with the panel on the left side.

4. Remove the ashtray. Remove the two screws which retain the ashtray bracket and remove the bracket.

5. On models so equipped, remove the two vent hoses from the heater assembly adapters.

6. Unscrew the two screws, and remove the heater assembly bracket.

7. Remove the two assembly mounting nuts from the cowl top panel. Then, pull the assembly rearward until the two core connections clear the openings in the bulkhead. Disconnect the plug for the blower motor.

8. Slide the assembly to the right and pull it out from under the dash. Remove tape from the core connections and tilt the unit to drain the coolant from the core.

9. Remove the two screws from the core cover, and then slide the core out of the assembly.

10. To install, slide the core back into the heater assembly with coolant lines upward and install the two attaching screws into the cover.

One of the heater assembly mounting nuts

Heater core cover screws

Installing the heater core

11. Install the assembly from the right, making sure the foam gaskets are in proper position. Connect the motor lead. Then, install the two assembly mounting nuts.

12. Be sure Bowden control cables are not kinked, and install the heater assembly bracket and secure with the two mounting screws.

13. If the car is equipped with vent hoses, slide them onto the adapters.

14. Install the ashtray bracket and insert the ashtray.

15. Install the foam gasket around the two coolant connections and against the bulkhead from the engine compartment, and then put the cover plate into position over it. Install the two mounting screws.

16. Connect the water hose coming from the intake manifold to the bottom connection and the hose coming from the water pump to the top. Tighten the clamps.

17. Reconnect the battery. Fill the radiator. Run the engine and complete the radiator filling operation after air has been expelled from the system.

18. After checking the function of all controls, install the trim panels under the dash.

RADIO

REMOVAL AND INSTALLATION

1. Disconnect both battery cables. Pull the knobs off the front of the radio.

2. Remove the four bezel retaining screws.

3. Unplug the aerial wire and disconnect the power wire at the back of the radio. Also disconnect any suppressor wires.

4. Unscrew the rear brace mounting screws, and remove the brace.

5. Unscrew the two shaft nuts, and pull the radio rearward, down, and out from under the dash.

6. Install in reverse order. Check radio operation and set the selector buttons, as necessary.

WINDSHIELD WIPERS

Wiper Arm and Wiper Blade Assembly

REMOVAL AND INSTALLATION

1. Lift the wiper arm away from the windshield. Lift the tab on the end of the wiper arm, and pull the blade assembly off the arm.

2. Lift the slot in the spring hook at the end of the blade retainer, and slide the blade and retainer out of the arm.

3. To install, slide the new rubber in, making sure the retainer engages every bridge on the arm. Make sure the end of the

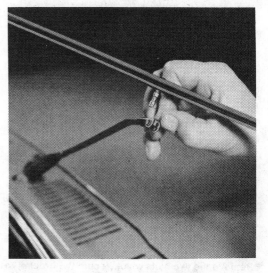

Replacing the wiper blade assembly

blade engages the slot at the end of the spring hook.

4. Install the blade assembly onto the wiper arm.

Front Wiper Motor
REMOVAL AND INSTALLATION

1. Disconnect the battery cables. Disconnect the two electrical connectors at the wiper motor.

2. Remove the three mounting bracket bolts and pull the motor and bracket assembly out far enough to make the linkage accessible. Disconnect the linkage and remove the motor and bracket assembly.

3. Remove the mounting bolt which retains the operating arm from the motor, *making sure that the torque is taken by the operating arm and not the motor gears.* To do this, hold the assembly by the arm and not the motor while applying torque.

4. Pull the arm off, remove the three bolts which hold the motor onto the mounting bracket, and remove the motor.

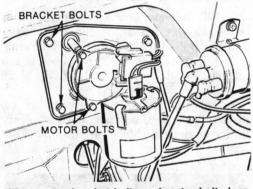

Wiper motor bracket bolts and motor bolts locations

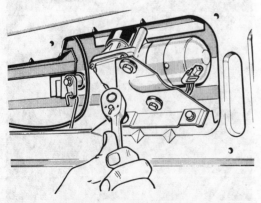

Remove the two bolts which secure the bracket to the rear door

5. To install, reverse the above procedures, noting the following points:

a. When installing the motor to the bracket, ensure that the sealing grommet is in place.

b. Ensure that the flat washer is adjacent to the motor and the waved washer adjacent to the operating arm when installing the arm. Also, make sure the arm takes the torque reaction when installing the nut, as when loosening it.

c. Apply a light mastic waterproofing sealer to the bracket when installing it to the bulkhead, to prevent water leaks.

Rear Wiper Motor
REMOVAL AND INSTALLATION

1. Disconnect the battery.

2. Remove the rear wiper arm assembly.

3. Remove the plastic cap, nut, metal washer, spacer and rubber washer securing the pivot shaft.

4. Remove the rear door trim panel by carefully prying out the attaching clips and removing the panel.

5. Remove the two bolts which secure the motor bracket to the rear door.

6. Remove the screw securing the ground lead to the bracket. Disconnect the electrical connector, and then pull the motor and bracket out of the door.

7. Remove the two mounting bolts and remove the motor from the bracket.

8. To install, reverse the removal procedure, noting the following points:

a. Make sure the motor bracket rubber grommets are correctly positioned.

b. Make sure the rubber washer is installed on the motor spindle before installing the pivot shaft.

Windshield Wiper Drive Linkage
REMOVAL AND INSTALLATION

1. Disconnect the battery. Disconnect the wiper motor connectors. Remove the three motor mounting bracket bolts.

2. Remove the wiper arm and blade assemblies as described above.

3. Remove the lower bolt from the ignition coil mounting bracket. Loosen the other bolt slightly. Then, push the back end of the coil downward so the coil pivots into a vertical position (with connectors at the top—see the dashed portion of the illustration).

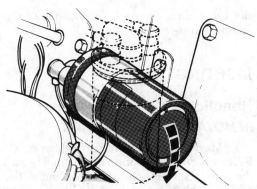

Move the coil as shown to gain access to the hood lock plate

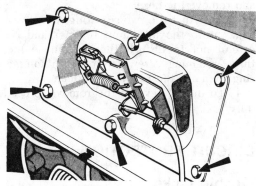

Hood lock plate mounting bolts (arrowed)

You might need to tighten the one mounting bolt to hold the coil in this position.

4. Remove the six hood lock plate retaining bolts, and remove the lock plate.

5. Remove the plastic sleeves, spindle arm nuts, and washers from the linkage. Then, disconnect the motor linkage at the spindle center arm. Remove the linkage through the opening created by removal of the hook lock plate.

6. Remove the motor and disconnect the motor linkage at the motor operating arm.

7. To install, first apply sealer to the mating surface of the flange on the center spindle.

8. Connect the linkage and install the spindle arm nuts, washers, and plastic sleeves.

9. Connect the wiper motor linkage to the motor operating arm. Put the motor mounting bracket in position and install the three bolts.

10. Connect the motor electrical connectors. Reconnect the motor linkage at the linkage spindle center arm.

11. Apply a light coating of a mastic-type

of waterproof sealer to the mating surface of the hood lock mounting plate, and reinstall the plate.

12. Reposition the ignition coil, install the bolt that was removed, and tighten the other bolt.

13. Reconnect the battery.

INSTRUMENT CLUSTER

REMOVAL AND INSTALLATION

1. Disconnect the battery cables. Remove the steering column upper shroud (A). Where applicable, remove the two screws from below the lower dashboard storage space, and drop the lower panel (B).

2. From behind the instrument cluster, grasp the speedometer cable and press the grooved section on the cable locking latch with your thumb, and pull the cable off the cluster.

3. Carefully pull off the bezel, using the fingertip access slots (A).

4. Remove the four phillips screws from

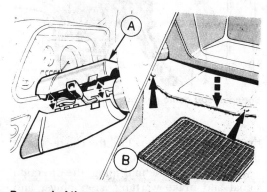

Removal of the upper steering column shroud (A) and the lower dash panel (B)

Removal of the cluster bezel—fingertip access is provided at "A"

The upper end of the speedometer cable

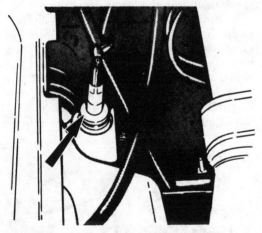

Speedometer cable gearbox attachment

the front of the cluster. Pull the cluster out of the dash.

5. Disconnect the multiplug, the direction signal and brake warning lamp plugs, and remove the cluster.

6. Installation is the reverse of removal.

SPEEDOMETER CABLE REPLACEMENT

1. Disconnect the battery cables. Remove the two screws from below the underdash parcel shelf, and lower the shelf and remove it.

2. Then, from behind the instrument cluster, hold the speedometer cable with your fingers and, with your thumb, press the grooved section on the cable locking catch and release the cable from the cluster.

3. From the left side of the engine compartment, remove the cable from the choke cable strap, unscrew the knurled ring, and disconnect the cable from the gearbox. Detach the grommet from the firewall and pull

the cable through the hole and out of the engine compartment.

LIGHTING

Headlights
REMOVAL AND INSTALLATION

1. Make sure the headlight switch is off. From inside the engine compartment, pull the wiring connector *straight* back and off the prongs on the rear of the sealed beam unit.

2. Unscrew the three plastic bezel screws from the bezel surrounding the headlamp, and remove the bezel.

3. Note that the two adjusting screws are adjacent to the headlamp retainer and be careful not to disturb them. Remove the three retaining screws from the retaining ring. Remove the ring and headlamp.

4. To install, reverse the removal procedure.

CIRCUIT PROTECTION

Fusible Links
REPLACEMENT

1. Make sure the replacement link is the one specified for the model of Fiesta you're working on.

2. Disconnect the negative battery cable. If the particular application does not require the eyelet supplied with all replacement links, cut the eyelet off.

3. If the application uses an eyelet, disconnect it at the starter relay. Then, cut the link out of the wire at the original splice or splices, as necessary.

4. Crimp and solder the new link to the existing wiring. Use resin core solder. Then, wrap the splices carefully with electrician's tape.

5. If the link uses an eyelet, attach the eyelet to the battery terminal of the starter relay.

6. Route the wiring in its original position. Reconnect the battery.

Fuses and Flashers

The fuse box is located under the instrument panel, on the driver's side of the steering column. The hazard and direction signal flasher unit is located on a bracket welded to the

Lightbulb Chart

Application	1978	1979–80
Brake Warning	194	194
Cluster Light	D3RY-13466-A①	D3RY-13466-A①
Heated Backlight	D2RY-13466-H①	D2RY-13466-H①
Interior Lamp	1155	97
Instrument Panel	194	194
License Lamp	1816	1816
Marker Lamps Front	194	194
Rear	194	194
Rear Lamps	1155	97
Seat Belt Warning Lamp	194	194
Stoplight Lamp	1156	1156
Sealed Beam	6014	6014
Tail Light	1155	1156
Front Turn Signals	1157	1157

① This is the Ford part number rather than the auto lighting industry standard number.

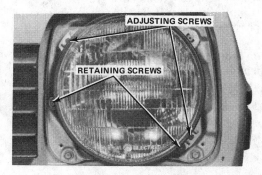

Headlight adjusting screws and retaining screws

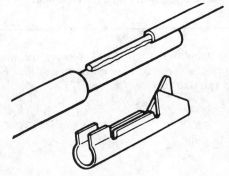

Solder and crimp the fusible link as shown

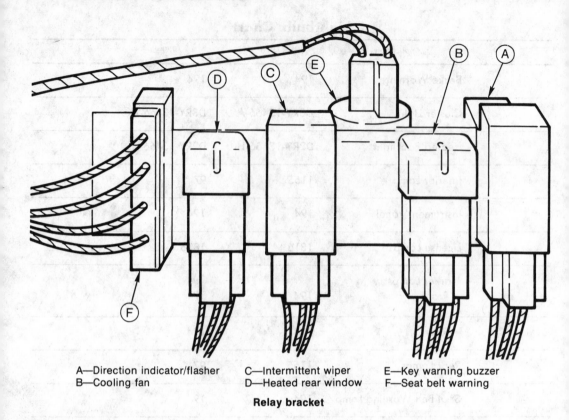

A—Direction indicator/flasher   C—Intermittent wiper   E—Key warning buzzer
B—Cooling fan   D—Heated rear window   F—Seat belt warning

Relay bracket

Fuses

1—Cigarette lighter, horn, interior light, flasher lights, stop lamp—16 amp
2—Windshield washer, seat belt control, heater blower, back-up lamp—8 amp
3—Wiper motor, brake warning lamp, instrument lights, rear window washer—8 amp
4—Right side tail light, right side marker lights, license plate lamp—8 amp
5—Instrument lights, left side tail light, left side side markers—8 amp
6—High beam—8 amp
7—Low beam—8 amp
8—Cooling fan switching circuit—8 amp
9—Blank

dash panel to the left of the steering column. There are three or four inline fuses, located and rated as follows:

Air Conditioner—in line behind glovebox—20 amp
Radio—in line behind radio—3 amp
Radiator Cooling Fan—in relay next to hazard flasher—16 amp
Heated Rear Window—in relay near hazard flasher—16 amp

WIRING DIAGRAMS

Wiring diagrams have been left out of this book. As cars have become more complex, and available with longer and longer option lists, wiring diagrams have grown in size and complexity also. It has become virtually impossible to provide a readable reproduction in a reasonable number of pages. Information on ordering wiring diagrams from the vehicle manufacturer can be found in the owners manual.

Clutch and Transaxle

TRANSAXLE

Identification

All Fiestas use a front-wheel drive transmission, called a "transaxle". The engine, gearbox, and final drive form a transversely mounted assembly. The gearbox and differential assemblies are both located in a light alloy housing, which is split into two parts when disassembly is required, and which is bolted to the engine.

REMOVAL AND INSTALLATION

In order to remove the transmission, it is necessary to fabricate an engine support bracket to the specifications shown in the illustration. Use the materials specified, as materials of lesser size and strength may fail—the unit is not overdesigned.

You will also need a special tool, a Tie Rod Remover Adapter and Main Tool, Ford Part Numbers T77F-3290-A and -C or equivalent.

1. Put the transmission in fourth gear to ensure proper gearshift linkage adjustment when it is reinstalled. Disconnect the battery cables.

2. Position the engine support bracket and support the engine with a cable as shown.

3. Unscrew the speedometer cable connection at the transmission.

4. Depress the clutch cable in the middle of the length that runs between the lever and cable support to get play into the cable. Then, unhook the cable from the release lever (a pair of pliers may help here).

5. Remove the four upper transmission flange bolts.

6. Jack up the vehicle and drain the transmission oil by removing the plunger retainer and spring. Make sure the plunger and spring stay together.

7. Remove the selector rod spring from the selector rod. Then, loosen the selector rod locating bolt and pull the selector rod off the shift shaft.

8. Unscrew the two inner nuts on the rubber coupling and engine support and reposition them as shown. Unscrew the locknut which is located on the stud, and screw it out of the transmission with an allen wrench. Allow the stabilizer and screw to be supported by the engine support bar.

9. Remove the six allen head bolts and three links at the coupling of the inner constant velocity joint on the left side driveshaft. Then, support the driveshaft out of the way.

10. Remove the six allen head bolts and three links from the inner constant velocity joint on the right side of the car. Unbolt the bearing collar from the support at the outer end of the primary shaft. Loosen the bearing support bracket at the engine. Support the

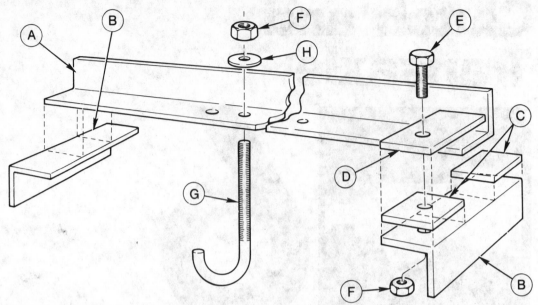

A—57 in. long "L" section 2 × 2 × ¼ in. (1 required)
B—6 in. long "L" section 2 × 2 × ¼ in. (2 required)
C—2 in. long flat bar 2 × ¼ in. (2 required)
D—3½ in. long flat bar 2 × ¼ in. (1 required)
E—⅜ in. bolt (1 required)
F—⅜ in. nut (2 required)
G—12 in. long round bar, ⅜ in. diameter (1 required)
H—7/16 in. (internal diameter) washer (1 required)

Dimensions of the engine support bracket

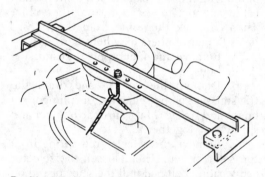

Positioning of the engine support bracket

Reposition inner stabilizer nuts on the rubber coupling and engine support as shown

driveshaft slightly out of the way, and then pull the primary shaft U-joint off the transmission stubshaft and remove the primary shaft.

11. Disconnect the starter motor wiring and remove the starter motor.

12. Remove the breather tube from its position on the side of the transmission.

13. Support the transmission securely. Then, remove the two lower flange bolts from the transmission and the three flange bolts from the engine mounting. Then, lower the transmission and remove it.

14. To install, grease the splines of the primary shaft U-joint and the right side stubshaft in the transmission.

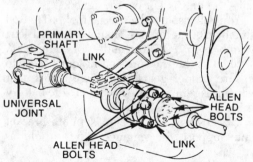

The figure identifies the Allen head bolts and primary shaft

15. Make sure the engine adapter plate is correctly seated on the engine guide bushings.

16. Raise the transmission into position. Install the two transmission flange bolts and tighten lightly. Then, correct the alignment of the engine adapter plate and hold it with two drivers.

17. Then, install the transmission and clutch adapter plate to the engine mounting, using three *new* self locking bolts.

18. Lower the engine, and then torque the selflocking engine mounting bolts to 65 ft lbs. Torque the two flange bolts to 30 ft lbs.

19 Install the plunger-retainer and spring into the plunger retainer hole.

NOTE: *Use a locking compound on the threads to ensure the plunger retainer will not come loose.*

20. Reinstall the starter motor.

21. Reinstall and reconnect the primary shaft, driveshafts, and bearing collar in reverse of the above. Tighten the bearing support bracket bolts at the engine after all other primary shaft parts are in place. Make sure to install the six allen head bolts and three links on each CV joint.

22. Connect the stabilizer bar to the trans-mission by installing the allen screw and locknut. Turn the allen screw in as far as the stop in the transmission housing and then tighten the locknut against the rubber coupling of the stabilizer. Then, bring the inner nut on the engine mounting into contact and torque the outer nut to 40 ft lbs.

23. Connect and adjust the gear selector rod to the shift shaft as follows:

    a. Check to make sure the shift shaft and shift lever are both in fourth gear position.

    b. Pull the selector rod down onto the shift shaft and align the hole in the selector housing with the shift lever. Then, lock it with a .16 in. pin.

    c. Insert a spacer 2.76 in. thick such as that shown between the floor pan and the selector rod as shown.

    d. Using a suitable arbor, turn the shift shaft clockwise against the stop. Then, tighten the selector rod locating both with the selector rod in this position.

    e. Install the selector rod spring into position hanging between the selector rod and the logitudinal member. Check gearshift linkage operation.

24. Refill the transmission with the required lubricant. Lower the vehicle.

25. Install the top transmission flange bolts and torque to 30 ft lbs.

26. Hook the clutch cable onto the release lever. Reconnect speedometer cable and battery cables. Release and remove the engine support bracket.

HALFSHAFT REMOVAL AND INSTALLATION

See "Driveshaft Removal and Installation" in Chapter 7.

Correct seating of the adapter plate on the engine

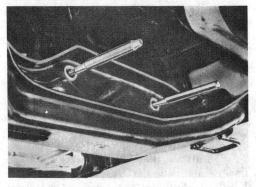

Correctly align and secure the adapter plate with two drivers

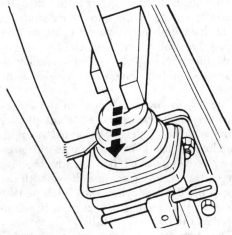

Adjusting selector rod

SHIFT LINKAGE ADJUSTMENT

To adjust the shift linkage, first put the transmission into fourth gear. Then, follow Step 7 of the Transmission Removal and Installation procedure above, but *do not* pull the selector rod off the shift shaft—just loosen the locating bolt. Finally, follow the lettered Steps of Step 23 of the Transmission Removal and Installation procedure.

CLUTCH

Understanding the Manual Transmission and Clutch

Because of the way the gasoline engine breathes, it can produce torque, or twisting force, only within a narrow speed range. Most modern engines must turn at about 2,500 rpm to produce their peak torque. By 4,500 rpm they are producing so little torque that continued increases in engine speed produce no power increases.

The transmission and clutch are employed to vary the relationship between engine speed and the speed of the wheels so that adequate engine power can be produced under all circumstances. The clutch allows engine torque to be applied to the transmission input shaft gradually, due to mechanical slippage. The car can, consequently, be started smoothly from a full stop.

The transmission changes the ratio between the rotating speeds of the engine and the wheels by the use of gears. Three-speed or four-speed transmissions are most common. The lower gears allow full engine power to be applied to the rear wheels during acceleration at low speeds.

The clutch driven plate is a thin disc, the center of which is splined to the transmission input shaft. Both sides of the disc are covered with a layer of material which is similar to brake lining and which is capable of allowing slippage without roughness or excessive noise.

The clutch cover is bolted to the engine flywheel and incorporates a diaphragm spring which provides the pressure to engage the clutch. The cover also houses the pressure plate. The driven disc is sandwiched between the pressure plate and the smooth surface of the flywheel when the clutch pedal is released, thus forcing it to turn at the same speed as the engine crankshaft.

The transmission contains a mainshaft which passes all the way through the transmission, from the clutch to the final drive gear in the transaxle. This shaft is separated at one point, so that front and rear portions can turn at different speeds.

Power is transmitted by a countershaft in the lower gears and reverse. The gears of the countershaft mesh with gears on the mainshaft, allowing power to be carried from one to the other. All the countershaft gears are integral with that shaft, while several of the mainshaft gears can either rotate independently of the shaft or be locked to it. Shifting from one gear to the next causes one of the gears to be freed from rotating with the shaft, and locks another to it. Gears are locked and unlocked by internal dog clutches which slide between the center of the gear and the shaft. The forward gears usually employ synchronizers: friction members which smoothly bring gear and shaft to the same speed before the toothed dog clutches are engaged.

The clutch is operating properly if:

1. It will stall the engine when released with the vehicle held stationary.

2. The shift lever can be moved freely between first and reverse gears when the vehicle is stationary and the clutch disengaged.

FREE PLAY ADJUSTMENT

The clutch pedal free play does not require periodic adjustment on the Fiesta. An automatic device (see the illustration) adjusts the linkage to compensate for wear as it occurs in the clutch disc and other moving parts of the system.

REMOVAL AND INSTALLATION

NOTE: *To remove and install the clutch, you'll need a special aligning tool, Ford Part No. T77F-7137-A or equivalent and will have to remove the transmission. See the Transmission Removal and Installation procedure above for further requirements.*

1. Remove the transmission from the car as described above. Then unscrew the six setscrews holding the pressure plate onto the flywheel. *The setscrews must be unscrewed alternately a little at a time so the pressure plate comes off while staying parallel to the flywheel.* Remove the setscrews and remove the pressure plate and disc.

2. To install, place the clutch disc on the flywheel *with the flat side of the disc facing the flywheel.* Insert the clutch aligning tool and center the disc.

3. With the aligning tool still in place, put

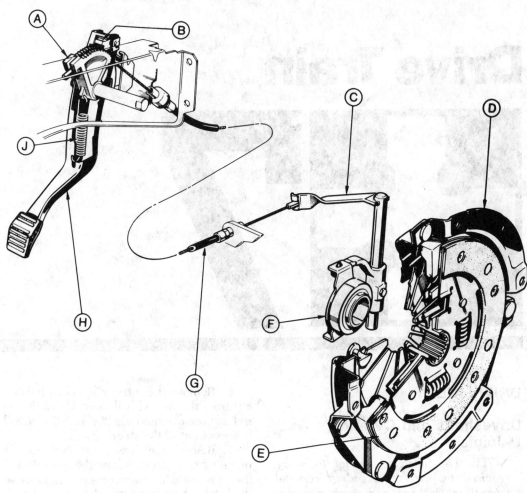

A—Toothed quadrant of the automatic adjusting device
B—Automatic adjusting device pawl
C—Release plate release shaft and lever
D—Pressure plate
E—Clutch disc
F—Release bearing and fork
G—Clutch cable
H—Clutch pedal
J—Toothed quadrant tension spring

The clutch assembly

Pulling the pressure plate off the flywheel

Centering the clutch plate with a special tool

the pressure plate onto the flywheel using the three locating dowels to center it. Start the setscrews and tighten alternately a little at a time to keep the pressure plate and flywheel parallel. When they come down tight, torque them to 13 ft lbs.

4. Remove the aligning tool. Install the transmission as described above.

Drive Train

7

DRIVELINE

Driveshafts and CV and U-Joints

NOTE: *The following special tools are required to perform driveshaft removal operations: Tie rod end removal tool—Ford part number T77F-3290-C or equivalent with adapter T77F-3290-A or equivalent. Front hub installer. Shaft seal remover T77F-6700-A or equivalent and shaft seal replacer T77F-3169-A or equivalent.*

LEFT HAND DRIVESHAFT REMOVAL AND INSTALLATION

1. Remove the hub cap and remove spindle shaft retaining nut and washer.

2. Loosen the wheel bolts, jack up the vehicle and put axle stands into position. Remove the wheel.

3. Remove the six allen head bolts and three links securing the inner CV joint to the stubshaft flange.

4. Remove the brake caliper retaining bolts and support the caliper away from the disc.

5. Remove the disc and hub assembly, if necessary by using a two legged puller. Keep dirt out of all exposed lubricated parts.

6. Remove the cotter pin and castellated nut from the tie rod ball joint. Using the tie rod end remover and adapter, pull the tie rod ball joint out of the steering arm.

7. Remove the lower arm-to-body mount retaining bolt and withdraw the inner end of the arm from the mounting point. Remove the ball joint-to-carrier clinch bolt and detach the outer end of the lower arm. **DO NOT** push the rear end of the bar downward during this operation.

8. Pull the driveshaft out of the spindle carrier and away from the vehicle.

9. Clean the old grease out of the inner CV joint. Repack it with about 1½ oz. of grease which meets Ford spec. ESA-M1C75-B.

10. Insert the outer end of the driveshaft through the spindle carrier. Loosely install the allen head bolts, links, and washers which connect the inner CV joint and stubshaft.

11. Reconnect the outer end of the lower arm assembly. Reconnect the ball joint to the spindle carrier and reinstall the clinch bolt. Position the inner end of the lower arm in the body mounting and install and torque the retaining bolt and nut. Torque to 30–33 ft lbs.

12. Reconnect the tie rod ball joint to the steering arm, install the castellated nut, and a new cotter pin.

13. Push the hub and rotor assembly onto the splined end of the driveshaft as far as possible by hand. Assemble a front hub installer to the driveshaft and seat the hub and rotor assembly on the driveshaft. Do not drive the hub onto the driveshaft without an installer as this will damage the CV joint.

14. Loosely fit the plain washer and a new hub retaining nut. Reinstall the brake caliper.

15. Torque the six CV-joint allen head bolts to 28–32 ft lbs.

16. Reinstall the wheels, lower the vehicle to the ground, and fully tighten wheel bolts.

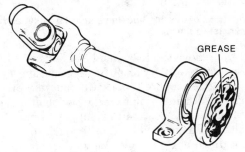

GREASE

Apply grease to CV-joints where shown

17. Torque the hub retaining nut to 180–200 ft lbs. Stake the nut by deforming it into the slot in the driveshaft with a center punch.

18. Reinstall the hubcap.

RIGHT HAND DRIVESHAFT REMOVAL AND INSTALLATION

1. Remove the hubcap and remove the hub retaining nut and washer.

2. Loosen the wheel bolts, raise the front of the vehicle, and put axle stands in place.

3. Remove the six allen head bolts and three links securing the inner CV-joint to the primary shaft flange.

4. Remove the wheel and then reinstall two wheel bolts to protect the disc retaining screw.

5. Have an assistant apply the foot brake to hold the hub still and remove the hub retaining nut and washer. Release the foot brake.

6. Remove the two wheel bolts.

7. Remove the two bolts securing the primary shaft bearing housing to the bracket.

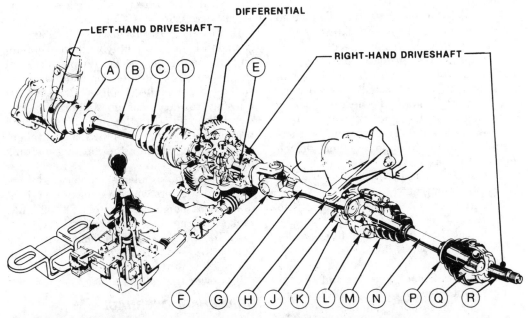

A—Left hand outer constant velocity (C.V.) joint
B—Left hand intermediate driveshaft
C—Left hand inner constant velocity (C.V.) joint
D—Left hand stubshaft
E—Right hand stubshaft
F—Universal joint
G—Primary shaft
H—Primary shaft bearing support bracket
J—Primary shaft support bearing
K—Primary shaft support bearing housing
L—Right-hand inner constant velocity (C.V.) joint
M—Bellows
N—Right-hand intermediate driveshaft
P—Bellows
Q—Right-hand outer constant velocity (C.V.) joint
R—Spindle shaft

Drive Train Parts

Allow the primary shaft and bearing assembly to rest clear of its normal position.

8. Withdraw the driveshaft assembly and spindle carrier from the vehicle.

9. Before installing the assembly, repack the CV-joint with 1½ oz. of a grease which meets Ford Spec. ESA-M1C75B. Then, check the following clearances:

a. Measure the clearance between the inner race of the intermediate bearing and the outer collar of the shaft. Replace the shaft and bearing assembly if the clearance is greater than .04 in. If a new shaft is used, put about 1 oz. of the grease specified above in the shaft flange cavity before installing it.

b. Check the bearing clearance between the dust shield and the bearing outer race. If the clearance is less than 104 in., the shaft and bearing assembly should be replaced.

10. Loosen two bolts on the engine block that hold the bearing support bracket in place. The bracket should still contact the mating surface, but be free to slide around on it.

11. Insert the outer end of the driveshaft through the spindle carrier.

12. Loosely install the six allen head bolts, three links, and washers to reconnect the inner joint to the primary shaft.

13. Position the primary shaft bearing housing against the support bracket with shafts aligned. Then, install the two allen head bolts which attach the bearing housing to the bracket and torque them to 14–16 ft lbs. Now, torque the upper support bracket-to-engine bolt to 45–50 ft lbs; then, do the same with the lower bolt.

14. Loosely install the plain washer and a *new* hub retaining nut.

15. Torque the CV joint retaining nuts to 28–32 ft lbs.

16. Install the wheel, lower the vehicle, and fully tighten wheel bolts.

17. Torque the hub retaining nut to 180–200 ft lbs. Then, stake the nut by deforming it into the slot in the driveshaft with a center punch. Install the hub cap.

PRIMARY SHAFT REMOVAL AND INSTALLATION

1. Raise the vehicle and install jackstands.

2. Remove the six allen head bolts, three links, and washers that secure the inner CV-joint to the flange of the primary shaft. *Support the driveshaft to avoid straining parts.*

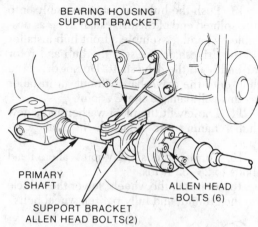

Locations of bearing housing support bracket and associated parts

3. Remove the two allen head bolts which secure the primary shaft bearing housing to the engine mounted bracket. Guide the primary shaft and U-joint off the stubshaft.

4. Loosen the bearing support bracket bolts at the engine block just enough to permit the bracket to slide around while the mating surfaces remain in contact.

5. Clean the inner CV-joint of old grease. Repack it with 1½ oz. of a grease meeting Ford Spec. ESA-M1C-75B.

6. To install the primary shaft, align the shaft and U-joint assembly with the stubshaft and engage the splines. Put the primary shaft bearing housing into position and loosely install the two allen head bolts which retain the housing to the bearing support bracket. Carefully shift the bearing housing and bracket as necessary until the shaft is in alignment. Then, torque the bearing housing bolts to 13–16 ft lbs.

7. Install the six allen head bolts and three links and washers which retain the CV-joint to the shaft flange and torque to 28–32 ft lbs. Make sure the shaft is perfectly aligned.

8. Torque the upper bracket mounting bolt on the engine to 48–55 ft lbs; repeat the operation with the lower bolt.

9. Lower the vehicle.

DRIVESHAFT OVERHAUL

1. Remove bellows at CV joints at either end and slide the bellows along the shaft (toward the center) to provide working clearance.

2. Remove the CV-joints from the shaft. Wipe off surplus grease, pry open the retaining clip, and pull the shaft out of each joint. Remove both bellows from the shaft.

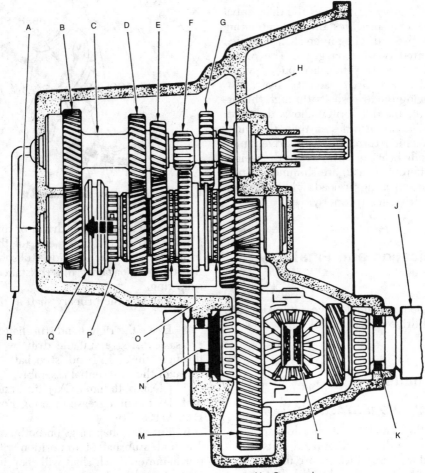

A—Output shaft (mainshaft)
B—4th speed gears
C—Input shaft
D—3rd speed gears
E—2nd speed gears
F—Reverse gear

G—Reverse idler gear
H—1st speed gears
J—Inner shaft
K—Oil seal
L—Snap ring
M—Final drive gear

N—Cup springs
O—1st/2nd speed synchronizer hub assembly,
   with reverse gear
P—3rd/4th speed synchronizer hub
Q—3rd/4th speed synchronizer ring
R—Breather tube

Transmission and final drive parts

3. Clean both joints thoroughly in a safe solvent to remove all old grease and dirt.

4. Inspect the retaining clips and replace if excessively fatigued or corroded. Inspect both bellows and replace if they are cracked or brittle. Repack each joint with 1½ oz. of grease meeting Ford Spec. EAS-M1C75-B.

5. Slide each bellows back onto the shaft. Reinstall the CV-joints onto the shaft by pushing the shaft into the joint until the clip engages.

6. Slide each bellows onto its CV-joint and install a new clamp. Tighten each clamp until it is finger tight, engage the clamp pin in the next hole, and then crimp the clamp to tighten fully.

TRANSAXLE FINAL DRIVE

Understanding the Final Drive

The final drive is a special type of transmission that reduces the speed of the drive from the engine and transmission and divides the power to the front wheels. Power enters the final drive from the transmission output shaft via the final drive gear. The transmission main shaft turns at slightly more than engine speed when the transmission is in fourth gear. The final drive gear turns much slower than the main shaft—the main shaft turns 3.55 times for each revolution of the drive gear. This reduces the speed but increases the force with which the drive axles turn.

The final drive gear drives the differential case. The case provides the two mounting points for the ends of a pinion shaft on which are mounted two pinion gears. The pinion gears drive the two side gears, one of which is located so as to drive each stubshaft.

By driving the axle shafts through this arrangement, the differential allows the outer drive wheel to turn faster than the inner drive wheel in a turn. The main drive pinion and the side bearings, which bear the weight of the differential case, are shimmed to provide proper bearing preload, and to position the final drive gear properly.

Identification and Final Drive Ratio

All Fiestas use the same 4 speed manual transmission and final drive transaxle unit. The final drive ratio is 3.58:1.

Stub Shafts

REMOVAL AND INSTALLATION

Support the vehicle front on axle stands.

1. Remove the six allen head bolts, three links, and washers which secure the left hand driveshaft to the left hand stubshaft. Support the driveshaft out of the way. Provide a drain pan to collect oil which will drain out when stubshafts are removed.

Levering out the left side stubshaft

2. Using a large screwdriver or tire iron as a lever, strike the outer end (of the lever) firmly to move the left side stubshaft out of the transaxle against the resistance of the snap ring.

3. Remove the primary shaft as described above.

4. Drive the right hand stubshaft from the transaxle using a suitable drift by going in through the left hand stubshaft aperture through the differential assembly.

5. Clean both inner CV-joints, and repack with 1½ oz. of a grease meeting Ford Spec. EAS-M1C-75B.

6. Put new snap rings on both stubshafts. Tap both stubshafts into position with a copper hammer. Each shaft will snap into position when the snap ring seats.

7. Reinstall the primary shaft and reconnect driveshafts in reverse of the above, torquing driveshaft bolts to 28–32 ft lbs.

Suspension and Steering

FRONT SUSPENSION

Description

The Fiesta uses a MacPherson strut front suspension, meaning the springs and shock absorbers are combined in a single, integral unit. The strut is bolted directly to the body at the top, thus saving several parts required in a conventional front suspension. Ball joints used in the lower suspension arms are retained in the spindle carriers by a clinch bolt, which makes ball joint replacement simpler for the home mechanic, and cheaper if the operation is done professionally.

Since the entire strut must turn as the vehicle is steered, the design of the bearing employed at the top of the strut can have a great effect on steering smoothness. If bearing action is rough, the spring can actually be wound up during turning of the steering wheel, increasing steering effort. The special phenolic resin bearing used in the Fiesta minimizes this effect.

Springs and MacPherson Struts

NOTE: *To remove the spring from the suspension strut, a front spring compressor, Ford Part No. T70P-5045 or an equivalent tool is required.*

REMOVAL AND INSTALLATION

1. Loosen the wheel bolts. Raise the vehicle and support on jackstands. Remove the wheel.
2. Remove the two bolts which retain the strut to the steering knuckle.

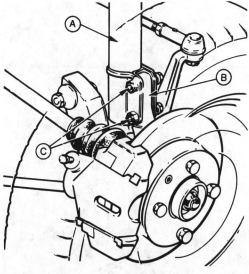

A—Strut
B—Knuckle
C—Strut-to-spindle carrier retaining nuts

Location of bolts retaining the strut to the steering knuckle

3. Remove the two top mount-to-body bolts from inside the engine compartment. Remove the strut assembly from the vehicle.

4. If using the Ford tool, mount the spring compressor in a vise and position the suspension strut so the spring seats in the tool jaws. Then, tighten the vise jaws to compress the spring. If using a standard spring compressor, mount the suspension strut in a vise with protected jaws by the portion of the base of the strut through which the strut-to-spindle bolts pass. Then position the spring compressors around the spring and tighten them alternately and evenly a little at a time until all pressure is taken off the spring retainer.

NOTE: *If the spring is not compressed so all pressure is relieved or the compressor is not in a secure position, a dangerous amount of force could be released as the retainer is removed!*

5. Install an offset box wrench on the top mount retaining nut. Then, insert a metric allen wrench into the top mount to keep it from turning as the retaining nut is removed. Remove the retaining nut.

6. Disassemble the top mount assembly, and separate the spring from the strut. Remove the spring compressor(s).

7. Compress the new spring as in Step 4 above. Position the spring on top of the strut. Install the various bearings, spacers and re-

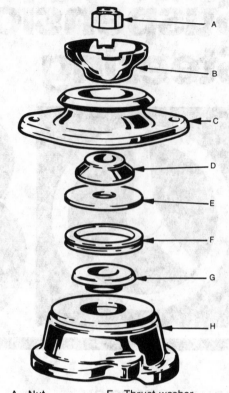

A—Nut   E—Thrust washer
B—Retainer   F—Rubber seal
C—Top mount G—Phenolic resin bearing
D—Spacer   H—Upper spring seat

Exploded view of the top mount

tainers in the exact sequence shown in the illustration. Tighten the retaining nut while holding the top mount stationary with the allen wrench as was done in disassembly. Torque to 30–38 ft lbs.

8. Remove the spring compressor(s) in reverse of the spring compression operation.

9. Position the suspension strut into the vehicle with the bolt holes in the top mount aligned with the holes in the body apron reinforcement. Install the top mount bolts and torque to 15–18 ft lbs.

10. Unless the strut has been removed and installed before, it will use production type bolts for strut attachment to the steering knuckle which do not precisely align the strut and knuckle. New precision ground bolts should be used unless it can be established that this type of bolt was installed previously. The special service type bolt has a knurled shank (see the illustration). Torque the bolts to 68–72 ft lbs.

11. Mount the wheel. Lower the vehicle and fully tighten the wheel bolts. Check and, if necessary, adjust toe-in.

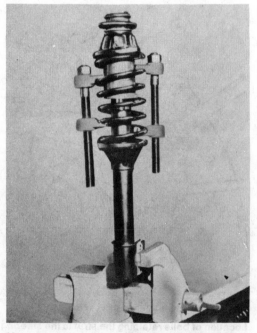

Mounting of the strut and spring compressors

Shock Absorbers

TESTING

The shock absorbers do not suspend the car, but limit the amount of jounce or rebound that comes from energy stored in the springs after hitting a good bump. Test the shocks' action by working the car up and down by the front bumper or the front of the hood. Move with the natural rhythm of the springs until the car is traveling up and down a good distance—as far as you can make it go. Release the car after pressing downward. It should come up, then drop back down to its normal riding height and stop. It it continues to

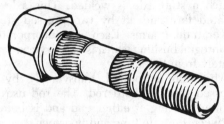

Service bolt with knurled shank

bounce, the shocks are probably weak. Another sign of shock trouble is fluid leakage from around the piston rod at the top of the strut.

REPLACING

The front shock absorbers in the Fiesta are integral with the MacPherson struts. Follow the procedure above for replacing the spring, but supply a new strut and re-use the old spring instead. Note that Fiestas with "S" type suspension use a different strut.

Ball Joints—Lower Suspension Arm

REMOVAL AND INSTALLATION

1. Support the front of the vehicle on axle stands.
2. Remove the clinch bolt (B) attaching the axle shaft carrier to the lower arm.
3. Remove the two ball joint-to-lower arm retaining nuts, and remove the ball joint.
4. To install, position the ball joint on the lower arm and install the retaining nuts, tightening only slightly.
5. Insert the stud of the ball joint with the axle shaft carrier. Install the clinch bolt and nut, and torque to 20–26 ft lbs.

6. Torque the ball joint-to-lower arm retaining nuts to 40–48 ft lbs.
7. Lower the vehicle.

Lower Control Arm

REMOVAL AND INSTALLATION

1. Raise the front of the vehicle and support on jack stands. Remove the lower arm inner pivot bolt (the arrowed bolt on the left side of the illustration).
2. Remove the clinch bolt (arrowed on the right side of the illustration) and disengage the ball joint from the spindle carrier.
3. Remove the two nuts which retain the lower arm and ball joint to the tie bar, and pull the lower arm and ball joint off the bolts.
4. To install, position the ball joint so the bolt holes line up with those in the lower arm. Then, slide the tie bar bolts through the lower arm and ball joint and install the retaining nuts loosely.
5. Insert the ball joint into the spindle carrier, and install the clinch bolt and nut, torquing to 20–26 ft lbs.
6. Position the lower arm's inner end into the mount on the side rail, line up bolt holes,

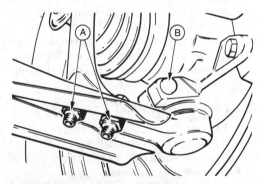

Replacing the lower arm ball joint

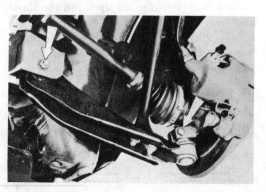

Locations of the lower arm pivot bolt and ball joint clinch bolt (both arrowed)

Wheel Alignment Specifications

Year	Model	CASTER		CAMBER		Toe-in (in.)
		Range (deg)	Preferred Setting (deg)	Range (deg)	Preferred Setting (deg)	
1978–80	All	¾N to 1⅓P	⅓P	1¼P to 3¼P	2¼P	¹⁄₁₀

install the pivot bolt and nut, and torque to 30–33 ft lbs.

7. Torque the ball joint and lower arm-to-tie bar retaining bolts to 40–48 ft lbs. Lower the vehicle.

Front End Alignment

Both caster and camber settings on the Fiesta are fixed by the design of the front suspension. A factory adjustment is made during original assembly as the lower MacPherson strut is attached to the spindle carrier. If this setting has been disturbed, proper settings can be restored by using special service type bolts. See the first procedure in this chapter ("Springs and MacPherson Struts Removal and Installation") for information on the appearance and installation of these bolts. If these bolts are installed, or the original setting has never been disturbed, improper caster or camber can be corrected only through replacement of worn or bent parts.

TOE-OUT ADJUSTMENT

1. Loosen the locknuts on the outer tie rod ends adjacent to the ball joints. Slacken the clamp on each side at the outer end of each steering gear bellows.

2. Rotate both tie rods in exactly equal amounts to get a toe-out of .1 in. *as measured at the wheel rim edge,* as shown in the illustration.

3. Tighten tie rod locknuts and reclip inner ends of steering gear bellows.

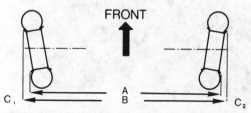

Setting toe-out. A is front, B is rear. C₁ + C₂ = toe-out

REAR SUSPENSION

Description

The rear suspension employs a transverse tubular steel member onto either end of which a stub axle is welded. This axle is located fore and aft by two pressed steel lower trailing arms. Each arm incorporates an integral bushing which is not serviced separately from the arm.

The axle is located transversely by a pressed steel panhard rod. The rod uses a rubber bushing at either end and is bolted between the axle tube and floor pan.

A strut is welded to each of the shock absorbers and fixed to the axle tube by a rubber bushed steel pin. This design keeps the axle from rotating axially. Coil springs are used.

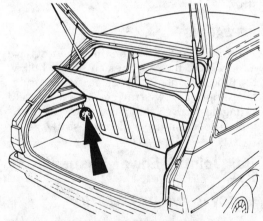

Location of the top mounting cap

Springs
REMOVAL AND INSTALLATION

CAUTION: *In performing this procedure, the vehicle must be securely supported, and a jack of adequate capacity must be positioned* squarely *under the rear axle. If the jack or vehicle should move forward or backward before both springs are fully ex-*

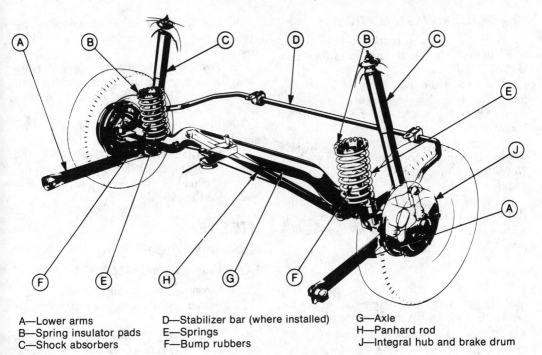

A—Lower arms
B—Spring insulator pads
C—Shock absorbers
D—Stabilizer bar (where installed)
E—Springs
F—Bump rubbers
G—Axle
H—Panhard rod
J—Integral hub and brake drum

Parts of the rear axle and suspension assembly

panded, energy stored up in the springs could be released violently.

1. Loosen the rear wheel bolts on both sides.

2. Raise the entire vehicle and support by the chassis.

3. Position a jack *squarely* under the center of the rear axle. Make sure the jack cannot roll.

4. Open the tailgate and raise the parcel tray out of the way.

5. Remove the retaining nut and washer and the plastic cap from the upper shock mounting on one side.

6. Remove the lower arm bolt at the axle on the same side.

7. If the car has a stabilizer bar, remove bolts from attachments on both sides.

8. Lower the jack until the spring is fully expanded and remove the spring and spring insulator pad.

9. Repeat Steps 5, 6 and 8 for the other side.

10. To install, seat the spring on the axle with the spring tang end butting the stop on the axle spring seat. Locate the insulating pad on the top of the spring with the spring end butting the stop on the pad.

11. Locate the spring and raise the axle until the lower arm bolt can be installed. Install the lower arm bolt for that side loosely.

12. If the car has a stabilizer bar, attach it to the body and torque nuts to 15–18 ft lbs.

13. Put the shock absorber upper mount into position and torque to 25–35 ft lbs. Replace the plastic cap.

14. Repeat Steps 10, 11, and 13 for the other side.

15. Lower the parcel tray, close to the tailgate, and install the wheels.

16. Lower the car to the ground. Torque the lower arm bolts to 40–48 ft lbs. Tighten the wheel bolts fully.

Shock Absorbers

TESTING

The shock absorbers do not suspend the car, but limit the amount of jounce or rebound that comes from energy stored in the springs after hitting a good bump. Test the shocks' action by working the car up and down by the rear bumper. Move with the natural rhythm of the springs until the car is traveling up and down a good distance—as far as you can make it go. Release the car after pressing downward. It should come up, then drop back down to its normal riding height and stop. If it continues to bounce, the shocks are probably weak. Another sign of shock trouble is fluid leakage.

REMOVAL AND INSTALLATION

1. Loosen wheel bolts on both sides. Raise the vehicle at both ends and support on chassis stands.

2. Remove the rear wheels. Position a jack squarely under the rear axle.

3. Open the tailgate and raise the parcel tray.

4. Remove the shock absorber cap, and remove the upper mounting nut and washer. Note the position of the upper insulator and remove it.

5. Remove the locknut and bolt from the shock absorber lower axle mounting. Then, with a lever, pry the shock off the locating peg. Clean the peg.

6. Repeat Steps 4 and 5 for the other side.

7. To install, lubricate the shock arm bushing and locating peg on one side with kerosene. Using a flat lever, flat washer, and a hollow tube to apply steady pressure, work the bushing onto the locating peg.

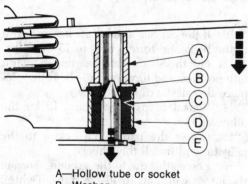

A—Hollow tube or socket
B—Washer
C—Rubber bushing
D—Rubber bushing housing
E—Peg base

Working the shock arm back onto the locating peg

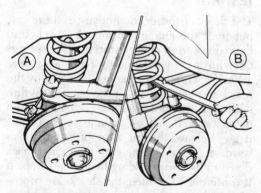

Using a lever to ("A") remove the shock arm; ("B") replace the shock arm

8. Position the lower shock mounting, install the nut and bolt and torque to 40–48 ft lbs.

9. Position the upper shock insulator, install the upper mounting nut and washer, and torque to 18–22 ft lbs. Replace the plastic cap.

10. Repeat Steps 7, 8, and 9 for the other shock.

11. Reinstall the wheels. Remove the jack and lower the vehicle to the ground. Tighten wheel bolts. Lower the parcel tray and close the tailgate.

STEERING
Steering Wheel
REMOVAL AND INSTALLATION

1. Disconnect the battery cables.

2. Pry out the steering wheel center insert.

3. Remove the steering wheel retaining nut. Lift the steering wheel and direction indicator cam off the steering shaft.

4. To install, install the direction signal indicator cam and bearing ring, and then position the steering wheel so the spokes are correctly aligned in relation to the position of the front wheels.

5. Install the wheel, and install the retaining nut, torquing to 30–37 ft lbs.

6. Install the steering wheel center insert and reconnect the battery.

Turn Signal Switch/Lever Assembly
REMOVAL AND INSTALLATION

1. Disconnect both battery cables. Remove both upper and lower shrouds from the steering column.

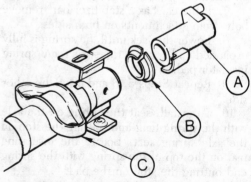

Steering shaft components: A—Direction indicator cam, B—Steering column tube, C—Steering column lock assembly

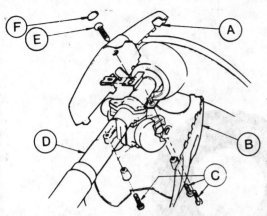

A—Upper shroud
B—Lower shroud
C—Retaining screws
D—Steering column tube
E—Retaining screw
F—Retaining screw cap

Parts of the steering column shroud

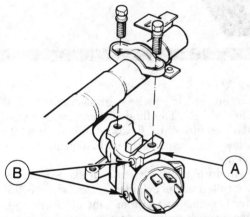

The steering column lock assembly ("A") and ignition switch retaining screws ("B")

2. Remove the steering column upper shroud, screw cap, retaining screw or clips, and shroud.

3. Remove the lower steering column shroud.

4. Remove the two attaching screws, located above and below the switch unit. Disconnect the lever multiplugs at the base of the switch, and remove the switch.

5. Installation is the reverse of removal.

Ignition Switch

REMOVAL AND INSTALLATION

1. Disconnect both battery cables.

2. Remove the steering column upper shroud, screw cap, retaining screw or clips, and shroud.

3. Loosen the switch retaining screws

("B") from the column lock assembly ("A"), and remove the ignition switch.

4. To install the switch, align the switch to the bracket and install the mounting screws. Reverse the remaining removal procedures.

Tie Rod Ends

REMOVAL AND INSTALLATION

NOTE: *A tool suitable for pressing tie rod ends out of a steering arm such as Ford Tools T77F-3290-A and T77F-3290-C is required.*

1. Put the steering wheel in the straight ahead position. Raise the front of the vehicle and support it on jack stands.

2. Remove the cotter pin ("E") and loosen, but do not remove the castellated nut ("O") attaching the ball joint to the steering arm.

3. Install the tool so the forked, upper portion slides in between the ball joint ("A") and the steering arm, and the adapter will rest against the ball joint castellated nut. Turn the tool bolt to force the ball joint out of the arm. Then, remove the tool and take off the castellated nut.

4. Loosen the ball joint locknut ("O") and remove the ball joint, *counting the number of turns required.*

5. Install the new tie rod end by screwing it onto the tie rod ("C") the same number of turns required during removal.

6. Drop the threaded portion of the ball joint through the steering arm. Install the castellated nut and torque to just over 18 ft lbs. Turn the nut farther, as necessary, until the slots in the nut line up with the cotter pin hole. Then, install a new cotter pin and bend over both legs.

7. Torque the tie rod end locknut to 42–50 ft lbs.

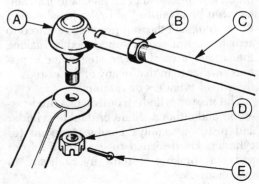

Tie rod outer ball joint

Brakes

BRAKE SYSTEM

Understanding the Brakes
HYDRAULIC SYSTEM
Basic Operating Principles

Hydraulic systems are used to actuate the brakes of all modern automobiles. The system transports the power required to force the frictional surfaces of the braking system together from the pedal to the individual brake units at each wheel. A hydraulic system is used for two reasons. First, fluid under pressure can be carried to all parts of an automobile by small hoses—some of which are flexible—without taking up a significant amount of room or posing routing problems. Second, a great mechanical advantage can be given to the brake pedal end of the system, and the foot pressure required to actuate the brakes can be reduced by making the surface area of the master cylinder pistons smaller than that of any of the pistons in the wheel cylinders or calipers.

The master cylinder consists of a fluid reservoir and either a single or double cylinder and piston assembly. Double type master cylinders are designed to separate the front and rear braking systems hydraulically in case of a leak.

Steel lines carry the brake fluid to a point on the vehicle's frame near each of the vehicle's wheels. The fluid is then carried to the slave cylinders by flexible tubes in order to allow for suspension and steering movements.

In drum brake systems, the slave cylinders are called wheel cylinders. Each wheel cylinder contains two pistons, one at either end, which push outward in opposite directions. In disc brake systems, the slave cylinders are used to force the brake pads against the disc, but all cylinders contain one piston only. All slave cylinder pistons employ some type of seal, usually made of rubber, to minimize the leakage of fluid around the piston. A rubber dust boot seals the outer end of the cylinder against dust and dirt. The boot fits around the outer end of the piston disc brake calipers, and around the brake actuating rod on wheel cylinders.

The hydraulic system operates as follows: When at rest, the entire system, from the piston(s) in the master cylinder to those in the wheel cylinders or calipers, is full of brake fluid. Upon application of the brake pedal, fluid trapped in front of the master cylinder piston(s) is forced through the lines to the slave cylinders. Here, it forces the pistons outward, in the case of drum brakes, and inward toward the disc, in the case of disc brakes. The motion of the pistons is opposed by return springs mounted outside the cylinders in drum brakes, and by internal springs or spring seals in disc brakes.

Upon release of the brake pedal, a spring located inside the master cylinder immediately returns the master cylinder piston(s) to the normal position. The pistons contain check valves and the master cylinder has compensating ports drilled in it. These are uncovered as the pistons reach their normal position. The piston check valves allow fluid to flow toward the wheel cylinders or calipers as the pistons withdraw. Then, as the return springs force the brake pads or shoes into the released position, the excess fluid returns to the master cylinder fluid reservoir through the compensating ports. It is during the time the pedal is in the released position that any fluid that has leaked out of the system will be replaced through the compensating ports.

Dual circuit master cylinders employ two pistons, located one behind the other, in the same cylinder. The primary piston is actuated directly by mechanical linkage from the brake pedal. The secondary piston is actuated by fluid trapped between the two pistons. If a leak develops in front of the secondary piston, it moves forward until it bottoms against the front of the master cylinder, and the fluid trapped between the pistons will operate the rear brakes. If the rear brakes develop a leak, the primary piston will move forward until direct contact with the secondary piston takes place, and it will force the secondary piston to actuate the front brakes. In either case, the brake pedal moves farther when the brakes are applied, and less braking power is available.

All dual-circuit systems use a distributor switch to warn the driver when only half of the brake system is operational. This switch is located in a valve body which is mounted on the firewall or the frame below the master cylinder. A hydraulic piston receives pressure from both circuits, each circuit's pressure being applied to one end of the piston. When the pressures are in balance, the piston remains stationary. When one circuit has a leak, however, the greater pressure in that circuit during application of the brakes will push the piston to one side, closing the distributor switch and activating the brake warning light.

In disc brake systems, this valve body also contains a metering valve and, in some cases, a proportioning valve. The metering valve keeps pressure from traveling to the disc brakes on the front wheels until the brake shoes on the rear wheels have contacted the drums, ensuring that the front brakes will never be used alone. The proportioning valve throttles the pressure to the rear brakes so as to avoid rear wheel lock-up during very hard braking.

These valves may be tested by removing the lines to the front and rear brake systems and installing special brake pressure testing gauges. Front and rear system pressures are then compared as the pedal is gradually depressed. Specifications vary with the manufacturer and design of the brake system.

Brake system warning lights may be tested by depressing the brake pedal and holding it while opening one of the wheel cylinder bleeder screws. If this does not cause the light to go on, substitute a new lamp, make continuity checks, and, finally, replace the switch as necessary.

The hydraulic system may be checked for leaks by applying pressure to the pedal gradually and steadily. If the pedal sinks very slowly to the floor, the system has a leak. This is not to be confused with a springy or spongy feel due to the compression of air within the lines. If the system leaks, there will be a gradual change in the position of the pedal with a constant pressure.

Check for leaks along all lines and at wheel cylinders. If no external leaks are apparent, the problem is inside the master cylinder.

DISC BRAKES
Basic Operating Principles

Instead of the traditional expanding brakes that press outward against a circular drum, disc brake systems utilize a cast iron disc with brake pads positioned on either side of it. Braking effect is achieved in a manner similar to the way you would squeeze a spinning phonograph record between your fingers. The disc (rotor) is a one-piece casting with cooling fins between the two braking surfaces. This enables air to circulate between the braking surfaces making them less sensitive to heat buildup and more resistant to fade. Dirt and water do not affect braking action since contaminants are thrown off by the centrifugal action of the rotor or scraped off by the pads. Also, the equal clamping action of the two brake pads tends to ensure uniform, straightline stops. All disc brakes are inherently self-adjusting.

There are three general types of disc brake:

1) A fixed caliper, four-piston type.
2) A floating caliper, single piston type.
3) A sliding caliper, single piston type.

The fixed caliper design uses two pistons mounted on either side of the rotor (in each side of the caliper). The caliper is mounted rigidly and does not move.

The sliding and floating designs are quite similar. In fact, these two types are often lumped together. In both designs, the pad on the inside of the rotor is moved into contact with the rotor by hydraulic force. The caliper, which is not held in a fixed position, moves slightly, bringing the outside pad into contact with the rotor. There are various methods of attaching floating calipers. Some pivot at the bottom or top, and some slide on mounting bolts. In any event, the end result is the same.

HYDRAULIC SYSTEM

Master Cylinder

REMOVAL AND INSTALLATION

1. Siphon brake fluid out of the fluid reservoir. Then, unscrew the union nuts and detach all fluid lines. Install plugs to prevent entry of dirt.
2. Remove the spring clip ("A"), pull off the clevis pin ("B"), and remove the bushing from the brake master cylinder pushrod or booster linkage.
3. Remove the two nuts and lockwashers securing the master cylinder to the firewall or vacuum booster, and remove the master cylinder assembly.

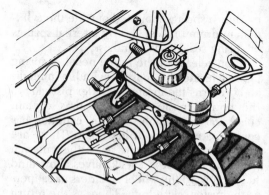

Removing the master cylinder

4. To install the master cylinder, position it on the firewall or booster, install the washers and nuts and torque to 13–28 ft lbs.
5. Screw in the fluid line union nuts and torque to 8–11 ft lbs.
6. Install the bushing into the pedal lever, then install the clevis pin. Then, install the spring clip.
7. Fill the master cylinder with fluid meeting DOT 3 standards. Bleed the brakes as described below.

OVERHAUL

1. Remove the fluid reservoir from the master cylinder and remove the rubber seals.

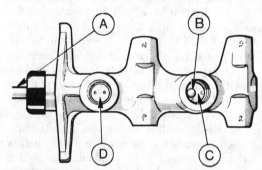

The parts involved in master cylinder disassembly

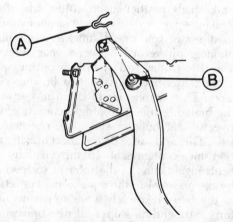

Removing the spring clip and clevis pin

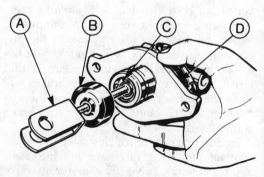

Removing the piston retaining clip

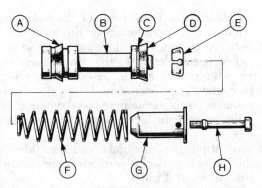

The primary piston assembly and associated parts

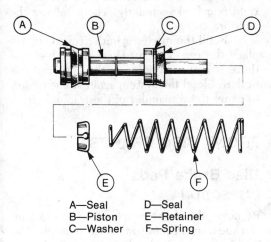

A—Seal   D—Seal
B—Piston   E—Retainer
C—Washer   F—Spring

The secondary piston assembly and associated parts

Then, mount the master cylinder assembly in a soft jawed vise.

2. Depress the pushrod ("A") to remove the pressure from the piston stop in ("B"). Then, remove the stop pin.

3. Pull the pushrod rubber boot back to expose the piston retaining clip ("C"), and remove the clip with a pair of pliers. Remove the pushrod and boot ("A" and "B") and the washer from the master cylinder assembly ("D"). Then, remove the boot from the operating rod.

4. Remove the primary piston assembly from the pushrod end of the cylinder.

5. Gently tap the pushrod end of the master cylinder against your hand to remove the secondary piston assembly.

6. Unscrew retaining screw "H" and withdraw the screw and sleeve ("G") from the primary piston assembly. Then, remove the spring ("F") retainer ("E"), and seal ("D"). Gently lever seal "A" from the pri-

mary piston. *Be careful not to damage the piston in doing this.*

7. Remove the secondary piston spring ("F"), retainer ("E") and seal "D". Gently lever seal "A" from the secondary piston, *taking care not to damage the piston.*

8. Examine the cylinder bores and pistons for score marks, ridges, and corrosion. Replace any parts that show such defects.

9. Clean the master cylinder and piston parts in alcohol or the brake fluid recommended for the car. Do not use mineral base solvents such as gasoline or kerosene or carbon tetrachloride as these will damage the rubber parts.

10. Install new secondary piston seals and secure them with the retainer. Install the spring. Make sure all seals are installed in the correct direction as shown in the illustration.

11. Dip the secondary piston assembly in clean brake fluid and slowly insert it into the bore of the master cylinder spring end first.

12. Install new primary piston seals and install the retainer, spring, sleeve, and retaining screws. Check to make sure the seals face in the the right direction (see illustration).

13. Dip the primary piston assembly in clean brake fluid and gently insert it into the cylinder bore, spring end first.

14. Install a new rubber boot and washer onto the pushrod and install the rod into the master cylinder. Install a new clip in front of the washer. Then, force the outer edge of the boot around the master cylinder.

15. Depress the pushrod and insert the piston stop pin into the secondary inlet port ("C" in the first master cylinder illustration).

16. Inspect the inlet port seals and replace if they are brittle or cracked. Install seals into the primary and secondary inlet ports ("C" and "D" in the first illustration). Install the fluid reservoir.

17. Install the master cylinder as described above and then fill and bleed the system as described below. The system should be tested by careful road test in a safe place

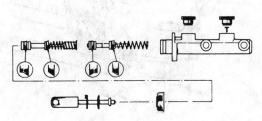

Install the seals in direction shown here

and by maintaining pressure on the brake pedal for ten seconds with the car stopped. There should be no change in the position of the pedal and no fluid leakage from the master cylinder.

BLEEDING

NOTE: *You'll need a rubber tube which will fit tightly around the brake bleed nipples ("A" in the figure), a glass jar half full of brake fluid, and a way to suspend the jar at least a foot above the bleed nipples (a small table).*

1. Raise the car and suspend it for access to the bleed nipples. The car must be suspended level all around on a lift or jack stands. You cannot perform the operation by raising one corner of the car at a time. Release the handbrake.

2. Remove the cap from the master cylinder reservoir and refill the reservoir with brake fluid which meets DOT 3 standards. The fluid level must be kept full throughout the operation; that is, it should be refilled each time a significant amount of air/fluid are expelled from a bleed nipple so that air cannot work its way into the system via the master cylinder.

3. Remove the dust cap from the right/front bleed nipple. Force the end of the bleeder tube over the nipple. Immerse the other end of the tube in a jar partly filled with the approved brake fluid so that the open end is completely covered. Make sure the jar is at least a foot above the bleed nipple so air cannot work its way back down the tube and into the system.

4. Unscrew the bleed nipple about half a turn. Have an assistant depress the brake pedal all the way and then release it as abruptly as possible. If no air or fluid is expelled, open the bleed nipple a little more and repeat the process. Repeat this until the

nipple is open. Then, continue the pumping operation, pausing for about three seconds between pumps, until the fluid which is expelled is completely air free. Remember to keep the master cylinder reservoir fairly full throughout the operation. When the fluid contains no air, tighten the bleed nipple to 8 ft lbs, remove the bleed tube and replace the cap.

5. Apply the handbrake and then bleed the left/rear brake by performing applicable parts of Steps 3 and 4.

6. Release the handbrake and bleed the left/front brake similarly.

7. Apply the handbrake and bleed the right/rear brake similarly. Then, release the handbrake.

8. Refill the master cylinder reservoir, replace the cap, and road test the vehicle. If there is any sponginess in the action of the brakes, bleed the system again at each point to expel the remainder of the trapped air.

FRONT DISC BRAKES

Disc Brake Pads

INSPECTION

Remove the front wheels and check the thickness of *braking material* (without the backing plate). It should be at least .060 in. thick, and must also pass any local inspection requirements.

REMOVAL AND INSTALLATION

1. Loosen the wheel bolts slightly and then raise and support the front of the car. Remove the front wheel.

2. Remove the piston housing retaining pins (arrowed) and discard them. Then, apply light pressure to the piston housing ("B") against the caliper tension springs ("C") and slide out the keys ("A").

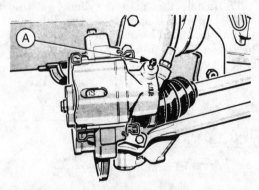

The bleed nipple is located at "A"

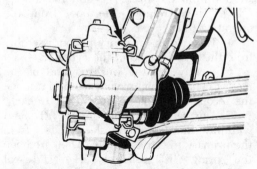

Location of piston housing retaining pins

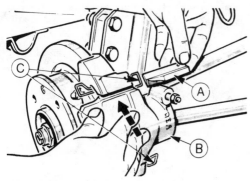

Sliding out keys

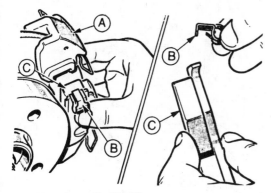

Installing the antirattle clips

3. Pull the piston housing away from the disc and suspend it securely (with wire) so the brake fluid hose is not stressed.

4. Withdraw the pads ("C") and antirattle clips ("B") from the pad housing ("A").

NOTE: *When replacing the pads, first inspect the new parts and make sure they are identical to the original equipment type. Make sure pads, antirattle clips, keys and the rotor are free from grease, oil, and dirt.*

5. Push the piston back into its bore by carefully applying pressure to the piston face (make sure you don't damage it). If necessary, siphon excess fluid out of the master cylinder.

6. Install new pads and new antirattle clips into the pad housing, with the clips attached to the top of the brake pad. Make sure all parts are exactly in place (see the illustration).

7. Remove the piston housing and position it, making sure it is above the caliper tension springs. Apply pressure on the piston housing to oppose the tension of the caliper tension springs and slide in new keys. Make sure the keys are positioned such that the retaining pin holes in caliper and the keys are lined up.

8. Insert new piston housing retaining pins and lock them securely.

9. Pump the brake pedal until pads are forced out against the disc so that the brakes will work properly when first applied.

10. Install the front wheels. Lower the vehicle and fully tighten wheel bolts. Road test the car in a safe place.

OVERHAUL

1. Follow Steps 1–4 of the procedure above to remove the piston housing from the caliper and remove brake pads from the housing.

2. Disconnect the hydraulic line at the piston housing and remove the housing from the car.

3. Apply a controllable source of air pressure to the piston via the brake fluid inlet port, and use the pressure to slowly remove the piston from the piston housing.

4. Remove the piston seal ("B") from its annular groove in the piston housing ("D").

5. Wash the piston and the bore of the piston housing with alcohol or the brake fluid approved for use in the car. *Do not use a mineral base solvent such as gasoline or kerosene.*

6. Be sure the piston and bore are free of score marks. Very light marks can be cleaned up with emery cloth. If there are heavy score marks or signs of severe corrosion, parts must be replaced.

7. Install a new piston seal in its annular groove in the piston housing.

8. Thoroughly lubricate the piston with clean brake fluid and carefully insert it into the cylinder bore as far down as it will go. Be careful not to cock the piston or otherwise permit the seal to be damaged in the operation.

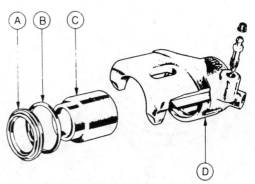

Removing the rubber bellows and seal from the piston

9. Install a new piston rubber bellows ("A) between the housing and piston.

10. Reinstall the pads to the piston housing and install the piston housing onto the caliper as described in Steps 6–8 in the procedure above.

11. Connect the brake hose to the piston housing and torque to 8–11 ft lbs. Then, bleed the entire system as described above. This will force the piston and caliper against the disc.

12. Install the road wheels, lower the car, and complete tightening of the wheel bolts. Road test the car in a safe place.

Brake Disc

REMOVAL AND INSTALLATION

1. Loosen the wheel bolts slightly, raise and support the vehicle securely, and remove the wheel.

2. Remove the two caliper mounting bolts (arrowed) and pull the caliper assembly off the disc. Hang the caliper securely with wire to avoid putting any stress on the brake hose.

3. Remove the rotor retaining screw (at "A") and pull the rotor off the front hub.

4. Clean all mating surfaces of any dirt or other foreign matter.

5. Put the rotor into position and install the retaining screw.

6. Slide the caliper into position, install the two retaining bolts, and torque them to 38–45 ft lbs.

7. Install the front wheels, lower the vehicle, and tighten the wheel bolts.

CHECKING BRAKE ROTOR RUNOUT

1. Raise the vehicle and remove the wheel. Make spacers .75 in. long which will fit over the wheel bolts. Then, install the wheel bolts over the spacers ("E") and tighten.

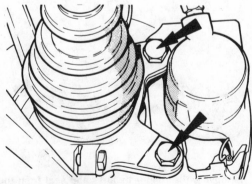

Location of the caliper retaining bolts

The rotor retaining screw ("A")

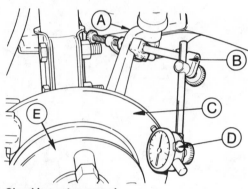

Checking rotor runout

2. Attach a dial indicator ("D") and holding fixture ("B") in the manner shown to the steering arm ("A"). Adjust the position of the holding fixture adjustments so the dial indicator is located against the rotor ("C"). Then, zero the dial indicator.

3. Turn the rotor with a speed wrench and socket via the wheel bearing nut at the center of the rotor. Watch the dial indicator and record the extremes in the readings. The difference should be within .15 mm or .006 in. If runout is excessive, the rotor should be replaced.

Wheel Bearings

ADJUSTMENT

No adjustment is required. The bearings must simply be assembled properly as described in the procedure below.

REMOVAL AND INSTALLATION– REPACKING

NOTE: *The following Ford special tools or equivalent are required to perform this operation:*

Tie Rod End Remover   T77F-3290-C
Tie Rod End Remover Adapter
*   T77F-3290-A*

Seal Remover	*T77F-6700-A*
Front Hub Bearing Cup	
Replacer	*T77F-1217-B*
with Handle	*T73T-815-A*
Front Hub Remover	*T71T-3010-P*
Slide Hammer	*T50T-100-A*
Bearing Cup Remover	*T77F-1102-A*
Front Hub Seal Replacer	*T77F-1190-A*
Puller	*T71T-3010-P*

1. Remove the center cap, hub retaining nut, and washer. Loosen the wheel lug bolts.

2. Raise the vehicle and support it safely. Remove the wheel.

3. Remove the caliper and hang it by wire from the body.

CAUTION: *Do not allow the caliper weight to hang from the brake hose.*

4. Remove the hub and disc assembly.

NOTE: *A puller may be needed to remove the hub from the shaft.*

5. Remove the cotter pin and castellated nut from the tie rod ball joint, and, using the appropriate tool, remove the tie rod end from the steering arm.

6. Remove the lower arm to body mounting retaining bolt and pull down the inner end of the arm.

7. Separate the ball joint from the knuckle by removal of the ball joint clinch bolt.

8. Remove the top mount to apron panel retaining bolts.

9. Support the driveshaft at the outer constant velocity joint and pull the knuckle clear of the drive shaft and out of the vehicle.

10. Mount the unit in a vise or other support with protective jaws and carefully remove the dust shield from the groove in the knuckle.

11. Using a slide hammer and seal remover, remove the inner and outer grease retainers and then lift out the bearings.

Removing the front hub

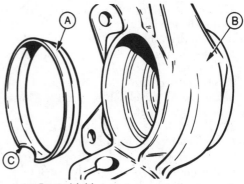

A—Dust shield
B—Knuckle
C—Cut out (must be positioned at bottom)

Lifting out the bearings

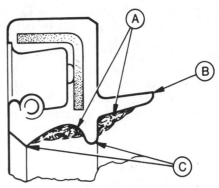

A—Apply grease as shown
B—Axial sealing lip
C—Radial sealing lips

Cross section of the grease retainer

12. Drive out the bearing cups with a flat-punch. Do not raise burrs on the cup seats. Use a bearing cup remover if necessary.

13. Install new bearing cups into the knuckle using a bearing cup replacer. Make sure the cups are properly seated by viewing the cup seating face from the rear.

14. Pack the new bearings with grease and install them in their races. Make sure the cavities between rollers are filled, but that no grease enters the cavity between inner and outer bearings or between grease retainers and bearings.

15. Apply grease to the sealing lips of the grease retainers, and using a seal driver, install the grease retainers.

16. Gently tap the dust shield into position in the groove on the inner face of the knuckle.

NOTE: *Align the cutout portion of the shield at the bottom, in line with the ball joint.*

17. Grease driveshaft spines and position the knuckle assembly in the vehicle over the end of the driveshaft.

18. Install the top mount in the apron panel and install two bolts.

19. Reconnect the lower ball joint to the knuckle. Install the clinch bolt and the lower arm inner pivot bolt.

20. Reinstall the tie rod end to the steering arm. Tighten and install a new cotter pin.

21. Install the splined end of the driveshaft through the hub and disc assembly. Draw the hub and disc on until seated with a puller.

22. Loosely install the plain washer and a *new* hub retaining nut.

23. Mount the brake caliper and install the retaining bolts, torquing to 38–45 ft lbs.

24. Install two wheel bolts to the hub. Apply the foot brake, and then torque the hub retaining nut to 150–175 ft lbs.

25. Stake the retaining nut ("A") to hold it in place by deforming it into the slot in the driveshaft ("B") with a pin punch.

26. Install the wheels, lower the vehicle to the ground, and torque wheel bolts.

Rear Drum Brakes
BRAKE DRUMS
Removal and Installation

1. Loosen the wheel bolts slightly. Support the car securely. Remove the wheel bolts and remove the wheel.

2. Make sure the handbrake is all the way off.

3. Remove the spindle and bearing dust cap, cotter pin, adjusting nut retainer, adjusting nut, washer, and outer bearing. Slide the drum/hub assembly off the spindle.

4. To replace the drum, slide it onto the spindle. Check the condition of the outer bearing, and replace it, if necessary. If the bearing is replaced, grease it thoroughly. Install the outer bearing, washer, and adjusting nut.

5. Adjust the bearing by torquing the nut to 15–18 ft lbs while spinning the drum counterclockwise. Then, loosen the nut ½ turn, and retorque it to 4–7 in. lb. Install the nut retainer, a new cotter pin, and the dust cap.

6. Install the wheel and tire. Lower the vehicle to the ground, and then fully tighten the wheel bolts.

Brake Shoes
REMOVAL AND INSTALLATION

NOTE: *Brake wear produces dust which is usually deposited on the insides of the drums and as a fine film over the various parts of the linings and actuating mechanism. You should be careful not to breathe in this dust. Use some sort of vacuum cleaner to remove the dust from the various parts rather than blowing it off with compressed air and be careful not to breathe the dust when emptying the vacuum cleaner's bag.*

1. Remove the brake drum as described above. Disconnect the handbrake cable ("B") from the actuating lever ("C") by removing the spring clip ("D") and withdrawing the clevis pin ("A"). Remove the operating lever rubber dust over from the brake carrier plate.

2. Remove the shoe hold-down spring ("B") from the secondary shoe ("C") by depressing and turning the washer 90 degrees. Remove the spring and washer and withdraw the pin from the carrier plate.

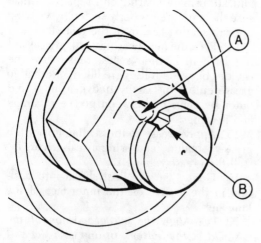

Staking the hub retaining nut

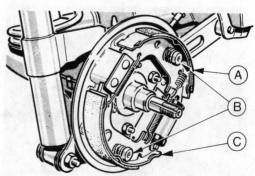

Removing the spring, washer, and pin

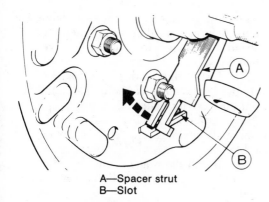

A—Spacer strut
B—Slot

Removing the spacer strut

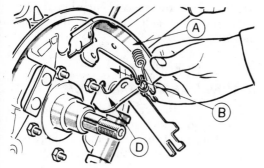

Removing the lever and shoe

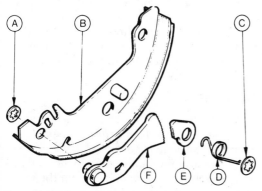

Secondary shoe and associated mounting parts

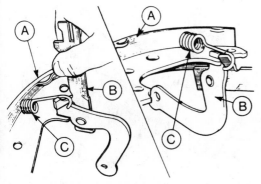

Assembling the primary shoe

3. Twist the shoe so the lining moves outward and then pull it upward and away from the carrier plate. Be careful not to damage the cylinder dust cover. Detach the shoe and remove the springs.

4. Remove the primary shoe hold-down spring from the shoe by depressing and turning the washer 90 degrees. Remove the spring and washer and withdraw the pin from the carrier plate.

5. Slide the lower end of the spacer strut out of the slot in the carrier plate.

6. Move the primary shoe ("A") upward and away from the carrier plate ("B") and remove the handbrake actuating lever ("D") and shoe assembly from the carrier plate.

7. Disassemble the secondary shoe as follows:

   a. Remove the spring washer ("A") and discard it, and separate the longer ratchet lever ("F") from the shoe ("B").

   b. Remove the spring washer ("C") from the shorter ratchet ("E") and discard it. Remove the spring ("D") and ratchet from the shoe.

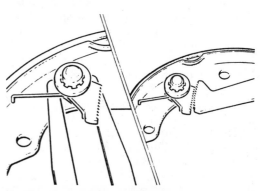

Position the ratchets as shown

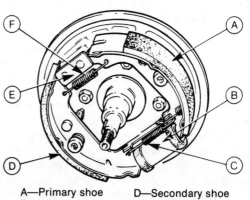

A—Primary shoe   D—Secondary shoe
B—Wheel cylinder   E—Pivot position
C—Spring   F—Spring

Installing the stronger of the two springs

8. Separate the primary shoe from the spacer strut by twisting it. Remove the spring.

NOTE: *In installation, make sure the handbrake actuating lever rotates freely relative to the spacer strut. The pin should rotate freely in the strut hole but be snugly riveted to the lever.*

9. To install, first assemble the primary shoe assembly as follows:

a. Install the actuating lever return spring ("C") to the brake shoe ("A").

b. Hook the spacer strut ("B") onto the spring and lever it into position.

10. Assemble the secondary shoe assembly as follows:

a. Position the smaller ratchet and spring on the shoe pivot. Slide two .008 in. feeler gauges between the brake shoe and ratchet and a new spring retainer washer. Make sure the retaining tabs are locked securely. Then, remove the gauges and check that the ratchet rotates on the pivot pin and returns freely with spring pressure.

b. Install the longer ratchet to the brake shoe and secure it with a new spring clip. Push the clip all the way on. The ratchet will still rotate freely.

c. The positions of the ratchets relative to each other should be such that they overlap as shown.

11. Insert the handbrake actuating lever through the carrier plate. Place the primary brake shoe against the wheel cylinder and upper pivot. Slide the spacer strut lower edge into the slot in the carrier plate.

12. Install the shoe hold-down spring to the primary shoe.

13. Install the stronger of the two springs located at "F" between the primary and secondary shoes at the pivot position with brake pliers.

14. Hook the secondary shoe under the pivot and position the shoe against the carrier plate. Check to make sure the slot in the long ratchet is engaged in the spacer strut and then place the shoe against the wheel cylinder (with the lining facing outward).

15. Install the shoe hold down spring for the secondary shoe.

16. Install the weaker of the two springs, located at "C", to the secondary shoe and then attach it to the primary shoe with brake pliers.

17. Pull the spring loaded ratchet back against its spring. Use a wire hook made from a piece of .06 in. diameter wire with one end bent to form a small hook and the other end secured to something that will serve as a handle.

18. Install the handbrake actuating lever rubber boot over the operating arm and fit it onto the carrier plate.

19. Assemble the handbrake cable clevis pin and retaining clip and reconnect the cable.

20. Install the brake drum and adjust the wheel bearing as described in the above procedure.

21. Adjust the brake by depressing the brake pedal several times. Install the wheel and tire, lower the car, and complete tightening of the wheel bolts. Road test the car in a safe spot.

Wheel Cylinders
REMOVAL AND INSTALLATION

1. Remove the rear brake drum and shoes as described in the procedure above.

2. Disconnect the brake line at the wheel cylinder, from behind the carrier plate, and install a plug.

3. Remove the two retaining bolts from behind the plate and remove the wheel cylinder.

4. To install locate the cylinder in its hole in the carrier plate and reverse the remaining removal procedures. Bleed the entire system as described above.

OVERHAUL

NOTE: *Be sure your hands and all working surfaces are clean before disassembling brake hydraulic component.*

1. Remove the rubber dust covers and piston assemblies ("D" and "E") from the cylinder bore, and separate the covers from the pistons.

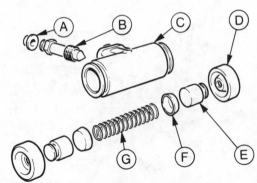

Exploded view of the wheel cylinder

2. Slide out the piston seals ("F") and remove the spring ("G") from the center of the cylinder bore.

3. Remove the bleed nipple cover ("A") and bleed nipple ("B").

4. Clean all metal parts in clean brake fluid or a non-mineral solvent such as alcohol. Replace all rubber parts. Make sure all rubbing surfaces—the cylinder bore and piston surfaces—are free of score marks. Replace parts if badly scored.

5. Assemble the dust covers to the pistons. Then, install one piston/dust cover assembly into the bore of the wheel cylinder.

6. From the opposite side, slide a new piston seal, spring, and a second new piston seal (make sure each seal faces in the proper direction—with open end toward the spring—into the cylinder bore.

7. Install the second piston and dust cover.

PARKING BRAKE

Cable

ADJUSTMENT

Be sure the handbrake is in the off position.

1. Raise the vehicle on a hoist or support it on jackstands. Check to make sure the cable is properly mounted in the cable guides.

2. Loosen the adjuster locknut ("B") and rotate the cable adjuster ("A") to slacken the cable ("C").

3. Tighten the cable by rotating the cable adjuster until the tension increases and the handbrake levers *just* begin to move off the back stops. Then, rotate the adjuster three turns further and tighten the locknut.

NOTE: *Check that the machined section ("D") must not protrude past the locknut.*

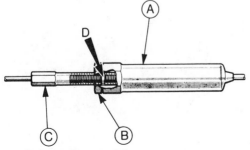

Handbrake adjuster parts

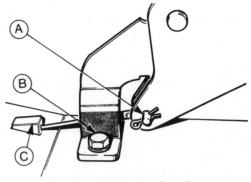

A—Clevis pin and spring clip
B—Lever retaining bolt
C—Cable guide

Disconnecting the handbrake cable

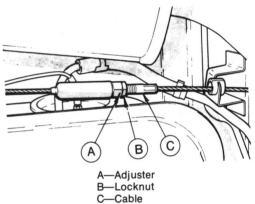

A—Adjuster
B—Locknut
C—Cable

Handbrake cable adjuster parts

REMOVAL AND INSTALLATION

1. Release the handbrake, and raise the vehicle and support it on jackstands.

2. Disconnect the cable from the brake lever by removing the clevis pin and spring clip ("A").

3. Disconnect the cable at the adjuster ("A").

4. Drive out the cable guide ("C") from the floorpan toward the rear. Remove the cable by pulling it to the rear through the hole in the floorpan.

5. To install a new cable, insert the cable and cable guide through the floorpan hole and push the cable guide securely into position.

6. Raise the handbrake lever all the way. Connect the cable to the lever and secure it with the clevis pin and spring clip. Release the brake lever.

7. Connect the cable to the adjuster and adjust it as described in the procedure above.

Brake Specifications

Model	Lug Nut Torque (ft/lb)	Master Cylinder Bore	Brake Disc		Brake Drum			Minimum Lining Thickness	
			Minimum Thickness	Maximum Run-Out •	Diameter	Max Machine O/S	Max Wear Limit	Front	Rear
All	63–85	—	.340	.006	7.0	①	①	.060	.060

① Refer to state inspection regulations

NOTE: *Minimum lining thickness is as recommended by the manufacturer. Because of variations in state inspection regulations, the minimum allowable thickness may be different than recommended by the manufacturer.*

Body
10

You can repair most minor auto body damage yourself. Minor damage usually falls into one of several categories: (1) small scratches and dings in the paint that can be repaired without the use of body filler, (2) deep scratches and dents that require body filler, but do not require pulling, or hammering metal back into shape and (3) rust-out repairs. The repair sequences illustrated in this chapter are typical of these types of repairs. If you want to get involved in more complicated repairs including pulling or hammering sheet metal back into shape, you will probably need more detailed instructions. Chilton's *Minor Auto Body Repair, 2nd Edition* is a comprehensive guide to repairing auto body damage yourself.

TOOLS AND SUPPLIES

The list of tools and equipment you may need to fix minor body damage ranges from very basic hand tools to a wide assortment of specialized body tools. Most minor scratches, dings and rust holes can be fixed using an electric drill, wire wheel or grinder attachment, half-round plastic file, sanding block, various grades of sandpaper (#36, which is coarse through #600, which is fine) in both wet and dry types, auto body plastic,

primer, touch-up paint, spreaders, newspaper and masking tape.

Most manufacturers of auto body repair products began supplying materials to professionals. Their knowledge of the best, most-used products has been translated into body repair kits for the do-it-yourselfer. Kits are available from a number of manufacturers and contain the necessary materials in the required amounts for the repair identified on the package.

Kits are available for a wide variety of uses, including:

- Rusted out metal
- All purpose kit for dents and holes
- Dents and deep scratches
- Fiberglass repair kit
- Epoxy kit for restyling.

Kits offer the advantage of buying what you need for the job. There is little waste and little chance of materials going bad from not being used. The same manufacturers also merchandise all of the individual products used—spreaders, dent pullers, fiberglass cloth, polyester resin, cream hardener, body filler, body files, sandpaper, sanding discs and holders, primer, spray paint, etc.

CAUTION: *Most of the products you will be using contain harmful chemicals, so be extremely careful. Always read the complete label before opening the containers. When*

*you put them away for future use, be sure
they are out of children's reach!*

Most auto body repair kits contain all the
materials you need to do the job right in the
kit. So, if you have a small rust spot or dent
you want to fix, check the contents of the kit
before you run out and buy any additional
tools.

ALIGNING BODY PANELS

Doors

There are several methods of adjusting
doors. Your vehicle will probably use one of
those illustrated.

Whenever a door is removed and is to be
reinstalled, you should matchmark the position of the hinges on the door pillars. The
holes of the hinges and/or the hinge attaching
points are usually oversize to permit alignment of doors. The striker plate is also
moveable, through oversize holes, permitting
up-and-down, in-and-out and fore-and-aft
movement. Fore-and-aft movement is made
by adding or subtracting shims from behind
the striker and pillar post. The striker should
be adjusted so that the door closes fully and
remains closed, yet enters the lock freely.

DOOR HINGES

Don't try to cover up poor door adjustment
with a striker plate adjustment. The gap on
each side of the door should be equal and
uniform and there should be no metal-to-
metal contact as the door is opened or closed.

1. Determine which hinge bolts must be
loosened to move the door in the desired direction.

2. Loosen the hinge bolt(s) just enough to
allow the door to be moved with a padded
pry bar.

3. Move the door a small amount and
check the fit, after tightening the bolts. Be
sure that there is no bind or interference
with adjacent panels.

4. Repeat this until the door is properly
positioned, and tighten all the bolts securely.

Hood, Trunk or Tailgate

As with doors, the outline of hinges should
be scribed before removal. The hood and
trunk can be aligned by loosening the hinge
bolts in their slotted mounting holes and
moving the hood or trunk lid as necessary.

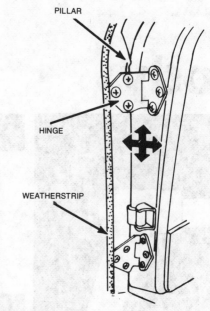

Door hinge adjustment

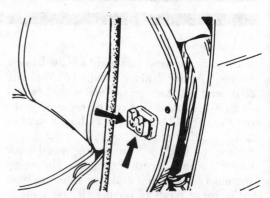

Move the door striker as indicated by arrows

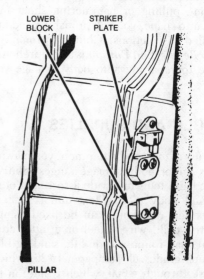

Striker plate and lower block

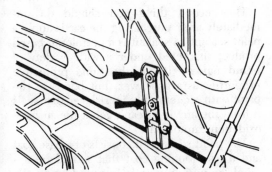

Loosen the hinge boots to permit fore-and-aft and horizontal adjustment

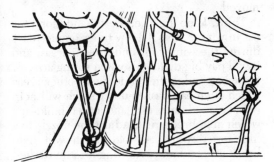

The hood is adjusted vertically by stop-screws at the front and/or rear

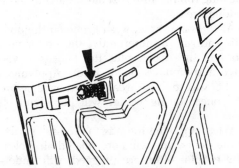

The hood pin can be adjusted for proper lock engagement

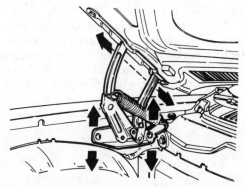

The height of the hood at the rear is adjusted by loosening the bolts that attach the hinge to the body and moving the hood up or down

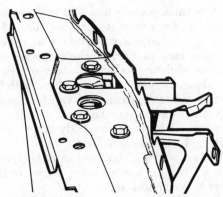

The base of the hood lock can also be repositioned slightly to give more positive lock engagement

The hood and trunk have adjustable catch locations to regulate lock engagement. Bumpers at the front and/or rear of the hood provide a vertical adjustment and the hood lockpin can be adjusted for proper engagement.

The tailgate on the station wagon can be adjusted by loosening the hinge bolts in their slotted mounting holes and moving the tailgate on its hinges. The latchplate and latch striker at the bottom of the tailgate opening can be adjusted to stop rattle. An adjustable bumper is located on each side.

RUST, UNDERCOATING, AND RUSTPROOFING

Rust

Rust is an electrochemical process. It works on ferrous metals (iron and steel) from the inside out due to exposure of unprotected surfaces to air and moisture. The possibility of rust exists practically nationwide—anywhere humidity, industrial pollution or chemical salts are present, rust can form. In coastal areas, the problem is high humidity and salt air; in snowy areas, the problem is chemical salt (de-icer) used to keep the roads clear, and in industrial areas, sulphur dioxide is present in the air from industrial pollution and is changed to sulphuric acid when it rains. The rusting process is accelerated by high temperatures, especially in snowy areas, when vehicles are driven over slushy roads and then left overnight in a heated garage.

Automotive styling also can be a contributor to rust formation. Spot welding of panels creates small pockets that trap moisture and form an environment for rust formation. Fortunately, auto manufacturers have been working hard to increase the corrosion protection of their products. Galvanized sheet metal enjoys much wider use, along with the increased use of plastic and various rust retardant coatings. Manufacturers are also designing out areas in the body where rust-forming moisture can collect.

To prevent rust, you must stop it before it gets started. On new vehicles, there are two ways to accomplish this.

First, the car or truck should be treated with a commercial rustproofing compound. There are many different brands of franchised rustproofers, but most processes involve spraying a waxy "self-healing" compound under the chassis, inside rocker panels, inside doors and fender liners and similar places where rust is likely to form. Prices for a quality rustproofing job range from $100–$250, depending on the area, the brand name and the size of the vehicle.

Ideally, the vehicle should be rustproofed as soon as possible following the purchase. The surfaces of the car or truck have begun to oxidize and deteriorate during shipping. In addition, the car may have sat on a dealer's lot or on a lot at the factory, and once the rust has progressed past the stage of light, powdery surface oxidation rustproofing is not likely to be worthwhile. Professional rustproofers feel that once rust has formed, rustproofing will simply seal in moisture already present. Most franchised rustproofing operations offer a 3–5 year warranty against rustthrough, but will not support that warranty if the rustproofing is not applied within three months of the date of manufacture.

Undercoating should not be mistaken for rustproofing. Undercoating is a black, tarlike substance that is applied to the underside of a vehicle. Its basic function is to deaden noises that are transmitted from under the car. It simply cannot get into the crevices and seams where moisture tends to collect. In fact, it may clog up drainage holes and ventilation passages. Some undercoatings also tend to crack or peel with age and only create more moisture and corrosion attracting pockets.

The second thing you should do immediately after purchasing the car is apply a paint sealant. A sealant is a petroleum based product marketed under a wide variety of brand names. It has the same protective properties as a good wax, but bonds to the paint with a chemically inert layer that seals it from the air. If air can't get at the surface, oxidation cannot start.

The paint sealant kit consists of a base coat and a conditioning coat that should be applied every 6–8 months, depending on the manufacturer. The base coat must be applied before waxing, or the wax must first be removed.

Third, keep a garden hose handy for your car in winter. Use it a few times on nice days during the winter for underneath areas, and it will pay big dividends when spring arrives. Spraying under the fenders and other areas which even car washes don't reach will help remove road salt, dirt and other build-ups which help breed rust. Adjust the nozzle to a high-force spray. An old brush will help break up residue, permitting it to be washed away more easily.

It's a somewhat messy job, but worth it in the long run because rust often starts in those hidden areas.

At the same time, wash grime off the door sills and, more importantly, the under portions of the doors, plus the tailgate if you have a station wagon or truck. Applying a coat of wax to those areas at least once before and once during winter will help fend off rust.

When applying the wax to the under parts of the doors, you will note small drain holes. These holes often are plugged with undercoating or dirt. Make sure they are cleaned out to prevent water build-up inside the doors. A small punch or penknife will do the job.

Water from the high-pressure sprays in car washes sometimes can get into the housings for parking and taillights, so take a close look. If they contain water merely loosen the retaining screws and the water should run out.

Repairing Scratches and Small Dents

Step 1. This dent (arrow) is typical of a deep scratch or minor dent. If deep enough, the dent or scratch can be pulled out or hammered out from behind. In this case no straightening is necessary

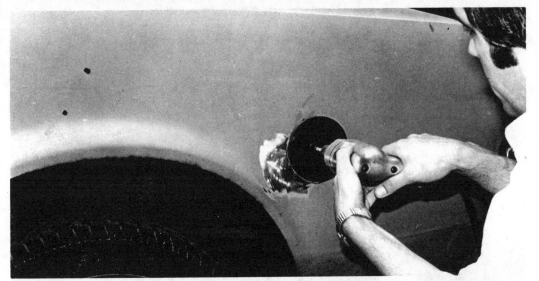

Step 2. Using an 80-grit grinding disc on an electric drill grind the paint from the surrounding area down to bare metal. This will provide a rough surface for the body filler to grab

Step 3. The area should look like this when you're finished grinding

Step 4. Mix the body filler and cream hardener according to the directions

Step 5. Spread the body filler evenly over the entire area. Be sure to cover the area completely

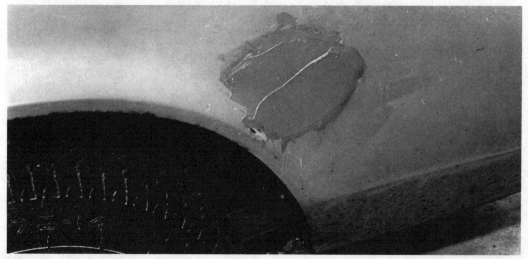

Step 6. Let the body filler dry until the surface can just be scratched with your fingernail

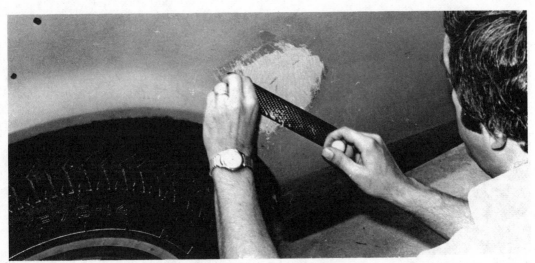

Step 7. Knock the high spots from the body filler with a body file

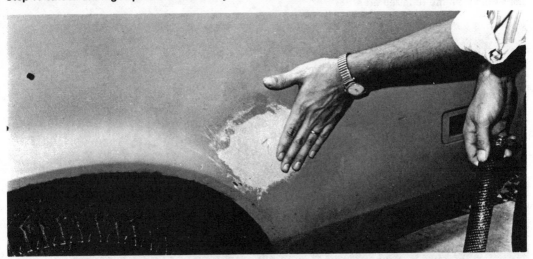

Step 8. Check frequently with the palm of your hand for high and low spots. If you wind up with low spots, you may have to apply another layer of filler

Step 9. Block sand the entire area with 320 grit paper

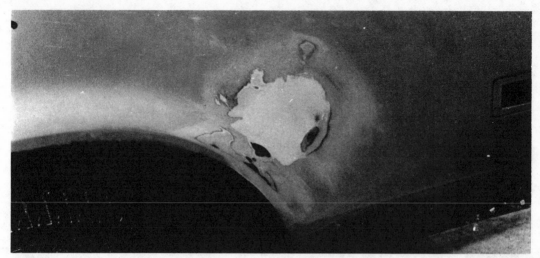

Step 10. When you're finished, the repair should look like this. Note the sand marks extending 2—3 inches out from the repaired area

Step 11. Prime the entire area with automotive primer

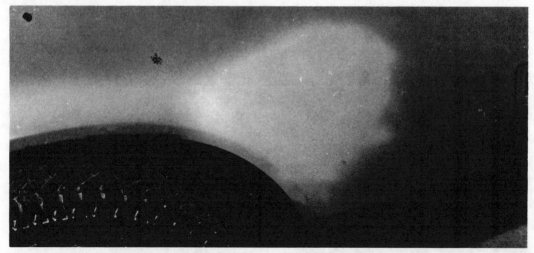

Step 12. The finished repair ready for the final paint coat. Note that the primer has covered the sanding marks (see Step 10). A repair of this size should be able to be spotpainted with good results

REPAIRING RUST HOLES

One thing you have to remember about rust: even if you grind away all the rusted metal in a panel, and repair the area with any of the kits available, *eventually* the rust will return. There are two reasons for this. One, rust is a chemical reaction that causes pressure under the repair from the inside out. That's how the blisters form. Two, the back side of the panel (and the repair) is wide open to moisture, and unpainted body filler acts like a sponge. That's why the best solution to rust problems is to remove the rusted panel and install a new one or have the rusted area cut out and a new piece of sheet metal welded in its place. The trouble with welding is the expense; sometimes it will cost more than the car or truck is worth.

One of the better solutions to do-it-yourself rust repair is the process using a fiberglass cloth repair kit (shown here). This will give a strong repair that resists cracking and moisture and is relatively easy to use. It can be used on large or small holes and also can be applied over contoured surfaces.

Step 1. Rust areas such as this are common and are easily fixed

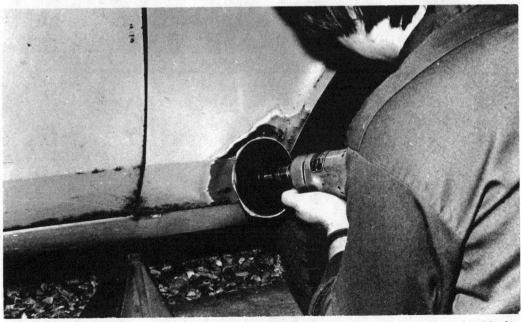

Step 2. Grind away all traces of rust with a 24-grit grinding disc. Be sure to grind back 3—4 inches from the edge of the hole down to bare metal and be sure all traces of rust are removed

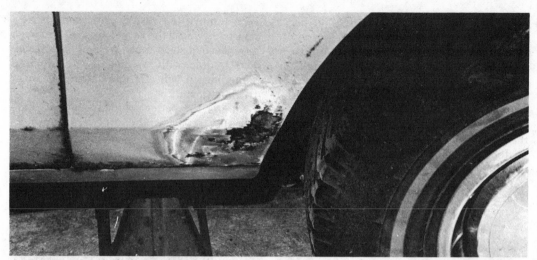

Step 3. Be sure all rust is removed from the edges of the metal. The edges must be ground back to un-rusted metal

Step 4. If you are going to use release film, cut a piece about 2″ larger than the area you have sanded. Place the film over the repair and mark the sanded area on the film. Avoid any unnecessary wrinkling of the film

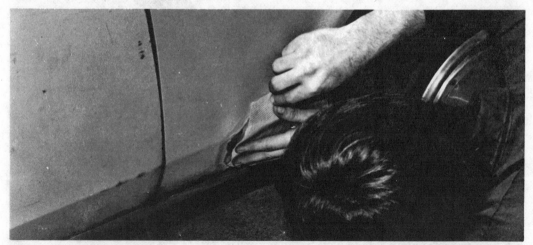

Step 5. Cut 2 pieces of fiberglass matte. One piece should be about 1″ smaller than the sanded area and the second piece should be 1″ smaller than the first. Use sharp scissors to avoid loose ends

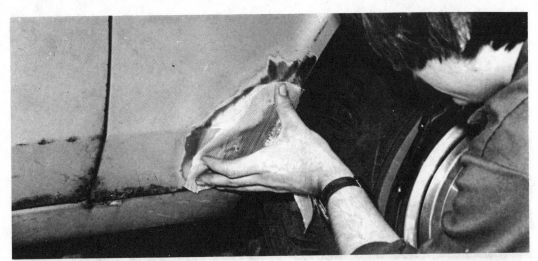

Step 6. Check the dimensions of the release film and cloth by holding them up to the repair area

Step 7. Mix enough repair jelly and cream hardener in the mixing tray to saturate the fiberglass material or fill the repair area. Follow the directions on the container

Step 8. Lay the release sheet on a flat surface and spread an even layer of filler, large enough to cover the repair. Lay the smaller piece of fiberglass cloth in the center of the sheet and spread another layer of repair jelly over the fiberglass cloth. Repeat the operation for the larger piece of cloth. If the fiberglass cloth is not used, spread the repair jelly on the release film, concentrated in the middle of the repair

Step 9. Place the repair material over the repair area, with the release film facing outward

Step 10. Use a spreader and work from the center outward to smooth the material, following the body contours. Be sure to remove all air bubbles

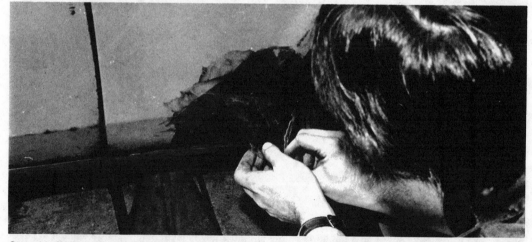

Step 11. Wait until the repair has dried tack-free and peel off the release sheet. The ideal working temperature is 65—90° F. Cooler or warmer temperatures or high humidity may require additional curing time

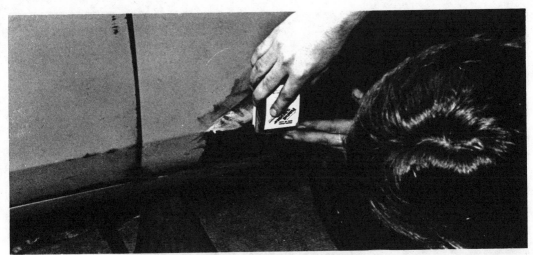

Step 12. Sand and feather-edge the entire area. The initial sanding can be done with a sanding disc on an electric drill if care is used. Finish the sanding with a block sander

Step 13. When the area is sanded smooth, mix some topcoat and hardener and apply it directly with a spreader. This will give a smooth finish and prevent the glass matte from showing through the paint

Step 14. Block sand the topcoat with finishing sandpaper

Step 15. To finish this repair, grind out the surface rust along the top edge of the rocker panel

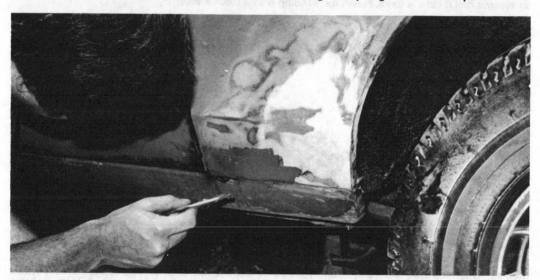

Step 16. Mix some more repair jelly and cream hardener and apply it directly over the surface

Step 17. When it dries tack-free, block sand the surface smooth

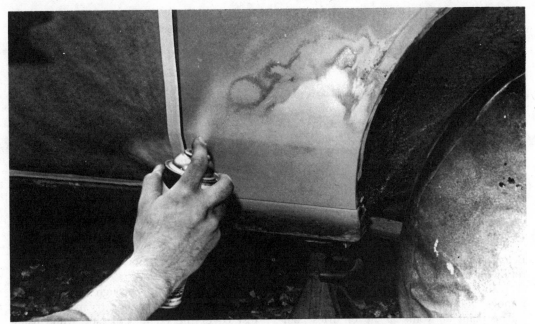

Step 18. If necessary, mask off adjacent panels and spray the entire repair with primer. You are now ready for a color coat

AUTO BODY CARE

There are hundreds—maybe thousands—of products on the market, all designed to protect or aid your car's finish in some manner. There are as many different products as there are ways to use them, but they all have one thing in common—the surface must be clean.

Washing

The primary ingredient for washing your car is water, preferably "soft" water. In many areas of the country, the local water supply is "hard" containing many minerals. The little rings or film that is left on your car's surface after it has dried is the result of "hard" water.

Since you usually can't change the local water supply, the next best thing is to dry the surface before it has a chance to dry itself.

Into the water you usually add soap. Don't use detergents or common, coarse soaps. Your car's paint never truly dries out, but is always evaporating residual oils into the air. Harsh detergents will remove these oils, causing the paint to dry faster than normal. Instead use warm water and a non-detergent soap made especially for waxed surfaces or a liquid soap made for waxed surfaces or a liquid soap made for washing dishes by hand.

Other products that can be used on painted surfaces include baking soda or plain soda water for stubborn dirt.

Wash the car completely, starting at the top, and rinse it completely clean. Abrasive grit should be loaded off under water pressure; scrubbing grit off will scratch the finish. The best washing tool is a sponge, cleaning mitt or soft towel. Whichever you choose, replace it often as each tends to absorb grease and dirt.

Other ways to get a better wash include:

• Don't wash your car in the sun or when the finish is hot.

• Use water pressure to remove caked-on dirt.

• Remove tree-sap and bird effluence immediately. Such substances will eat through wax, polish and paint.

One of the best implements to dry your car is a turkish towel or an old, soft bath towel. Anything with a deep nap will hold any dirt in suspension and not grind it into the paint.

Harder cloths will only grind the grit into the paint making more scratches. Always start drying at the top, followed by the hood and trunk and sides. You'll find there's always more dirt near the rocker panels and wheelwells which will wind up on the rest of the car if you dry these areas first.

Cleaners, Waxes and Polishes

Before going any farther you should know the function of various products.

Cleaners—remove the top layer of dead pigment or paint.

Rubbing or polishing compounds—used to remove stubborn dirt, get rid of minor scratches, smooth away imperfections and partially restore badly weathered paint.

Polishes—contain no abrasives or waxes; they shine the paint by adding oils to the paint.

Waxes—are a protective coating for the polish.

CLEANERS AND COMPOUNDS

Before you apply any wax, you'll have to remove oxidation, road film and other types of pollutants that washing alone will not remove.

The paint on your car never dries completely. There are always residual oils evaporating from the paint into the air. When enough oils are present in the paint, it has a healthy shine (gloss). When too many oils evaporate the paint takes on a whitish cast known as oxidation. The idea of polishing and waxing is to keep enough oil present in the painted surface to prevent oxidation; but when it occurs, the only recourse is to remove the top layer of "dead" paint, exposing the healthy paint underneath.

Products to remove oxidation and road film are sold under a variety of generic names—polishes, cleaner, rubbing compound, cleaner/polish, polish/cleaner, self-polishing wax, pre-wax cleaner, finish restorer and many more. Regardless of name there are two types of cleaners—abrasive cleaners (sometimes called polishing or rubbing compounds) that remove oxidation by grinding away the top layer of "dead" paint, or chemical cleaners that dissolve the "dead" pigment, allowing it to be wiped away.

Abrasive cleaners, by their nature, leave thousands of minute scratches in the finish, which must be polished out later. These should only be used in extreme cases, but are usually the only thing to use on badly oxidized paint finishes. Chemical cleaners are much milder but are not strong enough for severe cases of oxidation or weathered paint.

The most popular cleaners are liquid or paste abrasive polishing and rubbing compounds. Polishing compounds have a finer abrasive grit for medium duty work. Rubbing compounds are a coarser abrasive and for heavy duty work. Unless you are familiar with how to use compounds, be very careful. Excessive rubbing with any type of compound or cleaner can grind right through the paint to primer or bare metal. Follow the directions on the container—depending on type, the cleaner may or may not be OK for your paint. For example, some cleaners are not formulated for acrylic lacquer finishes.

When a small area needs compounding or heavy polishing, it's best to do the job by hand. Some people prefer a powered buffer for large areas. Avoid cutting through the paint along styling edges on the body. Small, hand operations where the compound is applied and rubbed using cloth folded into a thick ball allow you to work in straight lines along such edges.

To avoid cutting through on the edges when using a power buffer, try masking tape. Just cover the edge with tape while using power. Then finish the job by hand with the tape removed. Even then work carefully. The paint tends to be a lot thinner along the sharp ridges stamped into the panels.

Whether compounding by machine or by hand, only work on a small area and apply the compound sparingly. If the materials are spread too thin, or allowed to sit too long, they dry out. Once dry they lose the ability to deliver a smooth, clean finish. Also, dried out polish tends to cause the buffer to stick in one spot. This in turn can burn or cut through the finish.

WAXES AND POLISHES

Your car's finish can be protected in a number of ways. A cleaner/wax or polish/cleaner followed by wax or variations of each all provide good results. The two-step approach (polish followed by wax) is probably slightly better but consumes more time and effort. Properly fed with oils, your paint should never need cleaning, but despite the best polishing job, it won't last unless it's protected with wax. Without wax, polish must be renewed at least once a month to prevent oxidation. Years ago (some still swear by it today), the best wax was made from the Brazilian palm, the Carnuba, favored for its vegetable base and high melting point. However, modern synthetic waxes are harder, which means they protect against moisture better, and chemically inert silicone is used for a long lasting protection. The only problem with silicone wax is that it penetrates all layers of paint. To repaint or touch up a panel or car protected by silicone wax, you have to completely strip the finish to avoid "fish-eyes."

Under normal conditions, silicone waxes will last 4–6 months, but you have to be careful of wax build-up from too much waxing. Too thick a coat of wax is just as bad as no wax at all; it stops the paint from breathing.

Combination cleaners/waxes have become popular lately because they remove the old layer of wax plus light oxidation, while putting on a fresh coat of wax at the same time. Some cleaners/waxes contain abrasive cleaners which require caution, although many cleaner/waxes use a chemical cleaner.

Applying Wax or Polish

You may view polishing and waxing your car as a pleasant way to spend an afternoon, or as a boring chore, but it has to be done to keep the paint on your car. Caring for the paint doesn't require special tools, but you should follow a few rules.

1. Use a good quality wax.

2. Before applying any wax or polish, be sure the surface is completely clean. Just because the car looks clean, doesn't mean it's ready for polish or wax.

3. If the finish on your car is weathered, dull, or oxidized, it will probably have to be compounded to remove the old or oxidized paint. If the paint is simply dulled from lack of care, one of the non-abrasive cleaners known as polishing compounds will do the trick. If the paint is severely scratched or really dull, you'll probably have to use a rubbing compound to prepare the finish for waxing. If you're not sure which one to use, use the polishing compound, since you can easily ruin the finish by using too strong a compound.

4. Don't apply wax, polish or compound in direct sunlight, even if the directions on the can say you can. Most waxes will not cure properly in bright sunlight and you'll probably end up with a blotchy looking finish.

5. Don't rub the wax off too soon. The result will be a wet, dull looking finish. Let the wax dry thoroughly before buffing it off.

6. A constant debate among car enthusiasts is how wax should be applied. Some maintain pastes or liquids should be applied in a circular motion, but body shop experts have long thought that this approach results in barely detectable circular abrasions, especially on cars that are waxed frequently. They advise rubbing in straight lines, especially if any kind of cleaner is involved.

7. If an applicator is not supplied with the wax, use a piece of soft cheesecloth or very soft lint-free material. The same applies to buffing the surface.

SPECIAL SURFACES

One-step combination cleaner and wax formulas shouldn't be used on many of the special surfaces which abound on cars. The one-step materials contain abrasives to achieve a clean surface under the wax top coat. The abrasives are so mild that you could clean a car every week for a couple of years without fear of rubbing through the paint. But this same level of abrasiveness might, through repeated use, damage decals used for special trim effects. This includes wide stripes, wood-grain trim and other appliques.

Painted plastics must be cleaned with care. If a cleaner is too aggressive it will cut through the paint and expose the primer. If bright trim such as polished aluminum or chrome is painted, cleaning must be performed with even greater care. If rubbing compound is being used, it will cut faster than polish.

Abrasive cleaners will dull an acrylic finish. The best way to clean these newer finishes is with a non-abrasive liquid polish. Only dirt and oxidation, not paint, will be removed.

Taking a few minutes to read the instructions on the can of polish or wax will help prevent making serious mistakes. Not all preparations will work on all surfaces. And some are intended for power application while others will only work when applied by hand.

Don't get the idea that just pouring on some polish and then hitting it with a buffer will suffice. Power equipment speeds the operation. But it also adds a measure of risk. It's very easy to damage the finish if you use the wrong methods or materials.

Caring for Chrome

Read the label on the container. Many products are formulated specifically for chrome, but others contain abrasives that will scratch the chrome finish. If it isn't recommended for chrome, don't use it.

Never use steel wool or kitchen soap pads to clean chrome. Be careful not to get chrome cleaner on paint or interior vinyl surfaces. If you do, get it off immediately.

Troubleshooting

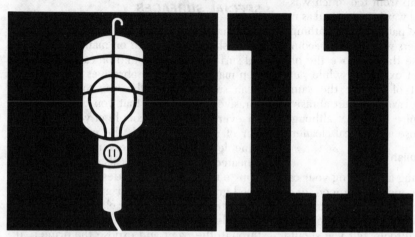

11

This section is designed to aid in the quick, accurate diagnosis of automotive problems. While automotive repairs can be made by many people, accurate troubleshooting is a rare skill for the amateur and professional alike.

In its simplest state, troubleshooting is an exercise in logic. It is essential to realize that an automobile is really composed of a series of systems. Some of these systems are interrelated; others are not. Automobiles operate within a framework of logical rules and physical laws, and the key to troubleshooting is a good understanding of all the automotive systems.

This section breaks the car or truck down into its component systems, allowing the problem to be isolated. The charts and diagnostic road maps list the most common problems and the most probable causes of trouble. Obviously it would be impossible to list every possible problem that could happen along with every possible cause, but it will locate MOST problems and eliminate a lot of unnecessary guesswork. The systematic format will locate problems within a given system, but, because many automotive systems are interrelated, the solution to your particular problem may be found in a number of systems on the car or truck.

USING THE TROUBLESHOOTING CHARTS

This book contains all of the specific information that the average do-it-yourself mechanic needs to repair and maintain his or her car or truck. The troubleshooting charts are designed to be used in conjunction with the specific procedures and information in the text. For instance, troubleshooting a point-type ignition system is fairly standard for all models, but you may be directed to the text to find procedures for troubleshooting an individual type of electronic ignition. You will also have to refer to the specification charts throughout the book for specifications applicable to your car or truck.

TOOLS AND EQUIPMENT

The tools illustrated in Chapter 1 (plus two more diagnostic pieces) will be adequate to troubleshoot most problems. The two other tools needed are a voltmeter and an ohmmeter. These can be purchased separately or in combination, known as a VOM meter.

In the event that other tools are required, they will be noted in the procedures.

Troubleshooting Engine Problems

See Chapters 2, 3, 4 for more information and service procedures.

Index to Systems

System	To Test	Group
Battery	Engine need not be running	1
Starting system	Engine need not be running	2
Primary electrical system	Engine need not be running	3
Secondary electrical system	Engine need not be running	4
Fuel system	Engine need not be running	5
Engine compression	Engine need not be running	6
Engine vacuum	Engine must be running	7
Secondary electrical system	Engine must be running	8
Valve train	Engine must be running	9
Exhaust system	Engine must be running	10
Cooling system	Engine must be running	11
Engine lubrication	Engine must be running	12

Index to Problems

Problem: Symptom	Begin at Specific Diagnosis, Number ____
Engine Won't Start:	
Starter doesn't turn	1.1, 2.1
Starter turns, engine doesn't	2.1
Starter turns engine very slowly	1.1, 2.4
Starter turns engine normally	3.1, 4.1
Starter turns engine very quickly	6.1
Engine fires intermittently	4.1
Engine fires consistently	5.1, 6.1
Engine Runs Poorly:	
Hard starting	3.1, 4.1, 5.1, 8.1
Rough idle	4.1, 5.1, 8.1
Stalling	3.1, 4.1, 5.1, 8.1
Engine dies at high speeds	4.1, 5.1
Hesitation (on acceleration from standing stop)	5.1, 8.1
Poor pickup	4.1, 5.1, 8.1
Lack of power	3.1, 4.1, 5.1, 8.1
Backfire through the carburetor	4.1, 8.1, 9.1
Backfire through the exhaust	4.1, 8.1, 9.1
Blue exhaust gases	6.1, 7.1
Black exhaust gases	5.1
Running on (after the ignition is shut off)	3.1, 8.1
Susceptible to moisture	4.1
Engine misfires under load	4.1, 7.1, 8.4, 9.1
Engine misfires at speed	4.1, 8.4
Engine misfires at idle	3.1, 4.1, 5.1, 7.1, 8.4

Sample Section

Test and Procedure	Results and Indications	Proceed to
4.1—Check for spark: Hold each spark plug wire approximately ¼″ from ground with gloves or a heavy, dry rag. Crank the engine and observe the spark.	→ If no spark is evident:	→ 4.2
	→ If spark is good in some cases:	→ 4.3
	→ If spark is good in all cases:	→ 4.6

Specific Diagnosis

This section is arranged so that following each test, instructions are given to proceed to another, until a problem is diagnosed.

Section 1—Battery

Test and Procedure	Results and Indications	Proceed to
1.1—Inspect the battery visually for case condition (corrosion, cracks) and water level.	If case is cracked, replace battery:	**1.4**
	If the case is intact, remove corrosion with a solution of baking soda and water (**CAUTION:** *do not get the solution into the battery*), and fill with water:	**1.2**

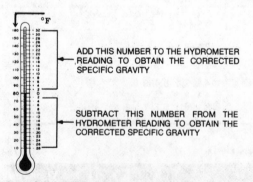

DIRT ON TOP OF BATTERY
PLUGGED VENT
CORROSION
LOOSE CABLE OR POSTS
CRACKS
LOW WATER LEVEL

Inspect the battery case

Test and Procedure	Results and Indications	Proceed to
1.2—Check the battery cable connections: Insert a screwdriver between the battery post and the cable clamp. Turn the headlights on high beam, and observe them as the screwdriver is gently twisted to ensure good metal to metal contact.	If the lights brighten, remove and clean the clamp and post; coat the post with petroleum jelly, install and tighten the clamp:	**1.4**
	If no improvement is noted:	**1.3**

TESTING BATTERY CABLE CONNECTIONS USING A SCREWDRIVER

Test and Procedure	Results and Indications	Proceed to
1.3—Test the state of charge of the battery using an individual cell tester or hydrometer.	If indicated, charge the battery. **NOTE:** *If no obvious reason exists for the low state of charge (i.e., battery age, prolonged storage), proceed to:*	**1.4**

°F

ADD THIS NUMBER TO THE HYDROMETER READING TO OBTAIN THE CORRECTED SPECIFIC GRAVITY

SUBTRACT THIS NUMBER FROM THE HYDROMETER READING TO OBTAIN THE CORRECTED SPECIFIC GRAVITY

Specific Gravity (@ 80° F.)

Minimum	Battery Charge
1.260	100% Charged
1.230	75% Charged
1.200	50% Charged
1.170	25% Charged
1.140	Very Little Power Left
1.110	Completely Discharged

The effects of temperature on battery specific gravity (left) and amount of battery charge in relation to specific gravity (right)

Test and Procedure	Results and Indications	Proceed to
1.4—Visually inspect battery cables for cracking, bad connection to ground, or bad connection to starter.	If necessary, tighten connections or replace the cables:	**2.1**

Section 2—Starting System
See Chapter 3 for service procedures

Test and Procedure	Results and Indications	Proceed to
Note: Tests in Group 2 are performed with coil high tension lead disconnected to prevent accidental starting.		
2.1—Test the starter motor and solenoid: Connect a jumper from the battery post of the solenoid (or relay) to the starter post of the solenoid (or relay).	If starter turns the engine normally:	2.2
	If the starter buzzes, or turns the engine very slowly:	2.4
	If no response, replace the solenoid (or relay).	3.1
	If the starter turns, but the engine doesn't, ensure that the flywheel ring gear is intact. If the gear is undamaged, replace the starter drive.	3.1
2.2—Determine whether ignition override switches are functioning properly (clutch start switch, neutral safety switch), by connecting a jumper across the switch(es), and turning the ignition switch to "start".	If starter operates, adjust or replace switch:	3.1
	If the starter doesn't operate:	2.3
2.3—Check the ignition switch "start" position: Connect a 12V test lamp or voltmeter between the starter post of the solenoid (or relay) and ground. Turn the ignition switch to the "start" position, and jiggle the key.	If the lamp doesn't light or the meter needle doesn't move when the switch is turned, check the ignition switch for loose connections, cracked insulation, or broken wires. Repair or replace as necessary:	3.1
	If the lamp flickers or needle moves when the key is jiggled, replace the ignition switch.	3.3

Checking the ignition switch "start" position

STARTER RELAY
(IF EQUIPPED)

Test and Procedure	Results and Indications	Proceed to
2.4—Remove and bench test the starter, according to specifications in the engine electrical section.	If the starter does not meet specifications, repair or replace as needed:	3.1
	If the starter is operating properly:	2.5
2.5—Determine whether the engine can turn freely: Remove the spark plugs, and check for water in the cylinders. Check for water on the dipstick, or oil in the radiator. Attempt to turn the engine using an 18" flex drive and socket on the crankshaft pulley nut or bolt.	If the engine will turn freely only with the spark plugs out, and hydrostatic lock (water in the cylinders) is ruled out, check valve timing:	9.2
	If engine will not turn freely, and it is known that the clutch and transmission are free, the engine must be disassembled for further evaluation:	Chapter 3

Section 3—Primary Electrical System

Test and Procedure	Results and Indications	Proceed to
3.1—Check the ignition switch "on" position: Connect a jumper wire between the distributor side of the coil and ground, and a 12V test lamp between the switch side of the coil and ground. Remove the high tension lead from the coil. Turn the ignition switch on and jiggle the key.	If the lamp lights:	3.2
	If the lamp flickers when the key is jiggled, replace the ignition switch:	3.3
	If the lamp doesn't light, check for loose or open connections. If none are found, remove the ignition switch and check for continuity. If the switch is faulty, replace it:	3.3

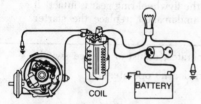

Checking the ignition switch "on" position

3.2—Check the ballast resistor or resistance wire for an open circuit, using an ohmmeter. See Chapter 3 for specific tests.	Replace the resistor or resistance wire if the resistance is zero. **NOTE:** *Some ignition systems have no ballast resistor.*	3.3

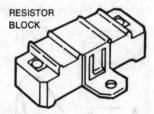

Two types of resistors

3.3—On point-type ignition systems, visually inspect the breaker points for burning, pitting or excessive wear. Gray coloring of the point contact surfaces is normal. Rotate the crankshaft until the contact heel rests on a high point of the distributor cam and adjust the point gap to specifications. On electronic ignition models, remove the distributor cap and visually inspect the armature. Ensure that the armature pin is in place, and that the armature is on tight and rotates when the engine is cranked. Make sure there are no cracks, chips or rounded edges on the armature.	If the breaker points are intact, clean the contact surfaces with fine emery cloth, and adjust the point gap to specifications. If the points are worn, replace them. On electronic systems, replace any parts which appear defective. If condition persists:	3.4

Test and Procedure	Results and Indications	Proceed to
3.4—On point-type ignition systems, connect a dwell-meter between the distributor primary lead and ground. Crank the engine and observe the point dwell angle. On electronic ignition systems, conduct a stator (magnetic pickup assembly) test. See Chapter 3.	On point-type systems, adjust the dwell angle if necessary. **NOTE:** *Increasing the point gap decreases the dwell angle and vice-versa.*	3.6
	If the dwell meter shows little or no reading;	3.5
	On electronic ignition systems, if the stator is bad, replace the stator. If the stator is good, proceed to the other tests in Chapter 3.	

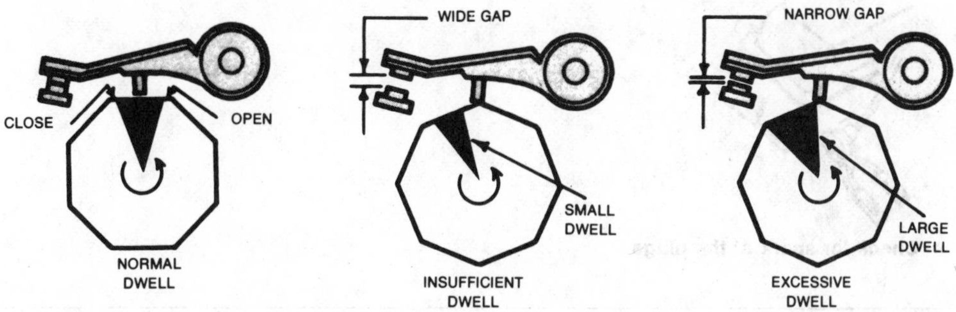

WIDE GAP   NARROW GAP

CLOSE   OPEN

NORMAL DWELL

SMALL DWELL   LARGE DWELL

INSUFFICIENT DWELL   EXCESSIVE DWELL

Dwell is a function of point gap

3.5—On the point-type ignition systems, check the condenser for short: connect an ohmeter across the condenser body and the pigtail lead.	If any reading other than infinite is noted, replace the condenser	3.6

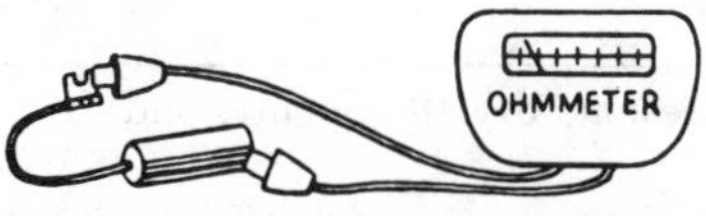

OHMMETER

Checking the condenser for short

3.6—Test the coil primary resistance: On point-type ignition systems, connect an ohmmeter across the coil primary terminals, and read the resistance on the low scale. Note whether an external ballast resistor or resistance wire is used. On electronic ignition systems, test the coil primary resistance as in Chapter 3.	Point-type ignition coils utilizing ballast resistors or resistance wires should have approximately 1.0 ohms resistance. Coils with internal resistors should have approximately 4.0 ohms resistance. If values far from the above are noted, replace the coil.	4.1

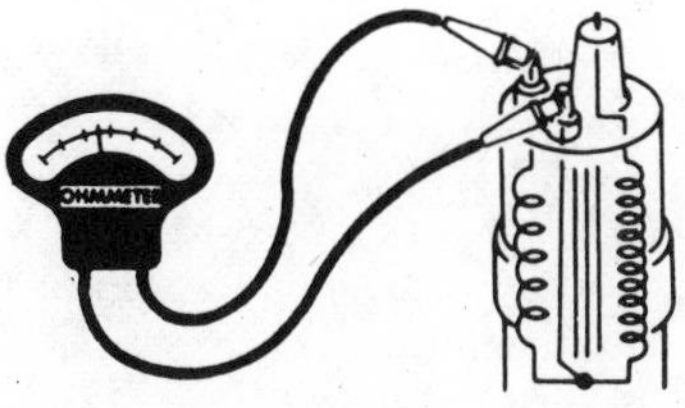

OHMMETER

Check the coil primary resistance

Section 4—Secondary Electrical System
See Chapters 2–3 for service procedures

Test and Procedure	Results and Indications	Proceed to
4.1—Check for spark: Hold each spark plug wire approximately ¼″ from ground with gloves or a heavy, dry rag. Crank the engine, and observe the spark.	If no spark is evident:	**4.2**
	If spark is good in some cylinders:	**4.3**
	If spark is good in all cylinders:	**4.6**

Check for spark at the plugs

4.2—Check for spark at the coil high tension lead: Remove the coil high tension lead from the distributor and position it approximately ¼″ from ground. Crank the engine and observe spark. **CAUTION:** *This test should not be performed on engines equipped with electronic ignition.*	If the spark is good and consistent:	**4.3**
	If the spark is good but intermittent, test the primary electrical system starting at 3.3:	**3.3**
	If the spark is weak or non-existent, replace the coil high tension lead, clean and tighten all connections and retest. If no improvement is noted:	**4.4**
4.3—Visually inspect the distributor cap and rotor for burned or corroded contacts, cracks, carbon tracks, or moisture. Also check the fit of the rotor on the distributor shaft (where applicable).	If moisture is present, dry thoroughly, and retest per 4.1:	**4.1**
	If burned or excessively corroded contacts, cracks, or carbon tracks are noted, replace the defective part(s) and retest per 4.1:	**4.1**
	If the rotor and cap appear intact, or are only slightly corroded, clean the contacts thoroughly (including the cap towers and spark plug wire ends) and retest per 4.1:	
	If the spark is good in all cases:	**4.6**
	If the spark is poor in all cases:	**4.5**

Inspect the distributor cap and rotor

Test and Procedure	Results and Indications	Proceed to

4.4—Check the coil secondary resistance: On point-type systems connect an ohmmeter across the distributor side of the coil and the coil tower. Read the resistance on the high scale of the ohmmeter. On electronic ignition systems, see Chapter 3 for specific tests.

The resistance of a satisfactory coil should be between 4,000 and 10,000 ohms. If resistance is considerably higher (i.e., 40,000 ohms) replace the coil and retest per 4.1. **NOTE:** *This does not apply to high performance coils.*

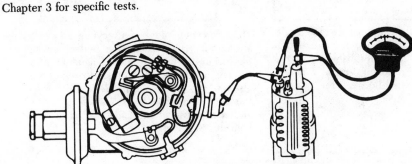

Testing the coil secondary resistance

4.5—Visually inspect the spark plug wires for cracking or brittleness. Ensure that no two wires are positioned so as to cause induction firing (adjacent and parallel). Remove each wire, one by one, and check resistance with an ohmmeter.

Replace any cracked or brittle wires. If any of the wires are defective, replace the entire set. Replace any wires with excessive resistance (over 8000 Ω per foot for suppression wire), and separate any wires that might cause induction firing.

4.6

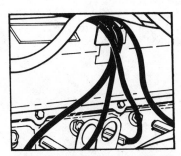

Misfiring can be the result of spark plug leads to adjacent, consecutively firing cylinders running parallel and too close together

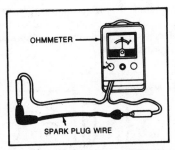

On point-type ignition systems, check the spark plug wires as shown. On electronic ignitions, do not remove the wire from the distributor cap terminal; instead, test through the cap

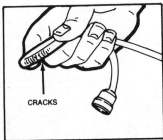

Spark plug wires can be checked visually by bending them in a loop over your finger. This will reveal any cracks, burned or broken insulation. Any wire with cracked insulation should be replaced

4.6—Remove the spark plugs, noting the cylinders from which they were removed, and evaluate according to the color photos in the middle of this book.

See following.

See following.

Test and Procedure	Results and Indications	Proceed to
4.7—Examine the location of all the plugs.	The following diagrams illustrate some of the conditions that the location of plugs will reveal.	4.8

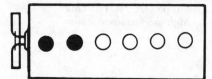

Two adjacent plugs are fouled in a 6-cylinder engine, 4-cylinder engine or either bank of a V-8. This is probably due to a blown head gasket between the two cylinders

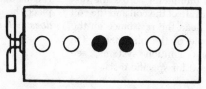

The two center plugs in a 6-cylinder engine are fouled. Raw fuel may be "boiled" out of the carburetor into the intake manifold after the engine is shut-off. Stop-start driving can also foul the center plugs, due to overly rich mixture. Proper float level, a new float needle and seat or use of an insulating spacer may help this problem

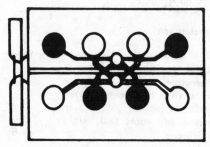

An unbalanced carburetor is indicated. Following the fuel flow on this particular design shows that the cylinders fed by the right-hand barrel are fouled from overly rich mixture, while the cylinders fed by the left-hand barrel are normal

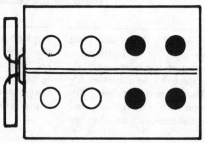

If the four rear plugs are overheated, a cooling system problem is suggested. A thorough cleaning of the cooling system may restore coolant circulation and cure the problem

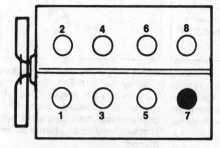

Finding one plug overheated may indicate an intake manifold leak near the affected cylinder. If the overheated plug is the second of two adjacent, consecutively firing plugs, it could be the result of ignition cross-firing. Separating the leads to these two plugs will eliminate cross-fire

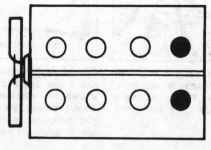

Occasionally, the two rear plugs in large, lightly used V-8's will become oil fouled. High oil consumption and smoky exhaust may also be noticed. It is probably due to plugged oil drain holes in the rear of the cylinder head, causing oil to be sucked in around the valve stems. This usually occurs in the rear cylinders first, because the engine slants that way

Test and Procedure	Results and Indications	Proceed to
4.8—Determine the static ignition timing. Using the crankshaft pulley timing marks as a guide, locate top dead center on the compression stroke of the number one cylinder.	The rotor should be pointing toward the No. 1 tower in the distributor cap, and, on electronic ignitions, the armature spoke for that cylinder should be lined up with the stator.	**4.8**
4.9—Check coil polarity: Connect a voltmeter negative lead to the coil high tension lead, and the positive lead to ground (**NOTE: Reverse the hook-up for positive ground systems**). Crank the engine momentarily.	If the voltmeter reads up-scale, the polarity is correct:	**5.1**
	If the voltmeter reads down-scale, reverse the coil polarity (switch the primary leads):	**5.1**

Checking coil polarity

Section 5—Fuel System

See Chapter 4 for service procedures

Test and Procedure	Results and Indications	Proceed to
5.1—Determine that the air filter is functioning efficiently: Hold paper elements up to a strong light, and attempt to see light through the filter.	Clean permanent air filters in solvent (or manufacturer's recommendation), and allow to dry. Replace paper elements through which light cannot be seen:	**5.2**
5.2—Determine whether a flooding condition exists: Flooding is identified by a strong gasoline odor, and excessive gasoline present in the throttle bore(s) of the carburetor.	If flooding is not evident:	**5.3**
	If flooding is evident, permit the gasoline to dry for a few moments and restart. If flooding doesn't recur:	**5.7**
	If flooding is persistent:	**5.5**

If the engine floods repeatedly, check the choke butterfly flap

Test and Procedure	Results and Indications	Proceed to
5.3—Check that fuel is reaching the carburetor: Detach the fuel line at the carburetor inlet. Hold the end of the line in a cup (not styrofoam), and crank the engine.	If fuel flows smoothly:	**5.7**
	If fuel doesn't flow (**NOTE: Make sure that there is fuel in the tank**), or flows erratically:	**5.4**

Check the fuel pump by disconnecting the output line (fuel pump-to-carburetor) at the carburetor and operating the starter briefly

Test and Procedure	Results and Indications	Proceed to
5.4—Test the fuel pump: Disconnect all fuel lines from the fuel pump. Hold a finger over the input fitting, crank the engine (with electric pump, turn the ignition or pump on); and feel for suction.	If suction is evident, blow out the fuel line to the tank with low pressure compressed air until bubbling is heard from the fuel filler neck. Also blow out the carburetor fuel line (both ends disconnected):	5.7
	If no suction is evident, replace or repair the fuel pump: NOTE: *Repeated oil fouling of the spark plugs, or a no-start condition, could be the result of a ruptured vacuum booster pump diaphragm, through which oil or gasoline is being drawn into the intake manifold (where applicable).*	5.7
5.5—Occasionally, small specks of dirt will clog the small jets and orifices in the carburetor. With the engine cold, hold a flat piece of wood or similar material over the carburetor, where possible, and crank the engine.	If the engine starts, but runs roughly the engine is probably not run enough. If the engine won't start:	5.9
5.6—Check the needle and seat: Tap the carburetor in the area of the needle and seat.	If flooding stops, a gasoline additive (e.g., Gumout) will often cure the problem:	5.7
	If flooding continues, check the fuel pump for excessive pressure at the carburetor (according to specifications). If the pressure is normal, the needle and seat must be removed and checked, and/or the float level adjusted:	5.7
5.7—Test the accelerator pump by looking into the throttle bores while operating the throttle.	If the accelerator pump appears to be operating normally:	5.8
	If the accelerator pump is not operating, the pump must be reconditioned. Where possible, service the pump with the carburetor(s) installed on the engine. If necessary, remove the carburetor. Prior to removal:	5.8

Check for gas at the carburetor by looking down the carburetor throat while someone moves the accelerator

Test and Procedure	Results and Indications	Proceed to
5.8—Determine whether the carburetor main fuel system is functioning: Spray a commercial starting fluid into the carburetor while attempting to start the engine.	If the engine starts, runs for a few seconds, and dies:	5.9
	If the engine doesn't start:	6.1

Test and Procedure	Results and Indications	Proceed to
5.9—Uncommon fuel system malfunctions: See below:	If the problem is solved:	6.1
	If the problem remains, remove and recondition the carburetor.	

Condition	Indication	Test	Prevailing Weather Conditions	Remedy
Vapor lock	Engine will not restart shortly after running.	Cool the components of the fuel system until the engine starts. Vapor lock can be cured faster by draping a wet cloth over a mechanical fuel pump.	Hot to very hot	Ensure that the exhaust manifold heat control valve is operating. Check with the vehicle manufacturer for the recommended solution to vapor lock on the model in question.
Carburetor icing	Engine will not idle, stalls at low speeds.	Visually inspect the throttle plate area of the throttle bores for frost.	High humidity, 32–40° F.	Ensure that the exhaust manifold heat control valve is operating, and that the intake manifold heat riser is not blocked.
Water in the fuel	Engine sputters and stalls; may not start.	Pump a small amount of fuel into a glass jar. Allow to stand, and inspect for droplets or a layer of water.	High humidity, extreme temperature changes.	For droplets, use one or two cans of commercial gas line anti-freeze. For a layer of water, the tank must be drained, and the fuel lines blown out with compressed air.

Section 6—Engine Compression
See Chapter 3 for service procedures

6.1—Test engine compression: Remove all spark plugs. Block the throttle wide open. Insert a compression gauge into a spark plug port, crank the engine to obtain the maximum reading, and record.	If compression is within limits on all cylinders:	7.1
	If gauge reading is extremely low on all cylinders:	6.2
	If gauge reading is low on one or two cylinders: (If gauge readings are identical and low on two or more adjacent cylinders, the head gasket must be replaced.)	6.2

Checking compression

6.2—Test engine compression (wet): Squirt approximately 30 cc. of engine oil into each cylinder, and retest per 6.1.	If the readings improve, worn or cracked rings or broken pistons are indicated:	See Chapter 3
	If the readings do not improve, burned or excessively carboned valves or a jumped timing chain are indicated:	7.1
	NOTE: *A jumped timing chain is often indicated by difficult cranking.*	

Section 7—Engine Vacuum
See Chapter 3 for service procedures

Test and Procedure	Results and Indications	Proceed to
7.1—Attach a vacuum gauge to the intake manifold beyond the throttle plate. Start the engine, and observe the action of the needle over the range of engine speeds.	See below.	**See below**

 INDICATION: normal engine in good condition

Proceed to: 8.1

Normal engine
Gauge reading: steady, from 17–22 in./Hg.

 INDICATION: sticking valves or ignition miss

Proceed to: 9.1, 8.3

Sticking valves
Gauge reading: intermittent fluctuation at idle

 INDICATION: late ignition or valve timing, low compression, stuck throttle valve, leaking carburetor or manifold gasket

Proceed to: 6.1

Incorrect valve timing
Gauge reading: low (10–15 in./Hg) but steady

 INDICATION: improper carburetor adjustment or minor intake leak.

Proceed to: 7.2

Carburetor requires adjustment
Gauge reading: drifting needle

 INDICATION: ignition miss, blown cylinder head gasket, leaking valve or weak valve spring

Proceed to: 8.3, 6.1

Blown head gasket
Gauge reading: needle fluctuates as engine speed increases

 INDICATION: burnt valve or faulty valve clearance. Needle will fall when defective valve operates

Proceed to: 9.1

Burnt or leaking valves
Gauge reading: steady needle, but drops regularly

 INDICATION: choked muffler, excessive back pressure in system

Proceed to: 10.1

Clogged exhaust system
Gauge reading: gradual drop in reading at idle

 INDICATION: worn valve guides

Proceed to: 9.1

Worn valve guides
Gauge reading: needle vibrates excessively at idle, but steadies as engine speed increases

---

White pointer = steady gauge hand   Black pointer = fluctuating gauge hand

Test and Procedure	Results and Indications	Proceed to
7.2—Attach a vacuum gauge per 7.1, and test for an intake manifold leak. Squirt a small amount of oil around the intake manifold gaskets, carburetor gaskets, plugs and fittings. Observe the action of the vacuum gauge.	If the reading improves, replace the indicated gasket, or seal the indicated fitting or plug:	**8.1**
	If the reading remains low:	**7.3**
7.3—Test all vacuum hoses and accessories for leaks as described in 7.2. Also check the carburetor body (dashpots, automatic choke mechanism, throttle shafts) for leaks in the same manner.	If the reading improves, service or replace the offending part(s):	**8.1**
	If the reading remains low:	**6.1**

Section 8—Secondary Electrical System
See Chapter 2 for service procedures

Test and Procedure	Results and Indications	Proceed to
8.1—Remove the distributor cap and check to make sure that the rotor turns when the engine is cranked. Visually inspect the distributor components.	Clean, tighten or replace any components which appear defective.	**8.2**
8.2—Connect a timing light (per manufacturer's recommendation) and check the dynamic ignition timing. Disconnect and plug the vacuum hose(s) to the distributor if specified, start the engine, and observe the timing marks at the specified engine speed.	If the timing is not correct, adjust to specifications by rotating the distributor in the engine: (Advance timing by rotating distributor opposite normal direction of rotor rotation, retard timing by rotating distributor in same direction as rotor rotation.)	**8.3**
8.3—Check the operation of the distributor advance mechanism(s): To test the mechanical advance, disconnect the vacuum lines from the distributor advance unit and observe the timing marks with a timing light as the engine speed is increased from idle. If the mark moves smoothly, without hesitation, it may be assumed that the mechanical advance is functioning properly. To test vacuum advance and/or retard systems, alternately crimp and release the vacuum line, and observe the timing mark for movement. If movement is noted, the system is operating.	If the systems are functioning:	**8.4**
	If the systems are not functioning, remove the distributor, and test on a distributor tester:	**8.4**
8.4—Locate an ignition miss: With the engine running, remove each spark plug wire, one at a time, until one is found that doesn't cause the engine to roughen and slow down.	When the missing cylinder is identified:	**4.1**

Section 9—Valve Train
See Chapter 3 for service procedures

Test and Procedure	Results and Indications	Proceed to
9.1—Evaluate the valve train: Remove the valve cover, and ensure that the valves are adjusted to specifications. A mechanic's stethoscope may be used to aid in the diagnosis of the valve train. By pushing the probe on or near push rods or rockers, valve noise often can be isolated. A timing light also may be used to diagnose valve problems. Connect the light according to manufacturer's recommendations, and start the engine. Vary the firing moment of the light by increasing the engine speed (and therefore the ignition advance), and moving the trigger from cylinder to cylinder. Observe the movement of each valve.	Sticking valves or erratic valve train motion can be observed with the timing light. The cylinder head must be disassembled for repairs.	See Chapter 3
9.2—Check the valve timing: Locate top dead center of the No. 1 piston, and install a degree wheel or tape on the crankshaft pulley or damper with zero corresponding to an index mark on the engine. Rotate the crankshaft in its direction of rotation, and observe the opening of the No. 1 cylinder intake valve. The opening should correspond with the correct mark on the degree wheel according to specifications.	If the timing is not correct, the timing cover must be removed for further investigation.	See Chapter 3

Section 10—Exhaust System

Test and Procedure	Results and Indications	Proceed to
10.1—Determine whether the exhaust manifold heat control valve is operating: Operate the valve by hand to determine whether it is free to move. If the valve is free, run the engine to operating temperature and observe the action of the valve, to ensure that it is opening.	If the valve sticks, spray it with a suitable solvent, open and close the valve to free it, and retest. If the valve functions properly:	10.2
	If the valve does not free, or does not operate, replace the valve:	10.2
10.2—Ensure that there are no exhaust restrictions: Visually inspect the exhaust system for kinks, dents, or crushing. Also note that gases are flowing freely from the tailpipe at all engine speeds, indicating no restriction in the muffler or resonator.	Replace any damaged portion of the system:	11.1

Section 11—Cooling System
See Chapter 3 for service procedures

Test and Procedure	Results and Indications	Proceed to
11.1—Visually inspect the fan belt for glazing, cracks, and fraying, and replace if necessary. Tighten the belt so that the longest span has approximately ½″ play at its midpoint under thumb pressure (see Chapter 1).	Replace or tighten the fan belt as necessary:	**11.2**

Checking belt tension

Test and Procedure	Results and Indications	Proceed to
11.2—Check the fluid level of the cooling system.	If full or slightly low, fill as necessary:	**11.5**
	If extremely low:	**11.3**
11.3—Visually inspect the external portions of the cooling system (radiator, radiator hoses, thermostat elbow, water pump seals, heater hoses, etc.) for leaks. If none are found, pressurize the cooling system to 14–15 psi.	If cooling system holds the pressure:	**11.5**
	If cooling system loses pressure rapidly, reinspect external parts of the system for leaks under pressure. If none are found, check dipstick for coolant in crankcase. If no coolant is present, but pressure loss continues:	**11.4**
	If coolant is evident in crankcase, remove cylinder head(s), and check gasket(s). If gaskets are intact, block and cylinder head(s) should be checked for cracks or holes.	
	If the gasket(s) is blown, replace, and purge the crankcase of coolant:	**12.6**
	NOTE: *Occasionally, due to atmospheric and driving conditions, condensation of water can occur in the crankcase. This causes the oil to appear milky white. To remedy, run the engine until hot, and change the oil and oil filter.*	
11.4—Check for combustion leaks into the cooling system: Pressurize the cooling system as above. Start the engine, and observe the pressure gauge. If the needle fluctuates, remove each spark plug wire, one at a time, noting which cylinder(s) reduce or eliminate the fluctuation.	Cylinders which reduce or eliminate the fluctuation, when the spark plug wire is removed, are leaking into the cooling system. Replace the head gasket on the affected cylinder bank(s).	

Pressurizing the cooling system

Test and Procedure	Results and Indications	Proceed to
11.5—Check the radiator pressure cap: Attach a radiator pressure tester to the radiator cap (wet the seal prior to installation). Quickly pump up the pressure, noting the point at which the cap releases.	If the cap releases within ± 1 psi of the specified rating, it is operating properly:	**11.6**
	If the cap releases at more than ± 1 psi of the specified rating, it should be replaced:	**11.6**

Checking radiator pressure cap

Test and Procedure	Results and Indications	Proceed to
11.6—Test the thermostat: Start the engine cold, remove the radiator cap, and insert a thermometer into the radiator. Allow the engine to idle. After a short while, there will be a sudden, rapid increase in coolant temperature. The temperature at which this sharp rise stops is the thermostat opening temperature.	If the thermostat opens at or about the specified temperature:	**11.7**
	If the temperature doesn't increase: (If the temperature increases slowly and gradually, replace the thermostat.)	**11.7**
11.7—Check the water pump: Remove the thermostat elbow and the thermostat, disconnect the coil high tension lead (to prevent starting), and crank the engine momentarily.	If coolant flows, replace the thermostat and retest per 11.6:	**11.6**
	If coolant doesn't flow, reverse flush the cooling system to alleviate any blockage that might exist. If system is not blocked, and coolant will not flow, replace the water pump.	

Section 12—Lubrication
See Chapter 3 for service procedures

Test and Procedure	Results and Indications	Proceed to
12.1—Check the oil pressure gauge or warning light: If the gauge shows low pressure, or the light is on for no obvious reason, remove the oil pressure sender. Install an accurate oil pressure gauge and run the engine momentarily.	If oil pressure builds normally, run engine for a few moments to determine that it is functioning normally, and replace the sender.	—
	If the pressure remains low:	**12.2**
	If the pressure surges:	**12.3**
	If the oil pressure is zero:	**12.3**
12.2—Visually inspect the oil: If the oil is watery or very thin, milky, or foamy, replace the oil and oil filter.	If the oil is normal:	**12.3**
	If after replacing oil the pressure remains low:	**12.3**
	If after replacing oil the pressure becomes normal:	—

Test and Procedure	Results and Indications	Proceed to
12.3—Inspect the oil pressure relief valve and spring, to ensure that it is not sticking or stuck. Remove and thoroughly clean the valve, spring, and the valve body.	If the oil pressure improves: If no improvement is noted:	— **12.4**
12.4—Check to ensure that the oil pump is not cavitating (sucking air instead of oil): See that the crankcase is neither over nor underfull, and that the pickup in the sump is in the proper position and free from sludge.	Fill or drain the crankcase to the proper capacity, and clean the pickup screen in solvent if necessary. If no improvement is noted:	**12.5**
12.5—Inspect the oil pump drive and the oil pump:	If the pump drive or the oil pump appear to be defective, service as necessary and retest per 12.1:	**12.1**
	If the pump drive and pump appear to be operating normally, the engine should be disassembled to determine where blockage exists:	**See Chapter 3**
12.6—Purge the engine of ethylene glycol coolant: Completely drain the crankcase and the oil filter. Obtain a commercial butyl cellosolve base solvent, designated for this purpose, and follow the instructions precisely. Following this, install a new oil filter and refill the crankcase with the proper weight oil. The next oil and filter change should follow shortly thereafter (1000 miles).		

TROUBLESHOOTING EMISSION CONTROL SYSTEMS

See Chapter 4 for procedures applicable to individual emission control systems used on specific combinations of engine/transmission/model.

TROUBLESHOOTING THE CARBURETOR

See Chapter 4 for service procedures

Carburetor problems cannot be effectively isolated unless all other engine systems (particularly ignition and emission) are functioning properly and the engine is properly tuned.

Condition	Possible Cause
Engine cranks, but does not start	1. Improper starting procedure 2. No fuel in tank 3. Clogged fuel line or filter 4. Defective fuel pump 5. Choke valve not closing properly 6. Engine flooded 7. Choke valve not unloading 8. Throttle linkage not making full travel 9. Stuck needle or float 10. Leaking float needle or seat 11. Improper float adjustment
Engine stalls	1. Improperly adjusted idle speed or mixture **Engine hot** 2. Improperly adjusted dashpot 3. Defective or improperly adjusted solenoid 4. Incorrect fuel level in fuel bowl 5. Fuel pump pressure too high 6. Leaking float needle seat 7. Secondary throttle valve stuck open 8. Air or fuel leaks 9. Idle air bleeds plugged or missing 10. Idle passages plugged **Engine Cold** 11. Incorrectly adjusted choke 12. Improperly adjusted fast idle speed 13. Air leaks 14. Plugged idle or idle air passages 15. Stuck choke valve or binding linkage 16. Stuck secondary throttle valves 17. Engine flooding—high fuel level 18. Leaking or misaligned float
Engine hesitates on acceleration	1. Clogged fuel filter 2. Leaking fuel pump diaphragm 3. Low fuel pump pressure 4. Secondary throttle valves stuck, bent or misadjusted 5. Sticking or binding air valve 6. Defective accelerator pump 7. Vacuum leaks 8. Clogged air filter 9. Incorrect choke adjustment (engine cold)
Engine feels sluggish or flat on acceleration	1. Improperly adjusted idle speed or mixture 2. Clogged fuel filter 3. Defective accelerator pump 4. Dirty, plugged or incorrect main metering jets 5. Bent or sticking main metering rods 6. Sticking throttle valves 7. Stuck heat riser 8. Binding or stuck air valve 9. Dirty, plugged or incorrect secondary jets 10. Bent or sticking secondary metering rods. 11. Throttle body or manifold heat passages plugged 12. Improperly adjusted choke or choke vacuum break.
Carburetor floods	1. Defective fuel pump. Pressure too high. 2. Stuck choke valve 3. Dirty, worn or damaged float or needle valve/seat 4. Incorrect float/fuel level 5. Leaking float bowl

Condition	Possible Cause
Engine idles roughly and stalls	1. Incorrect idle speed 2. Clogged fuel filter 3. Dirt in fuel system or carburetor 4. Loose carburetor screws or attaching bolts 5. Broken carburetor gaskets 6. Air leaks 7. Dirty carburetor 8. Worn idle mixture needles 9. Throttle valves stuck open 10. Incorrectly adjusted float or fuel level 11. Clogged air filter
Engine runs unevenly or surges	1. Defective fuel pump 2. Dirty or clogged fuel filter 3. Plugged, loose or incorrect main metering jets or rods 4. Air leaks 5. Bent or sticking main metering rods 6. Stuck power piston 7. Incorrect float adjustment 8. Incorrect idle speed or mixture 9. Dirty or plugged idle system passages 10. Hard, brittle or broken gaskets 11. Loose attaching or mounting screws 12. Stuck or misaligned secondary throttle valves
Poor fuel economy	1. Poor driving habits 2. Stuck choke valve 3. Binding choke linkage 4. Stuck heat riser 5. Incorrect idle mixture 6. Defective accelerator pump 7. Air leaks 8. Plugged, loose or incorrect main metering jets 9. Improperly adjusted float or fuel level 10. Bent, misaligned or fuel-clogged float 11. Leaking float needle seat 12. Fuel leak 13. Accelerator pump discharge ball not seating properly 14. Incorrect main jets
Engine lacks high speed performance or power	1. Incorrect throttle linkage adjustment 2. Stuck or binding power piston 3. Defective accelerator pump 4. Air leaks 5. Incorrect float setting or fuel level 6. Dirty, plugged, worn or incorrect main metering jets or rods 7. Binding or sticking air valve 8. Brittle or cracked gaskets 9. Bent, incorrect or improperly adjusted secondary metering rods 10. Clogged fuel filter 11. Clogged air filter 12. Defective fuel pump

TROUBLESHOOTING FUEL INJECTION PROBLEMS

Each fuel injection system has its own unique components and test procedures, for which it is impossible to generalize. Refer to Chapter 4 of this Repair & Tune-Up Guide for specific test and repair procedures, if the vehicle is equipped with fuel injection.

TROUBLESHOOTING ELECTRICAL PROBLEMS

See Chapter 5 for service procedures

For any electrical system to operate, it must make a complete circuit. This simply means that the power flow from the battery must make a complete circle. When an electrical component is operating, power flows from the battery to the component, passes through the component causing it to perform its function (lighting a light bulb), and then returns to the battery through the ground of the circuit. This ground is usually (but not always) the metal part of the car or truck on which the electrical component is mounted.

Perhaps the easiest way to visualize this is to think of connecting a light bulb with two wires attached to it to the battery. If one of the two wires attached to the light bulb were attached to the negative post of the battery and the other were attached to the positive post of the battery, you would have a complete circuit. Current from the battery would flow to the light bulb, causing it to light, and return to the negative post of the battery.

The normal automotive circuit differs from this simple example in two ways. First, instead of having a return wire from the bulb to the battery, the light bulb returns the current to the battery through the chassis of the vehicle. Since the negative battery cable is attached to the chassis and the chassis is made of electrically conductive metal, the chassis of the vehicle can serve as a ground wire to complete the circuit. Secondly, most automotive circuits contain switches to turn components on and off as required.

Every complete circuit from a power source must include a component which is using the power from the power source. If you were to disconnect the light bulb from the wires and touch the two wires together (don't do this) the power supply wire to the component would be grounded before the normal ground connection for the circuit.

Because grounding a wire from a power source makes a complete circuit—less the required component to use the power—this phenomenon is called a short circuit. Common causes are: broken insulation (exposing the metal wire to a metal part of the car or truck), or a shorted switch.

Some electrical components which require a large amount of current to operate also have a relay in their circuit. Since these circuits carry a large amount of current, the thickness of the wire in the circuit (gauge size) is also greater. If this large wire were connected from the component to the control switch on the instrument panel, and then back to the component, a voltage drop would occur in the circuit. To prevent this potential drop in voltage, an electromagnetic switch (relay) is used. The large wires in the circuit are connected from the battery to one side of the relay, and from the opposite side of the relay to the component. The relay is normally open, preventing current from passing through the circuit. An additional, smaller, wire is connected from the relay to the control switch for the circuit. When the control switch is turned on, it grounds the smaller wire from the relay and completes the circuit. This closes the relay and allows current to flow from the battery to the component. The horn, headlight, and starter circuits are three which use relays.

It is possible for larger surges of current to pass through the electrical system of your car or truck. If this surge of current were to reach an electrical component, it could burn it out. To prevent this, fuses, circuit breakers or fusible links are connected into the current supply wires of most of the major electrical systems. When an electrical current of excessive power passes through the component's fuse, the fuse blows out and breaks the circuit, saving the component from destruction.

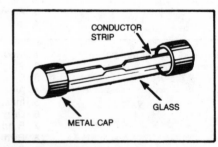

Typical automotive fuse

A circuit breaker is basically a self-repairing fuse. The circuit breaker opens the circuit the same way a fuse does. However, when either the short is removed from the circuit or the surge subsides, the circuit breaker resets itself and does not have to be replaced as a fuse does.

A fuse link is a wire that acts as a fuse. It is normally connected between the starter relay and the main wiring harness. This connection is usually under the hood. The fuse link (if installed) protects all the

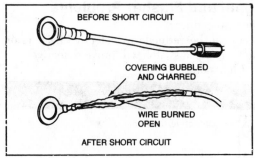

Most fusible links show a charred, melted insulation when they burn out

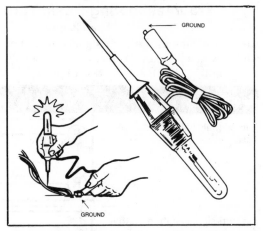

The test light will show the presence of current when touched to a hot wire and grounded at the other end

chassis electrical components, and is the probable cause of trouble when none of the electrical components function, unless the battery is disconnected or dead.

Electrical problems generally fall into one of three areas:

1. The component that is not functioning is not receiving current.

2. The component itself is not functioning.

3. The component is not properly grounded.

The electrical system can be checked with a test light and a jumper wire. A test light is a device that looks like a pointed screwdriver with a wire attached to it and has a light bulb in its handle. A jumper wire is a piece of insulated wire with an alligator clip attached to each end.

If a component is not working, you must follow a systematic plan to determine which of the three causes is the villain.

1. Turn on the switch that controls the inoperable component.

2. Disconnect the power supply wire from the component.

3. Attach the ground wire on the test light to a good metal ground.

4. Touch the probe end of the test light to the end of the power supply wire that was disconnected from the component. If the component is receiving current, the test light will go on.

NOTE: *Some components work only when the ignition switch is turned on.*

If the test light does not go on, then the problem is in the circuit between the battery and the component. This includes all the switches, fuses, and relays in the system. Follow the wire that runs back to the battery. The problem is an open circuit between the

battery and the component. If the fuse is blown and, when replaced, immediately blows again, there is a short circuit in the system which must be located and repaired. If there is a switch in the system, bypass it with a jumper wire. This is done by connecting one end of the jumper wire to the power supply wire into the switch and the other end of the jumper wire to the wire coming out of the switch. If the test light lights with the jumper wire installed, the switch or whatever was bypassed is defective.

NOTE: *Never substitute the jumper wire for the component, since it is required to use the power from the power source.*

5. If the bulb in the test light goes on, then the current is getting to the component that is not working. This eliminates the first of the three possible causes. Connect the power supply wire and connect a jumper wire from the component to a good metal ground. Do this with the switch which controls the component turned on, and also the ignition switch turned on if it is required for the component to work. If the component works with the jumper wire installed, then it has a bad ground. This is usually caused by the metal area on which the component mounts to the chassis being coated with some type of foreign matter.

6. If neither test located the source of the trouble, then the component itself is defective. Remember that for any electrical system to work, all connections must be clean and tight.

Troubleshooting Basic Turn Signal and Flasher Problems
See Chapter 5 for service procedures

Most problems in the turn signals or flasher system can be reduced to defective flashers or bulbs, which are easily replaced. Occasionally, the turn signal switch will prove defective.
F = Front   R = Rear   ● = Lights off   ○ = Lights on

Condition		Possible Cause
Turn signals light, but do not flash	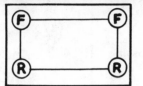	Defective flasher
No turn signals light on either side	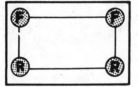	Blown fuse. Replace if defective. Defective flasher. Check by substitution. Open circuit, short circuit or poor ground.
Both turn signals on one side don't work	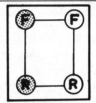	Bad bulbs. Bad ground in both (or either) housings.
One turn signal light on one side doesn't work	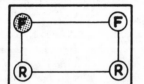	Defective bulb. Corrosion in socket. Clean contacts. Poor ground at socket.
Turn signal flashes too fast or too slowly	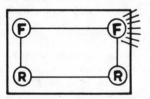	Check any bulb on the side flashing too fast. A heavy-duty bulb is probably installed in place of a regular bulb. Check the bulb flashing too slowly. A standard bulb was probably installed in place of a heavy-duty bulb. Loose connections or corrosion at the bulb socket.
Indicator lights don't work in either direction		Check if the turn signals are working. Check the dash indicator lights. Check the flasher by substitution.
One indicator light doesn't light		On systems with one dash indicator: See if the lights work on the same side. Often the filaments have been reversed in systems combining stoplights with taillights and turn signals. Check the flasher by substitution. On systems with two indicators: Check the bulbs on the same side. Check the indicator light bulb. Check the flasher by substitution.

Troubleshooting Lighting Problems
See Chapter 5 for service procedures

Condition	Possible Cause
One or more lights don't work, but others do	1. Defective bulb(s) 2. Blown fuse(s) 3. Dirty fuse clips or light sockets 4. Poor ground circuit
Lights burn out quickly	1. Incorrect voltage regulator setting or defective regulator 2. Poor battery/alternator connections
Lights go dim	1. Low/discharged battery 2. Alternator not charging 3. Corroded sockets or connections 4. Low voltage output
Lights flicker	1. Loose connection 2. Poor ground. (Run ground wire from light housing to frame) 3. Circuit breaker operating (short circuit)
Lights "flare"—Some flare is normal on acceleration—If excessive, see "Lights Burn Out Quickly"	High voltage setting
Lights glare—approaching drivers are blinded	1. Lights adjusted too high 2. Rear springs or shocks sagging 3. Rear tires soft

Troubleshooting Dash Gauge Problems
Most problems can be traced to a defective sending unit or faulty wiring. Occasionally, the gauge itself is at fault. See Chapter 5 for service procedures.

Condition	Possible Cause
COOLANT TEMPERATURE GAUGE	
Gauge reads erratically or not at all	1. Loose or dirty connections 2. Defective sending unit. 3. Defective gauge. To test a bi-metal gauge, remove the wire from the sending unit. Ground the wire for an instant. If the gauge registers, replace the sending unit. To test a magnetic gauge, disconnect the wire at the sending unit. With ignition ON gauge should register COLD. Ground the wire; gauge should register HOT.
AMMETER GAUGE—TURN HEADLIGHTS ON (DO NOT START ENGINE). NOTE REACTION	
Ammeter shows charge Ammeter shows discharge Ammeter does not move	1. Connections reversed on gauge 2. Ammeter is OK 3. Loose connections or faulty wiring 4. Defective gauge

Condition	Possible Cause

OIL PRESSURE GAUGE

| Gauge does not register or is inaccurate | 1. On mechanical gauge, Bourdon tube may be bent or kinked.
2. Low oil pressure. Remove sending unit. Idle the engine briefly. If no oil flows from sending unit hole, problem is in engine.
3. Defective gauge. Remove the wire from the sending unit and ground it for an instant with the ignition ON. A good gauge will go to the top of the scale.
4. Defective wiring. Check the wiring to the gauge. If it's OK and the gauge doesn't register when grounded, replace the gauge.
5. Defective sending unit. |

ALL GAUGES

| All gauges do not operate

All gauges read low or erratically
All gauges pegged | 1. Blown fuse
2. Defective instrument regulator
3. Defective or dirty instrument voltage regulator
4. Loss of ground between instrument voltage regulator and frame
5. Defective instrument regulator |

WARNING LIGHTS

| Light(s) do not come on when ignition is ON, but engine is not started

Light comes on with engine running | 1. Defective bulb
2. Defective wire
3. Defective sending unit. Disconnect the wire from the sending unit and ground it. Replace the sending unit if the light comes on with the ignition ON.
4. Problem in individual system
5. Defective sending unit |

Troubleshooting Clutch Problems

It is false economy to replace individual clutch components. The pressure plate, clutch plate and throwout bearing should be replaced as a set, and the flywheel face inspected, whenever the clutch is overhauled. See Chapter 6 for service procedures.

Condition	Possible Cause
Clutch chatter	1. Grease on driven plate (disc) facing 2. Binding clutch linkage or cable 3. Loose, damaged facings on driven plate (disc) 4. Engine mounts loose 5. Incorrect height adjustment of pressure plate release levers 6. Clutch housing or housing to transmission adapter misalignment 7. Loose driven plate hub
Clutch grabbing	1. Oil, grease on driven plate (disc) facing 2. Broken pressure plate 3. Warped or binding driven plate. Driven plate binding on clutch shaft
Clutch slips	1. Lack of lubrication in clutch linkage or cable (linkage or cable binds, causes incomplete engagement) 2. Incorrect pedal, or linkage adjustment 3. Broken pressure plate springs 4. Weak pressure plate springs 5. Grease on driven plate facings (disc)

Troubleshooting Clutch Problems (cont.)

Condition	Possible Cause
Incomplete clutch release	1. Incorrect pedal or linkage adjustment or linkage or cable binding 2. Incorrect height adjustment on pressure plate release levers 3. Loose, broken facings on driven plate (disc) 4. Bent, dished, warped driven plate caused by overheating
Grinding, whirring grating noise when pedal is depressed	1. Worn or defective throwout bearing 2. Starter drive teeth contacting flywheel ring gear teeth. Look for milled or polished teeth on ring gear.
Squeal, howl, trumpeting noise when pedal is being released (occurs during first inch to inch and one-half of pedal travel)	Pilot bushing worn or lack of lubricant. If bushing appears OK, polish bushing with emery cloth, soak lube wick in oil, lube bushing with oil, apply film of chassis grease to clutch shaft pilot hub, reassemble. NOTE: Bushing wear may be due to misalignment of clutch housing or housing to transmission adapter
Vibration or clutch pedal pulsation with clutch disengaged (pedal fully depressed)	1. Worn or defective engine transmission mounts 2. Flywheel run out. (Flywheel run out at face not to exceed 0.005″) 3. Damaged or defective clutch components

Troubleshooting Manual Transmission Problems
See Chapter 6 for service procedures

Condition	Possible Cause
Transmission jumps out of gear	1. Misalignment of transmission case or clutch housing. 2. Worn pilot bearing in crankshaft. 3. Bent transmission shaft. 4. Worn high speed sliding gear. 5. Worn teeth or end-play in clutch shaft. 6. Insufficient spring tension on shifter rail plunger. 7. Bent or loose shifter fork. 8. Gears not engaging completely. 9. Loose or worn bearings on clutch shaft or mainshaft. 10. Worn gear teeth. 11. Worn or damaged detent balls.
Transmission sticks in gear	1. Clutch not releasing fully. 2. Burred or battered teeth on clutch shaft, or sliding sleeve. 3. Burred or battered transmission mainshaft. 4. Frozen synchronizing clutch. 5. Stuck shifter rail plunger. 6. Gearshift lever twisting and binding shifter rail. 7. Battered teeth on high speed sliding gear or on sleeve. 8. Improper lubrication, or lack of lubrication. 9. Corroded transmission parts. 10. Defective mainshaft pilot bearing. 11. Locked gear bearings will give same effect as stuck in gear.
Transmission gears will not synchronize	1. Binding pilot bearing on mainshaft, will synchronize in high gear only. 2. Clutch not releasing fully. 3. Detent spring weak or broken. 4. Weak or broken springs under balls in sliding gear sleeve. 5. Binding bearing on clutch shaft, or binding countershaft. 6. Binding pilot bearing in crankshaft. 7. Badly worn gear teeth. 8. Improper lubrication. 9. Constant mesh gear not turning freely on transmission mainshaft. Will synchronize in that gear only.

Condition	Possible Cause
Gears spinning when shifting into gear from neutral	1. Clutch not releasing fully. 2. In some cases an extremely light lubricant in transmission will cause gears to continue to spin for a short time after clutch is released. 3. Binding pilot bearing in crankshaft.
Transmission noisy in all gears	1. Insufficient lubricant, or improper lubricant. 2. Worn countergear bearings. 3. Worn or damaged main drive gear or countergear. 4. Damaged main drive gear or mainshaft bearings. 5. Worn or damaged countergear anti-lash plate.
Transmission noisy in neutral only	1. Damaged main drive gear bearing. 2. Damaged or loose mainshaft pilot bearing. 3. Worn or damaged countergear anti-lash plate. 4. Worn countergear bearings.
Transmission noisy in one gear only	1. Damaged or worn constant mesh gears. 2. Worn or damaged countergear bearings. 3. Damaged or worn synchronizer.
Transmission noisy in reverse only	1. Worn or damaged reverse idler gear or idler bushing. 2. Worn or damaged mainshaft reverse gear. 3. Worn or damaged reverse countergear. 4. Damaged shift mechanism.

TROUBLESHOOTING AUTOMATIC TRANSMISSION PROBLEMS

Keeping alert to changes in the operating characteristics of the transmission (changing shift points, noises, etc.) can prevent small problems from becoming large ones. If the problem cannot be traced to loose bolts, fluid level, misadjusted linkage, clogged filters or similar problems, you should probably seek professional service.

Transmission Fluid Indications

The appearance and odor of the transmission fluid can give valuable clues to the overall condition of the transmission. Always note the appearance of the fluid when you check the fluid level or change the fluid. Rub a small amount of fluid between your fingers to feel for grit and smell the fluid on the dipstick.

If the fluid appears:	It indicates:
Clear and red colored	Normal operation
Discolored (extremely dark red or brownish) or smells burned	Band or clutch pack failure, usually caused by an overheated transmission. Hauling very heavy loads with insufficient power or failure to change the fluid often result in overheating. Do not confuse this appearance with newer fluids that have a darker red color and a strong odor (though not a burned odor).
Foamy or aerated (light in color and full of bubbles)	1. The level is too high (gear train is churning oil) 2. An internal air leak (air is mixing with the fluid). Have the transmission checked professionally.
Solid residue in the fluid	Defective bands, clutch pack or bearings. Bits of band material or metal abrasives are clinging to the dipstick. Have the transmission checked professionally.
Varnish coating on the dipstick	The transmission fluid is overheating

TROUBLESHOOTING DRIVE AXLE PROBLEMS

First, determine when the noise is most noticeable.

Drive Noise: Produced under vehicle acceleration.

Coast Noise: Produced while coasting with a closed throttle.

Float Noise: Occurs while maintaining constant speed (just enough to keep speed constant) on a level road.

External Noise Elimination

It is advisable to make a thorough road test to determine whether the noise originates in the rear axle or whether it originates from the tires, engine, transmission, wheel bearings or road surface. Noise originating from other places cannot be corrected by servicing the rear axle.

ROAD NOISE

Brick or rough surfaced concrete roads produce noises that seem to come from the rear axle. Road noise is usually identical in Drive or Coast and driving on a different type of road will tell whether the road is the problem.

TIRE NOISE

Tire noise can be mistaken as rear axle noise, even though the tires on the front are at fault. Snow tread and mud tread tires or tires worn unevenly will frequently cause vibrations which seem to originate elsewhere; *temporarily, and for test purposes only*, inflate the tires to 40–50 lbs. This will significantly alter the noise produced by the tires,

but will not alter noise from the rear axle. Noises from the rear axle will normally cease at speeds below 30 mph on coast, while tire noise will continue at lower tone as speed is decreased. The rear axle noise will usually change from drive conditions to coast conditions, while tire noise will not. Do not forget to lower the tire pressure to normal after the test is complete.

ENGINE/TRANSMISSION NOISE

Determine at what speed the noise is most pronounced, then stop in a quiet place. With the transmission in Neutral, run the engine through speeds corresponding to road speeds where the noise was noticed. Noises produced with the vehicle standing still are coming from the engine or transmission.

FRONT WHEEL BEARINGS

Front wheel bearing noises, sometimes confused with rear axle noises, will not change when comparing drive and coast conditions. While holding the speed steady, lightly apply the footbrake. This will often cause wheel bearing noise to lessen, as some of the weight is taken off the bearing. Front wheel bearings are easily checked by jacking up the wheels and spinning the wheels. Shaking the wheels will also determine if the wheel bearings are excessively loose.

REAR AXLE NOISES

Eliminating other possible sources can narrow the cause to the rear axle, which normally produces noise from worn gears or bearings. Gear noises tend to peak in a narrow speed range, while bearing noises will usually vary in pitch with engine speeds.

Noise Diagnosis

The Noise Is:	Most Probably Produced By:
1. Identical under Drive or Coast	Road surface, tires or front wheel bearings
2. Different depending on road surface	Road surface or tires
3. Lower as speed is lowered	Tires
4. Similar when standing or moving	Engine or transmission
5. A vibration	Unbalanced tires, rear wheel bearing, unbalanced driveshaft or worn U-joint
6. A knock or click about every two tire revolutions	Rear wheel bearing
7. Most pronounced on turns	Damaged differential gears
8. A steady low-pitched whirring or scraping, starting at low speeds	Damaged or worn pinion bearing
9. A chattering vibration on turns	Wrong differential lubricant or worn clutch plates (limited slip rear axle)
10. Noticed only in Drive, Coast or Float conditions	Worn ring gear and/or pinion gear

Troubleshooting Steering & Suspension Problems

Condition	Possible Cause
Hard steering (wheel is hard to turn)	1. Improper tire pressure 2. Loose or glazed pump drive belt 3. Low or incorrect fluid 4. Loose, bent or poorly lubricated front end parts 5. Improper front end alignment (excessive caster) 6. Bind in steering column or linkage 7. Kinked hydraulic hose 8. Air in hydraulic system 9. Low pump output or leaks in system 10. Obstruction in lines 11. Pump valves sticking or out of adjustment 12. Incorrect wheel alignment
Loose steering (too much play in steering wheel)	1. Loose wheel bearings 2. Faulty shocks 3. Worn linkage or suspension components 4. Loose steering gear mounting or linkage points 5. Steering mechanism worn or improperly adjusted 6. Valve spool improperly adjusted 7. Worn ball joints, tie-rod ends, etc.
Veers or wanders (pulls to one side with hands off steering wheel)	1. Improper tire pressure 2. Improper front end alignment 3. Dragging or improperly adjusted brakes 4. Bent frame 5. Improper rear end alignment 6. Faulty shocks or springs 7. Loose or bent front end components 8. Play in Pitman arm 9. Steering gear mountings loose 10. Loose wheel bearings 11. Binding Pitman arm 12. Spool valve sticking or improperly adjusted 13. Worn ball joints
Wheel oscillation or vibration transmitted through steering wheel	1. Low or uneven tire pressure 2. Loose wheel bearings 3. Improper front end alignment 4. Bent spindle 5. Worn, bent or broken front end components 6. Tires out of round or out of balance 7. Excessive lateral runout in disc brake rotor 8. Loose or bent shock absorber or strut
Noises (see also "Troubleshooting Drive Axle Problems")	1. Loose belts 2. Low fluid, air in system 3. Foreign matter in system 4. Improper lubrication 5. Interference or chafing in linkage 6. Steering gear mountings loose 7. Incorrect adjustment or wear in gear box 8. Faulty valves or wear in pump 9. Kinked hydraulic lines 10. Worn wheel bearings
Poor return of steering	1. Over-inflated tires 2. Improperly aligned front end (excessive caster) 3. Binding in steering column 4. No lubrication in front end 5. Steering gear adjusted too tight
Uneven tire wear (see "How To Read Tire Wear")	1. Incorrect tire pressure 2. Improperly aligned front end 3. Tires out-of-balance 4. Bent or worn suspension parts

HOW TO READ TIRE WEAR

The way your tires wear is a good indicator of other parts of the suspension. Abnormal wear patterns are often caused by the need for simple tire maintenance, or for front end alignment.

Excessive wear at the center of the tread indicates that the air pressure in the tire is consistently too high. The tire is riding on the center of the tread and wearing it prematurely. Occasionally, this wear pattern can result from outrageously wide tires on narrow rims. The cure for this is to replace either the tires or the wheels.

This type of wear usually results from consistent under-inflation. When a tire is under-inflated, there is too much contact with the road by the outer treads, which wear prematurely. When this type of wear occurs, and the tire pressure is known to be consistently correct, a bent or worn steering component or the need for wheel alignment could be indicated.

Feathering is a condition when the edge of each tread rib develops a slightly rounded edge on one side and a sharp edge on the other. By running your hand over the tire, you can usually feel the sharper edges before you'll be able to see them. The most common causes of feathering are incorrect toe-in setting or deteriorated bushings in the front suspension.

When an inner or outer rib wears faster than the rest of the tire, the need for wheel alignment is indicated. There is excessive camber in the front suspension, causing the wheel to lean too much putting excessive load on one side of the tire. Misalignment could also be due to sagging springs, worn ball joints, or worn control arm bushings. Be sure the vehicle is loaded the way it's normally driven when you have the wheels aligned.

Cups or scalloped dips appearing around the edge of the tread almost always indicate worn (sometimes bent) suspension parts. Adjustment of wheel alignment alone will seldom cure the problem. Any worn component that connects the wheel to the suspension can cause this type of wear. Occasionally, wheels that are out of balance will wear like this, but wheel imbalance usually shows up as bald spots between the outside edges and center of the tread.

Second-rib wear is usually found only in radial tires, and appears where the steel belts end in relation to the tread. It can be kept to a minimum by paying careful attention to tire pressure and frequently rotating the tires. This is often considered normal wear but excessive amounts indicate that the tires are too wide for the wheels.

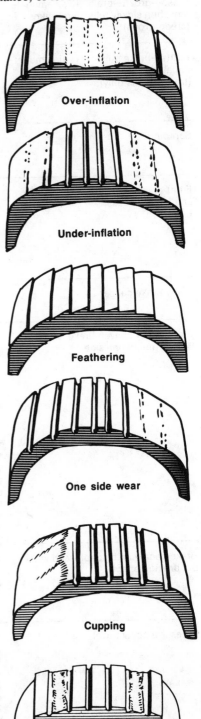

Over-inflation

Under-inflation

Feathering

One side wear

Cupping

Second-rib wear

Troubleshooting Disc Brake Problems

Condition	Possible Cause
Noise—groan—brake noise emanating when slowly releasing brakes (creep-groan)	Not detrimental to function of disc brakes—no corrective action required. (This noise may be eliminated by slightly increasing or decreasing brake pedal efforts.)
Rattle—brake noise or rattle emanating at low speeds on rough roads, (front wheels only).	1. Shoe anti-rattle spring missing or not properly positioned. 2. Excessive clearance between shoe and caliper. 3. Soft or broken caliper seals. 4. Deformed or misaligned disc. 5. Loose caliper.
Scraping	1. Mounting bolts too long. 2. Loose wheel bearings. 3. Bent, loose, or misaligned splash shield.
Front brakes heat up during driving and fail to release	1. Operator riding brake pedal. 2. Stop light switch improperly adjusted. 3. Sticking pedal linkage. 4. Frozen or seized piston. 5. Residual pressure valve in master cylinder. 6. Power brake malfunction. 7. Proportioning valve malfunction.
Leaky brake caliper	1. Damaged or worn caliper piston seal. 2. Scores or corrosion on surface of cylinder bore.
Grabbing or uneven brake action—Brakes pull to one side	1. Causes listed under "Brakes Pull". 2. Power brake malfunction. 3. Low fluid level in master cylinder. 4. Air in hydraulic system. 5. Brake fluid, oil or grease on linings. 6. Unmatched linings. 7. Distorted brake pads. 8. Frozen or seized pistons. 9. Incorrect tire pressure. 10. Front end out of alignment. 11. Broken rear spring. 12. Brake caliper pistons sticking. 13. Restricted hose or line. 14. Caliper not in proper alignment to braking disc. 15. Stuck or malfunctioning metering valve. 16. Soft or broken caliper seals. 17. Loose caliper.
Brake pedal can be depressed without braking effect	1. Air in hydraulic system or improper bleeding procedure. 2. Leak past primary cup in master cylinder. 3. Leak in system. 4. Rear brakes out of adjustment. 5. Bleeder screw open.
Excessive pedal travel	1. Air, leak, or insufficient fluid in system or caliper. 2. Warped or excessively tapered shoe and lining assembly. 3. Excessive disc runout. 4. Rear brake adjustment required. 5. Loose wheel bearing adjustment. 6. Damaged caliper piston seal. 7. Improper brake fluid (boil). 8. Power brake malfunction. 9. Weak or soft hoses.

Troubleshooting Disc Brake Problems (cont.)

Condition	Possible Cause
Brake roughness or chatter (pedal pumping)	1. Excessive thickness variation of braking disc. 2. Excessive lateral runout of braking disc. 3. Rear brake drums out-of-round. 4. Excessive front bearing clearance.
Excessive pedal effort	1. Brake fluid, oil or grease on linings. 2. Incorrect lining. 3. Frozen or seized pistons. 4. Power brake malfunction. 5. Kinked or collapsed hose or line. 6. Stuck metering valve. 7. Scored caliper or master cylinder bore. 8. Seized caliper pistons.
Brake pedal fades (pedal travel increases with foot on brake)	1. Rough master cylinder or caliper bore. 2. Loose or broken hydraulic lines/connections. 3. Air in hydraulic system. 4. Fluid level low. 5. Weak or soft hoses. 6. Inferior quality brake shoes or fluid. 7. Worn master cylinder piston cups or seals.

Troubleshooting Drum Brakes

Condition	Possible Cause
Pedal goes to floor	1. Fluid low in reservoir. 2. Air in hydraulic system. 3. Improperly adjusted brake. 4. Leaking wheel cylinders. 5. Loose or broken brake lines. 6. Leaking or worn master cylinder. 7. Excessively worn brake lining.
Spongy brake pedal	1. Air in hydraulic system. 2. Improper brake fluid (low boiling point). 3. Excessively worn or cracked brake drums. 4. Broken pedal pivot bushing.
Brakes pulling	1. Contaminated lining. 2. Front end out of alignment. 3. Incorrect brake adjustment. 4. Unmatched brake lining. 5. Brake drums out of round. 6. Brake shoes distorted. 7. Restricted brake hose or line. 8. Broken rear spring. 9. Worn brake linings. 10. Uneven lining wear. 11. Glazed brake lining. 12. Excessive brake lining dust. 13. Heat spotted brake drums. 14. Weak brake return springs. 15. Faulty automatic adjusters. 16. Low or incorrect tire pressure.

Condition	Possible Cause
Squealing brakes	1. Glazed brake lining. 2. Saturated brake lining. 3. Weak or broken brake shoe retaining spring. 4. Broken or weak brake shoe return spring. 5. Incorrect brake lining. 6. Distorted brake shoes. 7. Bent support plate. 8. Dust in brakes or scored brake drums. 9. Linings worn below limit. 10. Uneven brake lining wear. 11. Heat spotted brake drums.
Chirping brakes	1. Out of round drum or eccentric axle flange pilot.
Dragging brakes	1. Incorrect wheel or parking brake adjustment. 2. Parking brakes engaged or improperly adjusted. 3. Weak or broken brake shoe return spring. 4. Brake pedal binding. 5. Master cylinder cup sticking. 6. Obstructed master cylinder relief port. 7. Saturated brake lining. 8. Bent or out of round brake drum. 9. Contaminated or improper brake fluid. 10. Sticking wheel cylinder pistons. 11. Driver riding brake pedal. 12. Defective proportioning valve. 13. Insufficient brake shoe lubricant.
Hard pedal	1. Brake booster inoperative. 2. Incorrect brake lining. 3. Restricted brake line or hose. 4. Frozen brake pedal linkage. 5. Stuck wheel cylinder. 6. Binding pedal linkage. 7. Faulty proportioning valve.
Wheel locks	1. Contaminated brake lining. 2. Loose or torn brake lining. 3. Wheel cylinder cups sticking. 4. Incorrect wheel bearing adjustment. 5. Faulty proportioning valve.
Brakes fade (high speed)	1. Incorrect lining. 2. Overheated brake drums. 3. Incorrect brake fluid (low boiling temperature). 4. Saturated brake lining. 5. Leak in hydraulic system. 6. Faulty automatic adjusters.
Pedal pulsates	1. Bent or out of round brake drum.
Brake chatter and shoe knock	1. Out of round brake drum. 2. Loose support plate. 3. Bent support plate. 4. Distorted brake shoes. 5. Machine grooves in contact face of brake drum (Shoe Knock). 6. Contaminated brake lining. 7. Missing or loose components. 8. Incorrect lining material. 9. Out-of-round brake drums. 10. Heat spotted or scored brake drums. 11. Out-of-balance wheels.

Troubleshooting Drum Brakes (cont.)

Condition	Possible Cause
Brakes do not self adjust	1. Adjuster screw frozen in thread. 2. Adjuster screw corroded at thrust washer. 3. Adjuster lever does not engage star wheel. 4. Adjuster installed on wrong wheel.
Brake light glows	1. Leak in the hydraulic system. 2. Air in the system. 3. Improperly adjusted master cylinder pushrod. 4. Uneven lining wear. 5. Failure to center combination valve or proportioning valve.

Appendix

General Conversion Table

Multiply by	To convert	To	
2.54	Inches	Centimeters	.3937
30.48	Feet	Centimeters	.0328
.914	Yards	Meters	1.094
1.609	Miles	Kilometers	.621
6.45	Square inches	Square cm.	.155
.836	Square yards	Square meters	1.196
16.39	Cubic inches	Cubic cm.	.061
28.3	Cubic feet	Liters	.0353
.4536	Pounds	Kilograms	2.2045
3.785	Gallons	Liters	.264
.068	Lbs./sq. in. (psi)	Atmospheres	14.7
.138	Foot pounds	Kg. m.	7.23
1.014	H.P. (DIN)	H.P. (SAE)	.9861
—	To obtain	From	Multiply by

Note: 1 cm. equals 10 mm.; 1 mm. equals .0394".

Conversion—Common Fractions to Decimals and Millimeters

Common Fractions	Decimal Fractions	Millimeters (approx.)	Common Fractions	Decimal Fractions	Millimeters (approx.)	Common Fractions	Decimal Fractions	Millimeters (approx.)
1/128	.008	0.20	11/32	.344	8.73	43/64	.672	17.07
1/64	.016	0.40	23/64	.359	9.13	11/16	.688	17.46
1/32	.031	0.79	3/8	.375	9.53	45/64	.703	17.86
3/64	.047	1.19	25/64	.391	9.92	23/32	.719	18.26
1/16	.063	1.59	13/32	.406	10.32	47/64	.734	18.65
5/64	.078	1.98	27/64	.422	10.72	3/4	.750	19.05
3/32	.094	2.38	7/16	.438	11.11	49/64	.766	19.45
7/64	.109	2.78	29/64	.453	11.51	25/32	.781	19.84
1/8	.125	3.18	15/32	.469	11.91	51/64	.797	20.24
9/64	.141	3.57	31/64	.484	12.30	13/16	.813	20.64
5/32	.156	3.97	1/2	.500	12.70	53/64	.828	21.03
11/64	.172	4.37	33/64	.516	13.10	27/32	.844	21.43
3/16	.188	4.76	17/32	.531	13.49	55/64	.859	21.83
13/64	.203	5.16	35/64	.547	13.89	7/8	.875	22.23
7/32	.219	5.56	9/16	.563	14.29	57/64	.891	22.62
15/64	.234	5.95	37/64	.578	14.68	29/32	.906	23.02
1/4	.250	6.35	19/32	.594	15.08	59/64	.922	23.42
17/64	.266	6.75	39/64	.609	15.48	15/16	.938	23.81
9/32	.281	7.14	5/8	.625	15.88	61/64	.953	24.21
19/64	.297	7.54	41/64	.641	16.27	31/32	.969	24.61
5/16	.313	7.94	21/32	.656	16.67	63/64	.984	25.00
21/64	.328	8.33						

Conversion—Millimeters to Decimal Inches

mm	inches	mm	inches	mm	inches	mm	inches	mm	inches
1	.039 370	31	1.220 470	61	2.401 570	91	3.582 670	210	8.267 700
2	.078 740	32	1.259 840	62	2.440 940	92	3.622 040	220	8.661 400
3	.118 110	33	1.299 210	63	2.480 310	93	3.661 410	230	9.055 100
4	.157 480	34	1.338 580	64	2.519 680	94	3.700 780	240	9.448 800
5	.196 850	35	1.377 949	65	2.559 050	95	3.740 150	250	9.842 500
6	.236 220	36	1.417 319	66	2.598 420	96	3.779 520	260	10.236 200
7	.275 590	37	1.456 689	67	2.637 790	97	3.818 890	270	10.629 900
8	.314 960	38	1.496 050	68	2.677 160	98	3.858 260	280	11.032 600
9	.354 330	39	1.535 430	69	2.716 530	99	3.897 630	290	11.417 300
10	.393 700	40	1.574 800	70	2.755 900	100	3.937 000	300	11.811 000
11	.433 070	41	1.614 170	71	2.795 270	105	4.133 848	310	12.204 700
12	.472 440	42	1.653 540	72	2.834 640	110	4.330 700	320	12.598 400
13	.511 810	43	1.692 910	73	2.874 010	115	4.527 550	330	12.992 100
14	.551 180	44	1.732 280	74	2.913 380	120	4.724 400	340	13.385 800
15	.590 550	45	1.771 650	75	2.952 750	125	4.921 250	350	13.779 500
16	.629 920	46	1.811 020	76	2.992 120	130	5.118 100	360	14.173 200
17	.669 290	47	1.850 390	77	3.031 490	135	5.314 950	370	14.566 900
18	.708 660	48	1.889 760	78	3.070 860	140	5.511 800	380	14.960 600
19	.748 030	49	1.929 130	79	3.110 230	145	5.708 650	390	15.354 300
20	.787 400	50	1.968 500	80	3.149 600	150	5.905 500	400	15.748 000
21	.826 770	51	2.007 870	81	3.188 970	155	6.102 350	500	19.685 000
22	.866 140	52	2.047 240	82	3.228 340	160	6.299 200	600	23.622 000
23	.905 510	53	2.086 610	83	3.267 710	165	6.496 050	700	27.559 000
24	.944 880	54	2.125 980	84	3.307 080	170	6.692 900	800	31.496 000
25	.984 250	55	2.165 350	85	3.346 450	175	6.889 750	900	35.433 000
26	1.023 620	56	2.204 720	86	3.385 820	180	7.086 600	1000	39.370 000
27	1.062 990	57	2.244 090	87	3.425 190	185	7.283 450	2000	78.740 000
28	1.102 360	58	2.283 460	88	3.464 560	190	7.480 300	3000	118.110 000
29	1.141 730	59	2.322 830	89	3.503 903	195	7.677 150	4000	157.480 000
30	1.181 100	60	2.362 200	90	3.543 300	200	7.874 000	5000	196.850 000

To change decimal millimeters to decimal inches, position the decimal point where desired on either side of the millimeter measurement shown and reset the inches decimal by the same number of digits in the same direction. For example, to convert 0.001 mm to decimal inches, reset the decimal behind the 1 mm (shown on the chart) to 0.001; change the decimal inch equivalent (0.039″ shown) to 0.000039″.

Tap Drill Sizes

Screw & Tap Size	National Fine or S.A.E. Threads Per Inch	Use Drill Number
No. 5	44	.37
No. 6	40	.33
No. 8	36	.29
No. 10	32	.21
No. 12	28	.15
1/4	28	3
5/16	24	1
3/8	24	.Q
7/16	20	.W
1/2	20	29/64
9/16	18	33/64
5/8	18	37/64
3/4	16	11/16
7/8	14	13/16
1 1/8	12	1 3/64
1 1/4	12	1 11/64
1 1/2	12	1 27/64

Tap Drill Sizes

Screw & Tap Size	National Coarse or U.S.S. Threads Per Inch	Use Drill Number
No. 5	40	.39
No. 6	32	.36
No. 8	32	.29
No. 10	24	.25
No. 12	24	.17
1/4	20	8
5/16	18	.F
3/8	16	5/16
7/16	14	.U
1/2	13	27/64
9/16	12	31/64
5/8	11	17/32
3/4	10	21/32
7/8	9	49/64
1	8	7/8
1 1/8	7	63/64
1 1/4	7	1 7/64
1 1/2	6	1 11/32

Decimal Equivalent Size of the Number Drills

Drill No.	Decimal Equivalent	Drill No.	Decimal Equivalent	Drill No.	Decimal Equivalent
80	.0135	53	.0595	26	.1470
79	.0145	52	.0635	25	.1495
78	.0160	51	.0670	24	.1520
77	.0180	50	.0700	23	.1540
76	.0200	49	.0730	22	.1570
75	.0210	48	.0760	21	.1590
74	.0225	47	.0785	20	.1610
73	.0240	46	.0810	19	.1660
72	.0250	45	.0820	18	.1695
71	.0260	44	.0860	17	.1730
70	.0280	43	.0890	16	.1770
69	.0292	42	.0935	15	.1800
68	.0310	41	.0960	14	.1820
67	.0320	40	.0980	13	.1850
66	.0330	39	.0995	12	.1890
65	.0350	38	.1015	11	.1910
64	.0360	37	.1040	10	.1935
63	.0370	36	.1065	9	.1960
62	.0380	35	.1100	8	.1990
61	.0390	34	.1110	7	.2010
60	.0400	33	.1130	6	.2040
59	.0410	32	.1160	5	.2055
58	.0420	31	.1200	4	.2090
57	.0430	30	.1285	3	.2130
56	.0465	29	.1360	2	.2210
55	.0520	28	.1405	1	.2280
54	.0550	27	.1440		

Decimal Equivalent Size of the Letter Drills

Letter Drill	Decimal Equivalent	Letter Drill	Decimal Equivalent	Letter Drill	Decimal Equivalent
A	.234	J	.277	S	.348
B	.238	K	.281	T	.358
C	.242	L	.290	U	.368
D	.246	M	.295	V	.377
E	.250	N	.302	W	.386
F	.257	O	.316	X	.397
G	.261	P	.323	Y	.404
H	.266	Q	.332	Z	.413
I	.272	R	.339		

Anti-Freeze Chart

Temperatures Shown in Degrees Fahrenheit +32 is Freezing

Cooling System Capacity Quarts	Quarts of ETHYLENE GLYCOL Needed for Protection to Temperatures Shown Below													
	1	*2*	*3*	*4*	*5*	*6*	*7*	*8*	*9*	*10*	*11*	*12*	*13*	*14*
10	+24°	+16°	+ 4°	−12°	−34°	−62°								
11	+25	+18	+ 8	− 6	−23	−47								
12	+26	+19	+10	0	−15	−34	−57°							
13	+27	+21	+13	+ 3	− 9	−25	−45							
14			+15	+ 6	− 5	−18	−34							
15			+16	+ 8	0	−12	−26							
16			+17	+10	+ 2	− 8	−19	−34	−52°					
17			+18	+12	+ 5	− 4	−14	−27	−42					
18			+19	+14	+ 7	0	−10	−21	−34	−50°				
19			+20	+15	+ 9	+ 2	− 7	−16	−28	−42				
20				+16	+10	+ 4	− 3	−12	−22	−34	−48°			
21				+17	+12	+ 6	0	− 9	−17	−28	−41			
22				+18	+13	+ 8	+ 2	− 6	−14	−23	−34	−47°		
23				+19	+14	+ 9	+ 4	− 3	−10	−19	−29	−40		
24				+19	+15	+10	+ 5	0	− 8	−15	−23	−34	−46°	
25				+20	+16	+12	+ 7	+ 1	− 5	−12	−20	−29	−40	−50°
26					+17	+13	+ 8	+ 3	− 3	− 9	−16	−25	−34	−44
27					+18	+14	+ 9	+ 5	− 1	− 7	−13	−21	−29	−39
28					+18	+15	+10	+ 6	+ 1	− 5	−11	−18	−25	−34
29					+19	+16	+12	+ 7	+ 2	− 3	− 8	−15	−22	−29
30					+20	+17	+13	+ 8	+ 4	− 1	− 6	−12	−18	−25

For capacities over 30 quarts divide true capacity by 3. Find quarts Anti-Freeze for the 1/3 and multiply by 3 for quarts to add.

For capacities under 10 quarts multiply true capacity by 3. Find quarts Anti-Freeze for the tripled volume and divide by 3 for quarts to add.

To Increase the Freezing Protection of Anti-Freeze Solutions Already Installed

Cooling System Capacity Quarts	From +20° F. to					From +10° F. to					From 0° F. to			
	0°	−10°	−20°	−30°	−40°	0°	−10°	−20°	−30°	−40°	−10°	−20°	−30°	−40°
10	1¾	2¼	3	3½	3¾	¾	1½	2¼	2¾	3¼	¾	1½	2	2½
12	2	2¾	3½	4	4½	1	1¾	2½	3¼	3¾	1	1¾	2½	3¼
14	2¼	3¼	4	4¾	5½	1¼	2	3	3¾	4½	1	2	3	3½
16	2½	3½	4½	5¼	6	1¼	2½	3½	4¼	5¼	1¼	2¼	3¼	4
18	3	4	5	6	7	1½	2¾	4	5	5¾	1½	2½	3¾	4¾
20	3¼	4½	5¾	6¾	7½	1¾	3	4¼	5½	6½	1½	2¾	4¼	5¼
22	3½	5	6¼	7¼	8¼	1¾	3¼	4¾	6	7¼	1¾	3¼	4½	5½
24	4	5½	7	8	9	2	3½	5	6½	7½	1¾	3½	5	6
26	4¼	6	7½	8¾	10	2	4	5½	7	8¼	2	3¾	5½	6¾
28	4½	6¼	8	9½	10½	2¼	4¼	6	7½	9	2	4	5¾	7¼
30	5	6¾	8½	10	11½	2½	4½	6½	8	9½	2¼	4¼	6¼	7¾

Test radiator solution with proper hydrometer. Determine from the table the number of quarts of solution to be drawn off from a full cooling system and replace with undiluted anti-freeze, to give the desired increased protection. For example, to increase protection of a 22-quart cooling system containing Ethylene Glycol (permanent type) anti-freeze, from +20° F. to −20° F. will require the replacement of 6¼ quarts of solution with undiluted anti-freeze.

Index

A

Air cleaner, 3
Air conditioning
  Sight glass check, 5
Alternator, 25
Antifreeze, 6, 178
Axle
  Fluid recommendations, 6
  Lubricant level, 6
Axle ratio, 3
Axle shaft
  Bearings and seals, 87

B

Ball joints, 97
Battery
  Jump starting, 14
  Maintenance, 7
  Removal, 28
Belt tension adjustment, 4
Body, 116
Body work, 116
Brakes
  Bleeding, 106
  Caliper, 106
  Fluid level, 6
  Fluid recommendations, 6
  Front brakes, 106
  Master cylinder, 104
  Parking brake, 113
  Rear brakes, 110
Bulbs

C

Camber, 98
Camshaft and bearings, 38
Capacities, 7
Carburetor
  Adjustment, 72
  Overhaul, 75
  Replacement, 70
Caster, 98
Charging system, 22, 25
Chassis lubrication, 12
Choke, 73
Clutch
  Adjustment, 88
  Replacement, 88
Compression, 144
Connecting rod and bearings, 38
Control arm
  Lower, 97
Cooling system, 41
Crankcase ventilation (PCV), 3, 66
Cylinder head
  Removal and installation, 35
  Torque sequence, 35

D

Dents and scratches, 120
Distributor
  Removal and installation, 24
Door panels, 117
Drive axle, 91
Driveshaft, 90

E

Electrical
  Chassis, 21
  Engine, 21
Electronic ignition, 23
Emission controls, 66
Engine
  Camshaft, 38
  Cylinder head, 35
  Cylinder head torque sequence, 35
  Design, 29
  Exhaust manifold, 37
  Front cover, 37
  Identification, 3
  Intake manifold, 36
  Oil recommendations, 5
  Pistons and rings, 38
  Rebuilding, 44
  Removal and installation, 32
  Rocker arm (or shaft), 36
  Specifications, 30
  Timing chain (or gears), 37
  Tune-up, 15
Exhaust manifold, 37

F

Fan belt adjustment, 4
Firing order, 25
Fluid level checks
  Battery, 7
  Coolant, 6
  Engine oil, 5
  Master cylinder, 6
  Steering gear, 7
  Transaxle, 6
Fluid recommendations, 9
Front suspension
  Ball joints, 97
  Lower control arm, 97
  Springs and MacPherson struts, 95
  Wheel alignment, 98
Fuel filter, 8
Fuel pump, 70
Fuel system, 70
Fuel tank, 75
Fuses and flashers, 82
Fusible links, 82

G

Generator (see Alternator)

H

Hand brake, 113
Headlights, 82
Heater, 77

I

Identification
    Engine, 3
    Transmission, 3
    Vehicle, 2
Idle speed and mixture, 19, 20
Ignition switch, 101
Instrument cluster, 81
Intake manifold, 36

J

Jacking points, 14
Jump starting, 14

L

Light bulb specifications, 83
Lower control arm, 97
Lubrication
    Chassis, 12
    Engine, 9
    Transaxle, 6

M

Maintenance intervals, 9
Manifolds
    Intake, 36
    Exhaust, 37
Master cylinder, 6, 104
Model identification, 2

O

Oil and fuel recommendations, 9
Oil change, 11
Oil filter (engine), 11
Oil pan, 40
Oil pump, 41
Oil level (engine), 5

P

Parking brake, 113
Pistons and rings
    Installation, 38
    Positioning, 38
PCV valve, 3, 66

R

Radiator, 41
Radio, 79
Rear suspension, 98
Regulator, 26

Rear main oil seal, 40
Rings, 38
Rocker arm (or shaft), 36
Routine maintenance, 3
Rust spots, 118, 124

S

Scratches and dents, 120
Serial number location, 2
Shock absorbers
    Front, 95
    Rear, 99
Spark plugs, 15
Specifications
    Alternator and regulator, 25
    Battery and starter, 28
    Brakes, 114
    Capacities, 7
    Carburetor, 75
    Crankshaft and connecting rod, 31
    Fuses, 84
    General engine, 30
    Light bulb, 83
    Piston and ring, 30
    Torque, 30
    Tune-up, 15
    Valve, 31
    Wheel alignment, 98
Speedometer cable, 82
Springs
    Front, 95
    Rear, 98
Starter, 26
Steering
    Linkage, 101
    Wheel, 100
Stripped threads, 45

T

Thermostat, 42
Tie-rod ends, 101
Timing (ignition), 18
Tires, 7
Tools, 2
Towing, 13
Transaxle, 93
Troubleshooting, 133
Tune-up
    Procedures, 15
    Specifications, 15

U

U-joints, 90

V

Valves
    Adjustment, 19
    Service, 19

Specifications, 19, 31
Vehicle identification, 2

W

Water pump, 42
Wheel alignment, 98

Wheel bearings, 108
Wheel cylinders, 112
Windshield wipers
  Arm, 79
  Blade, 79
  Linkage, 80
  Motor, 80

Chilton's Repair & Tune-Up Guides

The complete line covers domestic cars, imports, trucks, vans, RV's and 4-wheel drive vehicles.

CODE	TITLE	CODE	TITLE
#7199	AMC 75–82; all models	#7171	Ford Vans 61–82
#7165	Alliance 1983	#7165	Fuego 82–83
#7323	Aries 81–82	#6935	GM Sub-compact 71–81 inc. Vega, Monza, Astre, Sunbird, Starfire & Skyhawk
#7344	Arrow 78–83		
#7193	Aspen/Volaré 76–80	#7311	Granada 78–83
#5902	Audi 70–73	#7204	Honda 73–82
#7028	Audi 4000/5000 77–81	#5912	International Scout 67–73
#6337	Audi Fox 73–75	#7136	Jeep CJ 1945–81
#5807	Barracuda 65–72	#6739	Jeep Wagoneer, Commando, Cherokee 66–79
#7203	Blazer 69–82	#7203	Jimmy 69–82
#5576	BMW 59–70	#7059	J-2000 1982
#7315	BMW 70–82	#7165	Le Car 76–83
#7308	Buick 75–83 all full sized models	#7323	Le Baron 1982
#7307	Buick Century/Regal 75–83	#7055	Lynx 81–82 inc. EXP & LN-7
#7045	Camaro 67–81	#6634	Maverick/Comet 70–77
#7317	Camaro 82–83	#7198	Mazda 71–82
#6695	Capri 70–77	#7031	Mazda RX-7 79–81
#7195	Capri 79–82	#6065	Mercedes-Benz 59–70
#7059	Cavalier 1982	#5907	Mercedes-Benz 68–73
#7309	Celebrity 82–83	#6809	Mercedes-Benz 74–79
#7309	Century 82–83	#7318	Mercury 68–83 all full sized models
#5807	Challenger 65–72	#7194	Mercury Mid-Size 71–82 inc. Continental, Cougar, XR-7 & Montego
#7343	Challenger (Import) 71–83		
#7344	Champ 78–83	#7173	MG 61–80
#6316	Charger/Coronet 71–75	#7311	Monarch 75–80
#7162	Chevette 76–82 inc. diesel	#7405	Mustang 65–73
#7313	Chevrolet 68–83 all full sized models	#6812	Mustang II 74–78
#7167	Chevrolet/GMC Pick-Ups 70–82	#7195	Mustang 79–82
#7169	Chevrolet/GMC Vans 67–82	#6841	Nova 69–79
#7310	Chevrolet S-10/GMC S-15 Pick-Ups 82–83	#7308	Oldsmobile 75–83 all full sized models
#7051	Chevy Luv 72–81 inc. 4wd	#7335	Omega 80–83
#7056	Chevy Mid-Size 64–81 inc. El Camino, Chevelle, Laguna, Malibu & Monte Carlo	#7191	Omni/Horizon 78–82
		#6575	Opel 71–75
#6841	Chevy II 62–79	#5982	Peugeot 70–74
#7309	Ciera 82–83	#7335	Phoenix 80–83
#7059	Cimarron 1982	#7027	Pinto/Bobcat 71–80
#7335	Citation 80–83	#8552	Plymouth 68–76 full sized models
#7343	Colt 71–83	#7168	Plymouth Vans 67–82
#7194	Continental 1982	#7308	Pontiac 75–83 all full sized models
#6691	Corvair 60–69 inc. Turbo	#7309	Pontiac 6000 82–83
#6576	Corvette 53–62	#5822	Porsche 69–73
#7192	Corvette 63–82	#7048	Porsche 924 & 928 77–81 inc. Turbo
#7405	Cougar 65–73	#7323	Reliant 81–82
#7190	Cutlass 70–82	#7165	Renault 75–83
#6324	Dart/Demon 68–76	#7383	S-10 Blazer 82–83
#5790	Datsun 61–72	#7383	S-15 Jimmy 82–83
#7196	Datsun F10, 310, Nissan Stanza 77–82	#5988	Saab 69–75
#7170	Datsun 200SX, 510, 610, 710, 810 73–82	#7344	Sapporo 78–83
#7197	Datsun 1200, 210/Nissan Sentra 73–82	#5821	Satellite/Roadrunner, Belvedere, GTX 68–73
#7172	Datsun Z & ZX 70–82	#7059	Skyhawk 1982
#7050	Datsun Pick-Ups 70–81 inc. 4wd	#7335	Skylark 80–83
#6554	Dodge 68–77 all full sized models	#7208	Subaru 70–82
#7323	Dodge 400 1982	#5905	Tempest/GTO/LeMans 68–73
#6486	Dodge Charger 67–70	#5795	Toyota 66–70
#7168	Dodge Vans 67–82	#7314	Toyota Celica & Supra 71–83
#7032	Dodge D-50/Plymouth Arrow Pick-Ups 77–81	#7316	Toyota Corolla, Carina, Tercel, Starlet 70–83
#7055	Escort 81–82 inc. EXP & LN-7	#7044	Toyota Corona, Cressida, Crown, Mark II 70–81
#6320	Fairlane/Torino 62–75	#7035	Toyota Pick-Ups 70–81
#7312	Fairmont 78–83	#5910	Triumph 69–73
#7042	Fiat 69–81	#7162	T-1000 1982
#6846	Fiesta 78–80	#6326	Valiant/Duster 68–76
#7046	Firebird 67–81	#5796	Volkswagen 49–71
#7345	Firebird 82–83	#6837	Volkswagen 70–81
#7059	Firenza 1982	#7339	Volkswagen Front Wheel Drive 74–83 inc. Dasher, GTI, Jetta, Quantum, Pick-Up, Rabbit, Scirocco
#7318	Ford 68–83 all full sized models		
#7140	Ford Bronco 66–81		
#7341	Ford Courier 72–82	#6529	Volvo 56–69
#7194	Ford Mid-Size 71–82 inc. Torino, Gran Torino, Ranchero, Elite, LTD II & Thunderbird	#7040	Volvo 70–80
		#7312	Zephyr 78–83
#7166	Ford Pick-Ups 65–82 inc. 4wd		

Chilton's Repair & Tune-Up Guides are available at your local retailer or by mailing a check or money order for **$10.95** plus **$1.00** to cover postage and handling to:

Chilton Book Company
Dept. DM
Radnor, PA 19089

NOTE: When ordering be sure to include your name & address, book code & title.